KOHUT, LOEWALD,
AND THE POSTMODERNS

Psychoanalytic Inquiry
Book Series

KOHUT, LOEWALD, AND THE POSTMODERNS

A Comparative Study of Self and Relationship

Judith Guss Teicholz

Routledge
Taylor & Francis Group
New York   London

First published by Lawrence Erlbaum Associates, Inc., Publishers
10 Industrial Avenue
Mahwah, New Jersey 07430

Reprinted 2009 by Routledge

Routledge

270 Madison Avenue
New York, NY 10016

2 Park Square, Milton Park
Abingdon, Oxon OX14 4RN, UK

Library of Congress Cataloging-in-Publication Data

Teicholz, Judith Guss.
   Kohut, Loewald, and the postmoderns : a comparative study of self
and relationship / Judith Guss Teicholz.
      p.   cm. — (Psychoanalytic inquiry book series ; v. 18)
   Includes bibliographical references and index.
   ISBN 0-88163-369-0
   1. Psychoanalysis.   2. Self psychology   3. Kohut, Heinz
   4. Leowald, Hans W., 1906-   . I. Title. II. Series.
   [DNLM: 1. Kohut, Heinz. 2. Loewald, Hans W., 1906-
   3. Self psychology.   W1 PS427F v. 18 1999
   BF175.5. S44T45 1999 First pbk printing 2001
   150.19′5′0922—dc21
   DNLM/DLC

for Library of Congress   98-47700
                                                           CIP

10 9 8 7 6 5 4 3 2 1

For Mildred Bassen Guss

And in Memory of

Benjamin R. Guss

Other worlds are no longer the stuff of dreams and philosophical musings. They are out there, beckoning, with the potential to change forever humanity's perspective on its place in the universe.

— John Noble Wilford

Because of the paradoxical rule of quantum mechanics, the bits in a quantum computer, called qubits, can be not only one or zero, but one and zero at the same time.

—George Johnson

Say a body. Where none. No mind. Where none.

—Samuel Beckett

CONTENTS

PREFACE

Although my final product may not be recognizable as such, this book had its origins in an invited address for the 19th Annual Conference on the Psychology of the Self, 1996, held in Washington, DC. The Conference Chair was Joseph D. Lichtenberg, who established a panel on psychoanalytic history and asked Malcolm O. Slavin, of Cambridge, MA, to chair it. Mal Slavin, in turn, asked me to participate on the historical panel with a paper looking comparatively at Kohut and Loewald. I had just published a series of papers in which I had clinically linked the ideas of Kohut and Loewald and had begun to investigate newer and more current trends in psychoanalysis-trends that, in fact, seemed to contain an implicit critique of some of Kohut's and Loewald's central contributions. I therefore decided to "flash forward" rather than backward in history, to look at the ideas of both Kohut and Loewald in comparison to those of a group of contemporary analytic authors who seemed to exemplify certain aspects of postmodern thought.

At the 1996 Self Psychology Conference, Arnold Goldberg and Joe Lichtenberg were among those who attended the historical panel and heard my presentation: Arnold Goldberg invited me to submit my paper for review by his Annual's editorial board for Progress in Self Psychology, where it has since been published as a chapter in Volume 14 (1998); Joe Lichtenberg suggested that I send a book proposal to The Analytic Press, with the idea that it become an addition to the Psychoanalytic Inquiry Book Series. This book is the result of that project, which has taken me far beyond the original paper.

In addition to thanking those already mentioned who encouraged me to write or to seek publication of my ideas, I wish to thank the several thriving psychoanalytic authors whom, throughout my book, I took the liberty of calling the "moderate postmoderns." Although I did not personally communicate with them in advance of writing the book, it was perhaps their writings, above all, that inspired me to undertake the project and that kept me enthralled with the ideas I was discussing from the first to the last words. These writers include Lewis Aron, Jessica Benjamin, Irwin Z. Hoffman, Stephen A. Mitchell, and Owen Renik. My book concerns itself, in addition to the ideas of those I labeled as moderate postmoderns, with the diverse concepts of subjectivity and intersubjectivity to be found in the writings of Daniel Stern, Thomas Ogden, Beatrice Beebe, Frank Lachmann, George Atwood, Bernard Brandchaft, and Robert Stolorow; and with more "radical" postmodern concepts to be found in the writings of Barnaby Barratt and Julia Kristeva. Although my selection of these authors for comparison reflects my admiration of their work, I know that it is a mixed blessing to have one's ideas discussed in a book while one is still writing and evolving one's thinking. For this reason, I wish to offer special acknowledgment to these writers, whose permission I did not seek, but without whose work I could not have written this book.

Of course, it is because of my ongoing work with my analysands that I keep struggling with any psychoanalytic ideas at all. My patients are a prime motivating force behind all my psychoanalytic theorizing, and they are the litmus test for any tentative "solutions" that I am led to through my writing and teaching. I am grateful to them for continuing to challenge me and for making any hint of theoretical complacency an impossibility in my life.

Paul Stepansky, Managing Director of The Analytic Press, was my editor over the course of the 18 months that it took me to write the book. But to call him my editor seems not to do justice to our interactions. I would say, rather, that our editorial relationship started out resembling something closer to a tutorial in writing and in the history of ideas (I was the student!), and then increasingly approached an ideal of pleasurable and mind-stretching collegial dialogue as the book progressed. When the initial writing project was complete, Eleanor Starke Kobrin (Lenni), also of The Analytic Press, walked me capably and gently through the final editing process and was an extraordinarily competent and patient teacher in introducing me to the ways of the book publishing world.

To my further delight and enlightenment, my son, Adam, wrote a paper on modern and postmodern thought for a college literature and philosophy course during the early stages of my writing project, and his research and our discussions were invaluable to me. Additionally, my sister Faith Guss, who lives in Oslo, was writing a multidisciplinary work on the topic of children's dramatic play during the same period that I began working on this book. In spite of the substantive differences in our topics, and the diverse intellectual disciplines from which we approached them (for instance, she included among her several sources writings from social anthropology and the theatre), we discovered enormous overlap in our focal issues, especially those pertaining to problems of subjectivity and intersubjectivity. These convergences further enhanced the pleasure that I derived from my own project. Although I have dedicated this book to my parents alone, I might easily have included all three of my siblings—Keren, Faith, and Jonathan-all of whom in different ways have contributed importantly to the complex web of feelings, aspirations, interests, and abilities that converged in my undertaking and completing this project.

I also thank my husband, Eric Teicholz, for his generous and unfailing emotional and technical support throughout the project and for repeatedly nudging me back to the broader sociocultural world many times when I could easily have disappeared entirely into my writing. Although I will not mention by name the other very important family members, friends, and colleagues who encouraged me along the way, I believe you all know who are are. Without your recognition of the book's importance to me, and without your acceptance of my antisocial trends during the writing process, I could not have enjoyed the project nearly as much as I did. As it was, however, the writing of the book was its own reward, and if others now find it interesting or worthwhile, I will feel most fortunate indeed.

INTRODUCTION

The Absent Authority and Ever-Present Subjectivity of the Author

---

*Every question, no matter how intellectual its content, reflects suffering.
. . . Let us try simply to be receptive to this suffering and if possible to
open our ears to meaning of a different kind.*

—Julia Kristeva

As the modern gradually moves into the postmodern, the earlier psychoanalytic focus on the suffering patient shifts imperceptibly to a focus on the unanswered and unanswerable questions of the analyst. We dare not ask: whose suffering is it, the analysand's or the analyst's?

Recent developments in Western thought and in psychoanalytic theory have heightened our awareness of lost authority and multiple subjectivities in our search for self-understanding and knowledge of the world. Since as analysts we are now more self-conscious than ever about the limitations of any one perspective, and more aware of the skewing effects of our own subjectivities, as writers we can be no less so. Thus I wonder what my idiosyncratic viewpoint can offer various readers, and I expect that my subjectivity will permeate the book in ways I cannot imagine. Still, I ask myself: why am I writing this book now, and how will my subjectivity shape its form and content? Any attempt to make a comprehensive response to these questions would detract from my intended subject matter, but I hope that a selective and brief response might at least warn the reader concerning certain of my *identifiable* biases, and perhaps also enhance an appreciation of the book's content.

The Author's Narrative

To this end, I presume to tell you something about the time and place of my (formal) introduction to psychoanalytic thought. My doctoral training in psychology took place in Boston, over the years from 1971 to 1977, the first and last of which happened to be the years of publication of Kohut's first two books, *The Analysis of the Self* and *The Restoration of the Self.* I read these two books, almost at the moment of their publication, in conjunction with my earliest studies of Freud and the history of psychoanalytic thought. I also read extensively on British and American object relations theories during this same six-year period. Besides Kohut's books and articles, a few other authors and their works significantly captured my imagination during the first years of my training. Among these were Winnicott's writings on the facilitating environment, Michael Balint's (1953) work on primary love, Arnold Modell's (1968) *Object Love and Reality*, Margaret Mahler's *The Psychological Birth of the Human Infant*, (Mahler, Pine, and Bergman, 1975), and some of the early interpersonal and existential literature. Thus, the critique of Freudian theory and practice that was implicit in these and other writings was something to which I was exposed at the moment of my first readings of Freud. In that context, the work of Hans Loewald was also of interest to me, because he seemed to remain allied with his classical background and milieu while struggling to integrate profoundly innovative (and potentially disruptive) ways of understanding human growth and change. Loewald's most original ideas might have fit more comfortably within the new framework that Kohut was in the process of developing, but Loewald seems to have been unable either to resolve the contradictions between the two theoretical frameworks or to make an explicit break with the classical tradition.

Kohut and Loewald may have been among the last generations of psychoanalysts to be trained in classical psychoanalytic theory at a time when there were few viable, alternative ways to get comprehensive and rigorous training (perhaps Jungian training was one of few exceptions to this Freudian exclusivity). Kohut and Loewald, each in his idiosyncratic way, may have arrived gradually at a sense of disequilibrium or "misfit" between their classical training, on one hand, and what they began to experience in their clinical work, on the other. In contrast to

Kohut and Loewald, who had the originality to construe things in ways that they had never been taught, those of us who trained three-quarters of the way through the century were taught multiple perspectives from the outset of our training: we never went through a stage of being deeply immersed in purely classical theory as the official (or only) version of the psychoanalytic story. For me personally, this meant that over the years of my training, my supervisors tried to teach me how to conduct a psychoanalytic psychotherapy according to classical principles, while I, in turn, tried to teach my supervisors what I thought I had learned from the writings of Kohut, Loewald, and some of the British object relations theorists.

In particular, I noticed, and tried to explain to my supervisors, that certain patients could not even tolerate my most ordinary *observation* of them, let alone my psychoanalytic interpretation. In those cases I felt compelled to come up with other ways for my patients and me to interact constructively. Additionally, I felt that with *all* my patients, I had no choice but to express in my clinical work some degree of an affective responsiveness that came naturally to me, the expression of which I felt was affirmed in Kohut's writings about empathic immersion and communication, as well as in Loewald's writings about the significance of the "real" external object in development and treatment. As an extension of my moderate self-expressiveness, I often felt that, regardless of my vigorous and ongoing integration of theory and practice, my patient and I were engaged in an existential encounter with only our own hearts and minds to guide us. I felt that all my theory and technique, all of our adherence to frame, could not protect my patient from me, nor me from my patient. We were two human beings meeting regularly together at a specified time and place, and, intentionally or not, I would become both an old and a new object to my patient, and my patient to me. Now, with the privilege of being a supervisor myself over the past 20 years, I have had the opportunity to continue my learning from my own supervisees, their patients, and, of course, my patients.

In the late 1980s, after a "multiply determined" delay, I resumed my formal study of psychoanalysis by becoming a training candidate at the Massachusetts Institute for Psychoanalysis (MIP). In the past five years, I have been engaged in teaching and supervising at MIP, which was founded on a commitment to comparative psychoanalysis, and fit well with my own leanings. I'm not, however, unaware of the hazards and pitfalls of theoretical comparisons, which can include tendencies toward diletantism, oversimplification, superficiality, and sometimes even the setting up of straw men for the purpose of knocking them down. Cooper (1996) suggests that comparative analysis also tends to yield caricature. I can only hope that, if in this book I lean toward caricature in my portrayal of any theorist, I do so in the Joseph Brodsky (1995) sense of accurately capturing the *essence* of that theory, while resisting the temptation to exaggerate that essence for effect.

To return to the late 1970s and early 80s in this brief narrative of my theoretical development: after the publication of Kohut's first two books, I was warmly sought out in some Boston circles for my appreciation of self psychology and the emerging relational theories. Being in Boston and not yet affiliated with any analytic institute, I was not part of a group of self psychologists or of any other cadre faithful to a particular analytic paradigm. I therefore felt free of professional constraints to search for what made sense to me *across* theories and was able to engage in a personal struggle toward theoretical integration. At the same time, I was aware that, among most classical analysts, the newer theories, and especially self psychology, were dismissed as passing trends or as not psychoanalytic (see, for example, Eagle, 1987). Then, over the next decade or so, I watched as *many of the new ideas seemed, one after the other, to be imperceptibly absorbed into mainstream psychoanalysis, even while paradoxically they continued to be the target of significant criticism.*

A Dual Shift in Psychoanalytic Discourse

Sometime over the course of the past decade, perhaps from the mid-80s to the mid-90s—I can't say exactly how or when—the theories that were considered heretical or revolutionary as recently as 1977 gradually shifted position such that they have now come to be seen, in significant ways, as outdated. My attempt to understand how this has happened, and why, is the theme of this book. My intent is also to search for prevailing validity in Kohut's and Loewald's ideas in the face of contemporary criticism of their work. The term postmodern, as I am using it in this book, refers specifically to the contemporary critique that has gradually nudged Kohut and Loewald's work from a revolutionary to a more or less outdated status.

On what basis do I say that Kohut's and Loewald's work has in significant ways become outdated, even while thousands of therapists and analysts throughout the world still read and study their writings and seek supervision based on their viewpoints? Although practice may indeed lag behind theoretical innovations, there has been a certain shift in specific theory *content*, at the same time as there has been a shift in how *theory*, in general, is regarded. Mitchell (1993) refers to these shifts as representing two revolutions: one in theory, the other in metatheory. In chapter 1 I suggest that there may be an inextricable interpenetration of these two revolutions. For the purposes of discussion in this book, I have identified five outstanding contemporary analytic writers who seem especially to exemplify, in different ways and to varying degrees, the second of these two shifts or revolutions, pertaining to metatheory. These are: Lewis Aron, Jessica Benjamin, Irwin Z. Hoffman, Stephen A. Mitchell, and Owen Renik. *Even where these writers have not directly addressed the ideas of Kohut and Loewald, the evocative quality of their writing, and many of their ideas, have in my mind become a questioning subtext to Kohut's and Loewald's works.* Although I am aware of the many problems involved in treating five highly original and divergent voices as a cohort, I am calling these five analysts the postmoderns and exploring how their writings, taken individually and together, might constitute an always implicit and sometimes explicit critique of certain aspects of Kohut's and Loewald's ideas, which themselves seemed to be revolutionary in the not so distant past. Although, owing to mutual influences, it will be in many regards difficult to separate out the feminist critique from these other contemporary commentaries on analytic theory, I also include a separate chapter on gender issues and the feminist contribution, for which I rely primarily on the writings of Jessica Benjamin and Nancy Chodorow.

Other Analysts' Ideas and This Author's Context

By examining Kohut's and Loewald's ideas in the light of the contemporary critique of their work, I have made an entire book out of other people's ideas. Any time that my own writing has ever been quoted or paraphrased in someone else's work, no matter how accurately, I always

ended up feeling vaguely uneasy: in every case I have felt that, regardless of bounteous intelligence and good will on the part of the other
writer, my meaning and my intent were subverted in the service of that
other writer's agenda. I know that, in spite of my best efforts to the contrary, my book will create a similar uneasiness in all those writers whose
work I'll be discussing and who are living and writing today. I may also
be at risk for doing violence to Kohut's and Loewald's thought, when
they are no longer here to correct my unintentional misrepresentations.
I will inevitably be discussing *my* Kohut, *my* Loewald, and *my* postmoderns! I therefore apologize in advance, to readers and writers alike,
for what will be the inevitable subversion of the work of others in the
service of my own agenda. I can only say that I have chosen to discuss
only those writers for whose work I have the profoundest respect and
admiration. I trust that my respect and admiration will be conveyed,
even as I unavoidably remove their words from their own contexts and
place them in mine.

One more note of caution and apology: over their lifetimes both
Kohut and Loewald created a large body of work. Not only did their
ideas evolve over time, but, even in different works written around the
same time, they often said things that seemed to contradict statements
they had made in other contexts. The same can be said for any open-
minded and productive theorist who commits his or her thoughts to the
page. But once a paper or book is published, it is frozen in time for others to use at their will. While recognizing that all creative psychoanalytic
writers move on in their thinking from what they have previously published, I have no choice but to use what has already been written as a
communal starting point—communal in the sense that others have also
had a chance to read and think about what has been written. Thus I am
aware that I will in some cases be citing earlier papers from authors who
may no longer entirely stand by what they have written in the past. When
this happens, I hope it will be understood that I am using earlier writings to represent a *stage* in the development of a particular author's thinking or, even more likely, as a "talking-point" for my own exposition. In
this way, I shall be using selected contemporary analysts' writings to
explore the late 20th-century critique of Kohut's and Loewald's work;
and I shall be undertaking that narrower task toward the larger purpose
of assessing the past and future revolutions in late 20th-century psychoanalytic thinking.

Kohut's and Loewald's Ideas and Their Reception: Mirror Images in Content and Style

In selecting Kohut and Loewald as representatives of a mid-century, partial revolution in psychoanalytic thought, I acknowledge that, in spite of important overlap, these two psychoanalytic giants had very different things to say and different ways of saying them. Although they both set out to elucidate aspects of human development and experience that they felt to be inadequately represented in Freud's theories, in a certain sense, Kohut's and Loewald's writings can be seen almost as constituting mirror images: Kohut elaborated a developmental theory of self that left certain (non-selfobject) aspects of the required relationship unarticulated; and Loewald began to elaborate a developmental theory of relationship that left certain aspects of the self unarticulated. Furthermore, the works of these two writers have met with very different fates in the psychoanalytic community. Loewald, who did not break with the classical tradition, nevertheless exerted a profoundly liberating influence on several generations of younger analysts through certain of his writings. His 1960 paper on therapeutic action was and continues to be one of the most widely cited papers in the history of psychoanalysis. While no new movement in analytic thought is specifically associated with Loewald's writings, he has commanded low-key but sustained and widespread respect and admiration over the course of nearly four decades.

In contrast to Loewald's quieter infusion into mainstream psychoanalytic thinking, there has been nothing low key in the response to Kohut's writings. Although starting out within a traditional Freudian framework, Kohut later made an explicit break with classical theory and offered what he claimed was an alternative depth psychology, the psychology of the self. Kohut's work has met with intense passions, both of a positive and negative valence. In the most simplistic rendering of this phenomenon, the positive passions may have been generated by the extent to which Kohut's work uniquely addressed problems and lacunae that over the years many analysts had felt to be inherent in Freud's theory, while at the same time capturing something essential in the *Zeitgeist*, the spirit of his own moment. Within psychoanalysis, Kohut's spirit of the moment had something to do with the rejection of Freud's drive theory, and it also intersected historically with the "age of narcissism" (Lasch, 1978), heralding the mass media's "me" generation.

Kohut's Theory of Narcissism and the Historical Moment

But Kohut's theory of narcissism seemed to turn both the Freudian concept and popular understandings of the phenomenon upside down. Freud (1914) described narcissism as the original state of the infant, to be followed in health by a transformation to obejct love. In contrast to this Freudian view, Kohut (1966) postulated a narcissism that would exist and develop side by side with object relatedness from birth onwards and that would itself be transformed into more mature forms throughout development. As for the lay understanding of narcissism, its primary feature was understood to be self-absorption and a lack of concern for others. Kohut's healthy and mature narcissism, in contrast, included in its very essence an intimate connection with and concern for others. Ultimately, in Kohut's theory, narcissism came to be synonymous with "the self" and thus could include the full range of qualities and experience associated with that concept.

This appropriation and change of meaning of a term long in use both within and outside of psychoanalysis may have accounted for some of the rejection, in the long run, that Kohut's new ideas received. But initially Kohut's (1971) work was hailed as a refreshing and much needed addition to psychoanalysis. Only upon the publication of his second book in 1977 did the full weight of his indictment of Freudian psychoanalysis become clear, perhaps to himself as well as to others. At least some of the negative passion in response to Kohut may have been engendered in those who felt the need to remain loyal to Freud's thinking and whose loyalty may have been threatened by the extent to which Kohut ultimately parted with Freud's ideas. This book, however, concentrates not on the Freudian, but on the *postmodern* critique of Kohut, which has come from analysts who are not at all struggling with their loyalty to Freud. This contemporary critique seems to emanate more from the ways in which Western thought in general has shifted and from the influence on psychoanalysis from such fields as feminist and literary criticism, revisionist history, philosophy, evolutionary biology, and, in a metaphorical sense, physics.

Transformations in Self Psychology, Post-Kohut

In addition to all the changes that are emergent across disciplines in Western thought, self psychology itself has undergone remarkable transformations in the past decade. Since Kohut's death, his new paradigm has become generative of at least three "subclasses" of self psychology, although several theorists might legitimately be classified in more than one of the subgroups.

One of these groups can be thought of as having stayed closer than the others to Kohut's own thinking, while developing certain of his ideas to make them more consistent with his break from classical theory (Brandchaft, 1983; Goldberg, 1983, 1985, 1990, 1995; P. Tolpin, 1983; Wolf, 1983, 1988, 1989, 1991, 1992, 1993; Ornstein and Ornstein, 1985; Fosshage, 1989, 1995a, b; Gedo, 1989; Lachmann, 1990, and 1991; Shane and Shane, 1988, 1990; Lichtenberg, 1983a 1988, 1990; A. Ornstein, 1988, 1990; P. Ornstein, 1991, 1993a, b; M. Tolpin, 1983, 1989, 1993; Lachmann and Beebe, 1996a, b). One example of this kind of shift was the move from a focus on *optimal frustration* in Kohut's work to an emphasis on *optimal responsiveness* in the evolving self psychology (A. Ornstein, 1988; Bacal, 1988; Terman, 1988; Shane and Shane, 1996); another example might be Fosshage's (1997) argument for an analytic stance that oscillates between positions inside and outside of the analysand's viewpoint, an attempt to add flexibility and range to Kohut's clinical recommendations. Perhaps the most radical shift to come from this subgroup within self psychology is the plea for a thoroughgoing questioning of psychoanalytic foundations (Goldberg, 1996) for which Kohut himself provided some of the groundwork.

A second group within self psychology has made a claim for five universal systems of motivation within the self (Lichtenberg, 1989), systems that seem to draw creatively from Freud's instinct theory, broad-based relational theories, and self psychology. Motivational Systems theory adds texture to Kohut's concept of the self and expands and enriches Kohut's proposal that individuals are motivated primarily by the need for self-coherence, continuity, and enhancement, to be met through mirroring, twinship and idealizing relationships. Motivational Systems theory brings added dimension to both self and relationship in Kohut's theory and has made a significant contribution by clarifying relevant clinical principles as well (Lichtenberg, 1998; Lichtenberg, Lachmann, and Fosshage, 1996).

A third group still affiliated with self psychology has moved from Kohut's central focus on the *analysand's* self-experience to an insistence on recognition of the *analyst's* self-experience as well, thus spawning a new psychoanalytic theory of intersubjectivity (Stolorow, Brandchaft, and Atwood, 1987). The initially unheralded shift, from preferential use of the term *self* to a preference for the term *subjectivity*, can perhaps be seen as an early indicator of perceptions among those with evolving psychoanalytic sensibilities. For them *self* implies an unacceptable degree of rigidity or "thing-ness" that *subjectivity* does not. This new intersubjectivity theory emphasizes above all the contextual nature of experience (Stolorow and Atwood, 1992). It reminds us that psychoanalysis takes place within the field constructed by the intersection of the subjectivities, respectively, of the analyst and analysand. From its originators (Stolorow et al., 1987), there is also a plea for understanding relationships as moving back and forth, in figure–ground constellations, between selfobject and other kinds of relating. Additionally, the intersubjectivists argue for an openness to the discovery of innumerable selfobject needs beyond Kohut's specified three. Intersubjectivity theory has had a tremendous impact on other relational theories that are further removed from self psychology. Furthermore, there are multiple versions of intersubjectivity theory: some of these claim origins quite outside of self psychology, such as the writings of Jessica Benjamin, which include a significant feminist dimension. The pivotal topic of intersubjectivity, as well as aspects of the feminist critique, are discussed in chapters of their own in this book.

Perhaps even a fourth "subgroup" of self psychology could be construed, made up of those doing infant observation research from a psychoanalytic perspective (Stechler and Kaplan, 1980; Lichtenberg, 1983b, 1987, and 1989; Stechler, 1983; Stern, 1983, 1985; Emde, 1980, 1981, 1983, 1988, 1990; Beebe and Lachmann, 1988a, b, 1994; Lachmann and Beebe, 1992a, b; Demos, 1988; Lyons-Ruth, 1991). The findings of these innovators in infant research overlap in important ways with all the other self psychology subgroups: with Kohut's original self psychology, with Lichtenberg's motivational theory (which originated in infant research), and with Stolorow et al.'s intersubjectivity theory. Some of the essential contributions of the infant research literature have centered on identifying earlier cognitive and psychological capacities in infants than were previously recognized, as well as an insistence on a greater degree of mutuality in parent–child interaction than has usually been acknowledged in the past. The findings concerning infant capacities are sometimes seen as support for the notion of a nascent self, or self-as-potential from birth onward; and the emphasis on mutuality is often seen as support for intersubjectivity and relational theories in psychoanalysis. Overall, infant observation research seems to meld with important aspects of the multiple self psychologies while at the same time introducing significant divergent emphases.

How might Kohut have responded to these changes and extensions to self psychology? We do know that he expressed reservations about Margaret Mahler's ground-breaking observation research. He questioned whether findings based on any mode of observation other than empathy could really be counted as "properly" psychological or psychoanalytic. We can only guess how he might have responded to each of these contemporary innovations by those who are still to some extent willing to shelter their theories under a broad and variegated self psychology umbrella.

It is clear that in each of the subclasses of contemporary self psychology just described, there are many highly individual voices, each adding substance, texture, dimension, and color to the whole. There are multiple overlaps and divergences. These and other new developments in self psychology are discussed at greater length in a later chapter, where I also bring in the unique viewpoint of evolutionary biology, a viewpoint that, while sympathetic to much of self psychology, simultaneously offers one of its more interesting critiques. In fact, *some of the contemporary developments within self psychology itself might be said to constitute a postmodern critique of Kohut's self psychology, while at the same time remaining part of the expanded self psychology movement.* What does it mean that certain paradigms seem almost to play a double role on the theoretical scene; they look somewhat like self-psychological theories while functioning as postmodern critiques of self psychology? One thing it might suggest is that Kohut's own self psychology expressed certain postmodern attitudes in nascent form and that many of his former colleagues and followers are facilitating the inevitable evolution of his ideas in a postmodern direction. And whatever else it might mean, it seems to reflect that we are in a period of great flux, with potential either to collapse into theoretical chaos or to realize exciting opportunities for constructive mutual influence among the multiple competing paradigms.

Theoretical Fusions and Confusions

The tendency to blur lines among some of the current theories may be nowhere more intriguing than in the debates concerning whether Kohut's self psychology is to be understood as a one-person or a two-person psychology (see Aron, 1990, 1996; Cooper, 1996; Gerson, 1996; Spezzano, 1996, on the one-person/two-person debate). Certainly, intersubjectivity theory is necessarily a two-person psychology, and, as I earlier noted, some theories of intersubjectivity were a direct outgrowth of self-psychological thinking; their originators currently include themselves at least partially under the broad umbrella of self psychology (Stolorow et al., 1987; Stolorow and Atwood, 1992; Stolorow, Atwood & Brandchaft, 1994). And yet, self psychology's emphasis on the individual self, with its selfobject needs and transferences, its ambitions, goals, and ideals, might suggest a one-person, more forcibly than a two-person, psychology, *even though self is understood to develop only within the self/selfobject matrix, and all selfobject needs are understood to be met only through relationship with another.*

Kohut's concept of self-and-selfobject might best be seen as transcending the one-person/two-person debate: Within Kohut's framework, the debate itself poses an inappropriate question. Just as Winnicott (1951) insisted that the question about whether the "object" was created or found should never be asked in relation to what is in transitional space, I imagine that Kohut might have insisted that *the question of whether there are one or two persons in the room should never be asked of an individual in a primary state of selfobject need.* The importance of not asking certain questions would apply to all babies with their caretakers and to certain patients at certain times with their analysts. In many discussions of this issue, the theoretical, the empirical, and the experiential are unfortunately confused, and the patient's and the analyst's separate experiences are conflated: on an empirical level of discourse, of course, there are two persons in the room; and on the basis of *most analysts' experience* most of the time, it might also be said that there are two persons in the room. But Kohut tells us that, out of deference to the infant's or the *patient's experience,* the question generally should not be asked. The theory has to contain or hold these multiple ways of understanding, and I suggest that Kohut's theory does so, though not explicitly. Technical considerations follow the theoretical:

postmodern analysts, arguing for a two-person theory, tend to insist on the expression of the analyst's separate subjectivity in the treatment situation; in contrast, Kohut emphasized the analyst's empathic resonance with the analysand's viewpoint and affect. What these technical recommendations have in common, and to what extent they are irreconcilible, is a matter for further discussion and is taken up later in this book.

The blurring of one-person and two-person phenomena and theories is echoed in other overlappings and interpenetrations among paradigms. For instance, self psychology itself is usually classified within the broad category of relational theories. We must ask whether self and relational paradigms can really be considered two distinct categories of theory at all, or whether they might better be thought of as occupying different points along a continuum. There seem to be theories that are primarily self theories, theories that are primarily relational theories, and perhaps the greatest number of perspectives in which the relative import of self and relationship cannot easily be discerned. (But dare I try to ascertain which authors fall within each of these three categories?) Still another example of the blurring phenomena can be seen by observing that not only the different subsets of self psychology, but also some of the authors whom I designate as postmoderns, have built their theories in part on implicit assumptions derived from certain tenets of self psychology. In these contemporary theories, some aspects of self psychology seem to be unattributed or taken for granted, some are explicitly articulated and embraced, while still others are met with a searing critique. I try to sort out some of these complexities when I take up specific ideas that originated differently with Kohut, Loewald, and the postmodern analysts, to see better how their ideas might interface and diverge.

The Unavoidable Arbitrariness of Chapters

For purposes of intelligibility and clarity, I have no choice but to isolate and break down these ideas into separate chapter headings. It will quickly become clear to the reader, though, that my attempt to discuss any of the major ideas of these authors in isolation from all of the others is fraught with serious difficulties. For example, I try to discuss the idea of self separately from the idea of subjectivity, the idea of subjectivity separately from intersubjectivity, intersubjectivity separately from mutuality, and self separately from relationship. All my chapter topics are inherently interconnected, and therefore my separate discussion of each will inevitably at times seem somewhat forced.

The Author's Book and the Changing World

Meanwhile, psychoanalytic discourse, like many other aspects of contemporary life, seems to be accelerating. There is a proliferation of journals, symposia, and viewpoints, some establishing dramatic differences from mainstream theory, others suggesting only subtle shadings of difference. The loss of a singular authority in psychoanalysis opens the possibility for many authoritative voices. Consequently, I am setting out, to some degree, with the feeling that the ground is constantly shifting under me as I undertake to write. To the extent that a book is a project executed over time, I believe the psychoanalytic world in which I finish this book will be very different from the world in which I started it. I also can't help but believe that this feeling itself is one more manifestation of what I call postmodern.

In this book, I use the first chapter to argue that there have been two partial and overlapping psychoanalytic revolutions in late 20th century theory and practice, with Kohut and Loewald spearheading the one and my selected group of postmoderns spearheading the other. In the second chapter, I present an overview of how the term postmodern has been used in psychoanalytic discourse, as well as *my own construction of Kohut and Loewald's work as a link or waystation between the modern and the postmodern.* In the remaining chapters, I discuss specific ideas that originated differentially with Kohut, Loewald, and the postmoderns. My aim in these discussions is to assess the current state of what I call the two partial revolutions in psychoanalysis. I suggest that Kohut's and Loewald's work represented a partial revolution and that the work of several contemporary analytic writers (the postmoderns) represents a continuation of that revolution. Nevertheless, the two partial revolutions, as I see them, are so intertwined in time, form, and subject matter that it is almost arbitrary to separate them for purposes of discussion. It remains unclear whether these revolutions will continue in their current direction or whether there will be a retrenchment before the seeming abyss. Without foundations, without representation, without coherence or continuity, perhaps even without drives or self or object, what will psychoanalysis be?

PART I

KOHUT'S AND LOEWALD'S WRITINGS AS FINALE TO THE MODERN AND OVERTURE TO THE POSTMODERN

THE ONE-HALF AND THREE-QUARTERS REVOLUTIONS

The Shift From Modern to Postmodern in Psychoanalysis

We cannot yet think outside of this tradition of precepts; we do not know what will develop beyond the modern episteme. But we surely know that this episteme, our old ways of thinking, is fast exhausting itself, and we know that we desperately need new ways of thinking and acting.

—Barnaby Barratt

Trying to capture the physicists' precise mathematical description of the quantum world with our crude words and mental images is like playing Chopin with a boxing glove on one hand and a catcher's mitt on the other.

—George Johnson

Mr. Sokal invites anybody who feels that physical laws are mere social constructs to defy them by leaping from his 21st story window.

—Edward Rothstein

Elucidating the Postmodern in Psychoanalysis

In *The Scientific Revolution*, Steven Shapin (1996) equates *modernity* with the "idea of science as the reliable product of disinterested and dispassionate inquiry [which goes] hand in hand with the idea that such knowledge [can] be a tool for improving the human lot" (quoted in

Gottlieb, 1996, p. 28). At this moment in history, no longer attributing to science the capacity to generate "reliable products," we are facing a crisis of confidence concerning our psychoanalytic "tool for improving the human lot." This crisis of confidence has engendered in many psychoanalysts an intensive search for alternative tools or methodologies for healing those who come to us for help, even when such concepts as tools or methodologies have fallen into a certain disrepute. Our search, therefore, involves not only a rigorous questioning of all that has been used or taken for granted in the past, but also a questioning of the very process of trying to find new ways of doing and understanding. *It is this questioning that I am calling the postmodern.*

The psychoanalytic literature has seen a recent upsurge in references to postmodern phenomena (Barratt, 1993, 1995; Mitchell, 1993; Sass, 1995; Aron, 1996; Elliott and Spezzano, 1996; Protter, 1996). In the psychoanalytic context, the term postmodern seems to refer sometimes to aspects of contemporary life and the human condition as we hurtle toward the millenium (Elliott and Spezzano, 1996); sometimes to current developments in art, philosophy, history, and literary or feminist criticism (Sass, 1995); sometimes to the metaphorical reverberations of quantum physics on psychoanalytic theorizing (Sucharov, 1994; Mayer, 1996b); and occasionally to specific trends in psychoanalytic thought and practice that are associated with any of these other experiential phenomena or intellectual disciplines (Mitchell, 1993). Less frequently, individual psychoanalysts identify themselves, or are identified by others, as postmodern analysts (Aron, 1996). In all these uses of the term, postmodern seems to encompass a multitude of meanings, this multiplicity of meanings being a postmodern phenomenon in and of itself.

In this book, my use of the term postmodern refers only to the last two of the foregoing uses: namely, to specific trends in contemporary psychoanalytic thought and practice and to a small group of contemporary analysts whose work in various ways seems to exemplify these trends, whether or not they identify themselves as postmodern or would welcome the term as descriptive of their thinking. The trends in question have broadly to do with a certain critique of previous psychoanalytic theorizing, along with a certain tentative and questioning attitude on the part of analytic writers toward their own theoretical efforts.

Barnaby Barratt (1993) has written a masterful treatise on postmodern thought in the Western world and its implications for psychoanalysis. For Barratt (1995), the term postmodern refers to "an impulse to critique that tries to disclose the limitations, insufficiencies, and distortions of reasoning of the modern episteme from within the monopoly of its epistemics" (pp. 139–140). Barratt proposes that Western thought is in the midst of a revolution in relation to which psychoanalysis has been both "instigator" and "reaction" (p. 137). According to Barratt (1993, 1995), Freud's early 20th-century notion of the unconscious and the method of free association played a pivotal role in starting a revolution in modern thought: unconscious processes, as expressed in free association, deconstruct and thereby liberate us from the confines of rational thought, its order, and its systems of meaning. Yet in spite of and perhaps because of this "irreducible equivocation and undecidability of meaning" (Barratt, 1995, p. 139), *psychoanalysis has spawned multiple systems of meaning*, meanings that psychoanalysts, starting with Freud, have read into the free associations of their analysands or have abstracted from the interactions between themselves and their analysands over the course of this century.

Freud himself articulated a multifaceted and complex system of meanings, which he believed were universal and which he interwove into his "discoveries" about the structure of the human psyche and its instincts. But to the extent that Freud imposed order on, and attributed meaning to, the form and content of the unconscious, he was ignoring or even opposing the more radical implications of his own innovation (Barratt, 1993, 1995). From this viewpoint, psychoanalysis has always held within itself the inevitability of its own deconstruction, a deconstruction that can be seen as a liberating source of vitality, even while it reflects and entails a loss: "the loss of a transcendental or foundational point of universal reference by which the diversities of thinking and communication, the plurivocality of human experiences and values, might be commonly anchored or organized as a unity" (Barratt, 1995, p. 137).

I suggest that, starting midway through the 20th century, a different kind of revolution began to get underway and build up momentum, smaller and more confined to psychoanalytic thinking itself, but nevertheless significant in its long-term effects. This mid-century, "part-revolution," which I will examine here through the writings of Kohut and Loewald, both expressed and influenced the ongoing unraveling of "foundations" that had been begun earlier by Freud's recognition of the unconscious. This part-revolution questioned many of Freud's universalist assumptions but offered some universalist or quasi-universalist assumptions of its own. Thus, while its carriers recognized and explicitly acknowledged the cultural-historical limitations of their own perspectives, they did not take the revolution to the radical postmodern position of questioning altogether the possibility of order or shared meaning in human experience. By rejecting important aspects of Freud's received teachings, and by attempting to place their own ideas in historical perspective, Kohut and Loewald were perhaps precursors to the postmodern "impulse to critique." But they stopped well short of the postmodern to the extent that they were still able, without epistemological misgivings, to elaborate alternative renderings of what might be primary and universal in human experience and development and to portray development and psychopathology in terms of cause-and-effect relationships.

Kohut and Loewald accepted and built on Freud's concept of the unconscious, but they construed the "content" and "organization" of the unconscious in ways that turned out to be radically different from what Freud believed himself to have "discovered." Even more significantly, Kohut and Loewald, each in a different way, began to shift psychoanalytic inquiry from an exclusive focus on the interior of the subject as a closed system to a focus on the arena between analytic subject and analyst; they no longer saw either "system" as closed. This shift in the focus of inquiry led to new ways of constructing psychoanalytic meaning: ultimately, Kohut (1959, 1966) and Loewald (1960) placed self and relationship at the center of human motivation and narrative and questioned Freud's notion of sexual and aggressive drives as the primary organizers of personality, experience, and psychopathology.

Simultaneously with Kohut and Loewald, other psychoanalysts in other parts of the world were launching parallel and overlapping "part-revolutions," as for example the British Middle or Independent school of psychoanalysis, among which the work of Winnicott stands out as the most compatible with aspects of Kohut and Loewald's thinking. Even during Freud's time, however, there had been voices which were discordant with some of his central ideas, voices that spoke of self, culture, or relationship, independent of the drives. These included Sullivan, Fromm, the Balints, Rank, Ferenczi, and Horney, among others. But in many instances these voices were suppressed or cordoned off from mainstream psychoanalysis (Aron, 1996), and some of them are only now enjoying a vigorous revival of interest. Most interestingly, some of the current interest in these previously ignored contemporaries of Freud's is being expressed by the very analysts whom I term postmodern. In fact, much of what we call postmodern today is profoundly resonant with the thinking of these contemporaries of Freud's who wished to emphasize aspects of human development and the psychoanalytic situation that Freud chose to downplay or ignore. Perhaps the most striking example of this phenomenon is the contemporary interest in Ferenczi's concept of mutual analysis (Aron and Harris, 1993; Aron, 1996).

To explore this protracted, 20th-century revolution toward the postmodern in psychoanalysis, started by Freud and looking very much as if it will continue into the 21st century, I compare in this book central tenets of the work of Kohut and Loewald with salient ideas from the writings of a selected group of contemporary American psychoanalysts who are currently in the process of forging new perspectives. I use the term postmodern—with several caveats both about the choice of label itself and about treating as a cohort—to describe a group of highly individual voices, each of whom has already made a significant and distinctive contribution to the development of psychoanalytic thinking and practice. As mentioned in the introduction, the analysts I have chosen to pay most attention to in this context are Lewis Aron, Jessica Benjamin, Irwin Hoffman, Stephen Mitchell, and Owen Renick. What these individual analysts seem to have in common is a sensitive and thoughtful recognition of the forces at work in the postmodern world and in postmodern thought that are pulling at the fabric of our psyches and our theories. But, for these writers, what seems to go hand in hand with this recognition is a desire and a determination not to yield to the nihilistic undertow of these forces in their work and in their thought.

Most of the new perspectives might be said to fit under a broad umbrella of relational, social-constructivist, or participant-observation theories (Spezzano, 1996), which have both significant convergences and divergences. In some cases, there is also a tentativeness and process quality to their theory-building that may be one of many ways in which they express their postmodern sensibilities. These analysts (Hoffman, 1983, 1991, 1994, 1996; Benjamin, 1988, 1995a, b; Mitchell, 1993, 1996a, b; Aron, 1991, 1992, 1996; Renik, 1993, 1995, 1996) have furthered the revolution in psychoanalysis but for the most part have not taken it beyond the limits of hermeneutics, a philosophical viewpoint that still allows for the construction of shared meanings (Brook, 1995; Steiner, 1995). *Thus, to the extent that we can call them postmodern at all, they are moderate postmoderns, as opposed to extreme postmoderns, and perhaps represent only a conservative, as opposed to a radical, revolution.* Of course there are many psychoanalysts other than those I have chosen, both mid- and late-20th century, whom I could have used to examine the state of this revolution in analytic thought; but to make the task manageable I must narrow the field by trying to find significant, if not totally representative, theorists. In fact, in the face of today's plethora of theoretical viewpoints, finding a group of writers who might be representative of a single psychoanalytic trend is an unattainable task. My choice of these particular analysts is therefore necessarily personal and subjective but one I hope serves my purpose well.

The field of hermeneutics studies the principles of interpretation and thereby highlights the possibility of multiple principles of interpretation and of multiple interpretations as well. But beyond hermeneutics lies a postmodern point of implosion: this is a point at which one would approach with "radical seriousness . . . the possibility that 'commonalities of understanding' should always be treated with suspicion for what they exclude, foreclose, or 'repress'" (Barratt, 1995, p. 139). At this point of implosion or deconstruction, it can be difficult to grasp why one would undertake to be in or to conduct a psychoanalysis, because the possibilities for the establishment of shared meanings and common understandings seem to have been questioned out of existence. It seems then that there is *only* the flux of the unconscious, and nothing else. It also seems that there would be little sense in trying to write a book about this or any topic (see also Harvey, 1990; Sass, 1995; Eagleton, 1996), since the writer would not be able to assume sufficient commonality of understanding to imagine a reading audience. But if we accept this line of thought (can there be a "line" of thought when thought is no longer accepted as linear?), we would be giving in to the Talking Heads, who sing: "Stop Making Sense." One way to express this postmodern dilemma is by asking, How do we permit ourselves to make sense, to ourselves and others, now that we have become aware of how arbitrary, and therefore in some ways *false*, any sense that we make must necessarily be? Is it really possible for us to do our work, once we undertake to examine and question every assumption? There is a tension in the psychoanalytic air between those who see the postmodern impulse to critique as tending toward chaos and nihilism and those who see it primarily as a challenge to free ourselves (Goldberg, 1990; Barratt, 1993, 1995), and thereby our patients as well, of unnecessary and even harmful constraints.

Actually, Barratt (1993, 1995) goes well beyond suggesting that an embrace of the postmodern will help only the community of analysts and their patients. He suggests that it has significantly been the *modern* outlook, with its blind faith in science, progress, and the perfectibility of mankind, that has made possible such catastrophes as the Holocaust(s) and the ecological destruction of the planet. In a similar vein, he views the modern concept of *identity* primarily in terms of foreclosure of alternative lives and selves. These foreclosures get in the way of achieving genuine empathy with others whose identities are different from ours and thus contribute to racial or social divisiveness and to gender polarization. Barratt insists that only by turning away from our modern structures, whether internal or external, and surrendering to a postmodern formlessness can we avoid continuing or repeating some of the worst disasters of the 20th century.

Among the group of analysts whom I call the postmoderns, Hoffman has explicitly expressed a preference to be seen not as a post modern but as a critical realist (Stepansky, 1997, personal communication). Aron (1996) also discusses his view of himself in regard to the postmodern classification. He writes that he wishes to embrace certain aspects of postmodern thinking while rejecting others, and he does this by identifying two contrasting trends within postmodern thought (he credits P. M. Resenau, 1992, with having originated this distinction, which he also acknowledges as being oversimplified). Aron *aligns himself only with the more moderate and "affirmative" of these two postmodern trends*, which he describes as follows:

> The more extreme, skeptical postmodernists tend to be influenced by Continental European philosophers, especially Heidegger and Nietzsche, and emphasize the dark side of postmodernism, despair, the demise of the subject, the end of the author, the impossibility of truth, radical uncertainty, and the destructive character of modernity. The more moderate, affirmative postmodernists tend to be indigenous to Anglo-North American culture and are more oriented to process, emphasizing a nondogmatic, tentative, and nonideological intellectual practice (p. 25).

By identifying himself and several of his contemporaries as allied with the moderate and affirmative trends in postmodern thought rather than with the radical, Aron suggests that he might more comfortably label himself a "critical modernist" (p. 26) than a "postmodernist" proper. Aron seems to choose this terminology in order to emphasize the perspectival and constructivist possibilities in postclassical thought, while attempting to avoid its nihilistic overtones. In my mind, however, Aron's and Hoffman's convergence on the adjective "critical" seems to bring them closer to the radical postmodern realm of Barratt's (1993) "impulse to critique" than either of these authors might wish. Aron (1996) struggles to maintain a position for himself (as analyst and as writer) somewhere between the now outmoded "rational and unified subject," on one hand, and the postmodern subject who is "socially and linguistically decentered and fragmented," on the other (p. 25). He clearly succeeds in maintaining this tension but also seems to be aware of a lurking darkness. Hoffman, likewise, struggles with the polarities: he places the dialectic at the center of his proposed "solution" and thereby urges us to live with a rather postmodern nonresolution.

Barratt (1993, 1995) acknowledges that the radical postmodern critique constitutes a crisis of Western thought, but he welcomes this crisis as an "unlocking" and a liberation from "imprisonment" within a false sense of order and shared meanings. In contrast to Barratt on this point, the individual analysts in my so-called postmodern group struggle to identify common principles of personal experience and relationships that might guide them (and their students, supervisees, and readers) in their work as analysts; at the same time they must avoid falling into the positions that they themselves have criticized: the positions of positing universals, of reifying and "privileging" particular aspects of human experience, or of seeming to claim that their particular viewpoints are the best ones possible, at least for now. The outcome of this struggle cannot now be predicted. At this moment, it may well be impossible to critique modern ways of thinking and being without falling prey to modern ways of thinking and being.

To the extent that, living in this time and place, we cannot avoid recognizing and expressing the postmodern "impulse to critique," we must ask how it has affected our current understandings of psychoanalytic theory. In general, "the loss of a foundational point of universal reference" (Barratt, 1995, p. 137) has taught us "to approach the history of ideas in any field with a heightened awareness of *cultural relativity, the subjectivity of the historian, and the nonlinearity of progress*" (Teicholz, 1998a, p. 267). Mitchell (1993) describes this evolving postmodern approach to theory, for which he sees evidence across all major intellectual disciplines: "all knowledge is regarded as perspectival, not incremental; constructed, not discovered, inevitably rooted in a particular historical and and cultural setting, not singular and additive; thoroughly contextual, not universal and absolute" (p. 20). Joining Mitchell, Aron, and Barratt in their expositions of what constitutes the postmodern in psychoanalysis, Protter (1996) equates it with an antiessentialist stance, "as opposed to the more representational, foundational views that have been referred to as modern" (p. 549).

Protter identifies three points on a continuum, moving from the modern to the postmodern. He calls his three points the "antiessentialist continuum" and labels them as follows: 1) the modern- humanistic sensibility, which takes primarily an *explanatory* approach to theory within an interpretive metapsychology (pp. 551–552); 2) the *radically descriptive* sensibility, in which there is an attempt to forego explanatory theory and to give up essentialist assumptions (pp. 552–553); and 3) the *normative-prescriptive* outlook, which constitutes "a more completely postmodern-historicist position" (p. 554) emphasizing not only the inevitable theoretical and methodical contamination inherent in any psychoanalytic observations, but also the larger cultural-historical influences as well.

Protter sees the antiessentialist continuum as an increasing progression toward postmodernism, from the first stage of modern-humanistic sensibility to the third, normative-prescriptive stage. But, in my view, his third continuum point, having to do with awareness of cultural-historical influences on one's thought and practice, is no more "advanced" toward the postmodern than is his second point, which attempts to do away with explanatory and universalist assumptions by maintaining a radically *descriptive* position. I would even suggest that in some ways, the cultural-historicist position might have a tendency to *lead* to the radically descriptive: with the loss of theoretical foundations that comes out of our recognition of multiple (cultural-historical) perspectives, we are left with nothing to do but attend to what happens within ourselves and between ourselves and our patients, and to try to describe it.

Perhaps most interesting for our discussion, however, Protter makes the point that the concept of the *self* has moved from being "the focus and raison d'etre of modern therapeutic culture" (p. 551) within the explanatory-theoretical viewpoint, to becoming increasingly a "problematic" in the radically descriptive and normative-prescriptive viewpoints. It is therefore not surprising that Kohut's and Loewald's ideas would fit most comfortably within Protter's first and earliest point on the continuum, which allows for explanatory theories of development, etiology, and structure. The contemporary analysts whom I term post-modern seem to aspire to the "values" of both the second and the third of Protter's three continuum points; they attempt to do away with "heavy handed essentialist assumptions" and explanations (Protter, 1996, p. 552) and to keep at the forefront of awareness the personal subjectivity and cultural-historical perspectives that they now know will necessarily cloud their vision. Aspirations and actual achievements in these efforts are, however, difficult to line up one with the other: all the postmodern analysts I have selected have difficulty escaping at least "light-handed" assumptions. Often, for instance, they replace self values with relational values; and, even as they insist on the cultural-historical limitations of their individual perspectives, in the end they (and we) have no choice but to try to articulate and persuade others of the "truths" of their individual, time-and-place-limited subjectivities, and to allow or encourage others to find the same kinds of truths about and for themselves.

But, even if there is no group of psychoanalysts who can either meet others' criteria for what is postmodern or wholeheartedly identify themselves as such, there are certain characteristics of contemporary life which have been labeled postmodern and that are generally thought to have had a profound impact on individual experience, affecting even the sense of *selfhood* on a global scale (Elliott and Spezzano, 1996). Describing this phenomenon, Anthony Elliott and Charles Spezzano point to the "compression of space, the mutation of time, and cataclysmic forms of change," as characteristics of post modern life which contribute to a widespread "sense of fragmentation and dislocation" (p. 59).

These authors seem to be describing, almost as a new norm, what Kohut would have understood as a *breakdown* of the self, arising out of failures in the sustaining self–selfobject matrix. If we were to translate Elliot and Spezzano's observations into the language of self psychology, they would seem to be saying that the destructive aspects of postmodern life are so powerful that they shatter the protective shield of self-selfobject relationships within the nuclear family or perhaps render most parents unable to function adequately as selfobjects for their children. Even if there were no changes in theory itself, this claim for such a *transformation of personal experience* would point to the deconstruction of previous psychoanalytic concepts (such as, for instance, the self) and make us self-conscious about using our old language in familiar ways.

If we could still allow ourselves to think in terms of what the analyst might "find" (as opposed to what she might construct, or coconstruct) as she listens to her patient, we might say, on the basis of Elliot and Spezanno's description of postmodern life and its effect on the human psyche, that late 20th-century analysts, listening to their patients, would be hearing and responding to a more fragmented self than did either Kohut or Loewald only 15, 20 or 25 years ago. Therefore, contemporary analysts might "find" something quite different in human nature and experience than even their quite recent predecessors did. Furthermore, we might say that the analyst herself, by virtue of her exposure to postmodern life and thought, is a more fragmented and decentered subject (Aron, 1996), less able to believe that she is capable of focusing her own attention and empathy on the other in the analytic dyad. Thus might we approach the differences between what Kohut and Loewald found and recommended and what Aron, Benjamin, Hoffman, Mitchell, and Renik now construct and recommend. However, our thinking in postmodern directions has taken us beyond these simple and unidimensional ways of understanding such differences, and I will be addressing these questions in more detail as I take up in the following chapters the specific tenets of thought in the writings of Kohut, Loewald and the postmoderns.

KOHUT AND LOEWALD

Way Stations on the Road to the Postmodern

Close examination reveals no precise, datable event when the world changed.

—Anthony Gottlieb

At the heart of natural dialectics . . . are three universal laws. . . . The law of the transformation of quantitative into qualitative change asserts that change occurs in qualitative leaps as a result of accumulated quantitative change. The law of the unity and contradiction of opposites holds that all entities are a combination of oppositions, whose mutual interaction drives change within such entities and in the world as a whole. The law of the negation of the negation posits that each successive stage of development contains within itself the seed of its own destruction and replacement by a new stage that contains elements, on a higher plane, of the stage preceding it.

—H. Lyman Miller

I have earlier suggested that the writings of Kohut and Loewald coincided with a certain moment in the history of psychoanalysis that looked both backward and forward: backward to the modern, and forward to the postmodern, and in many ways presaged the latter. As much as both men were steeped in psychoanalytic tradition, each had a vision that in many ways broke with the past.

Loewald was a profoundly innovative commentator on human development and on the psychoanalytic process. But he seemed to be of two minds about his own innovations. Throughout his career, he repeatedly went out on exhilarating theoretical or technical limbs, only to follow these moves with a seeming retreat to more traditional positions. He continued to use the language of classical metapsychology but consistently infused it with new meaning, often turning Freudian ideas inside out, without ever announcing that he was doing so.

As early as 1960, for instance, Loewald had subtly shifted Freud's concept of "neutrality" to his own concept of *positive neutrality*. In Loewald's elaboration of what he meant by positive neutrality, he included *the analyst's love for the individual* and for individual development. In the same paper, Loewald also suggested that *the analyst should make himself available to the patient as a new object*; that the analyst should help the patient negotiate reality by articulating his own perception of the patient's significant objects; and that the analyst should hold up for the patient an image of what the patient might become through the analysis.

Loewald never explicitly resolved the tensions between these radical ideas and the more traditional elements of his own theorizing. The contrasting elements remain unintegrated in his writings as a whole, making it possible for traditionalists and postmoderns alike to pick and choose according to their own belief systems while ignoring the strongly opposing currents in the larger body of his work (see Friedman, 1996). It may be this very failure to integrate his own contradictory ideas that has allowed Loewald not only to remain within the fold of classical American psychoanalysis, but to be studied and admired both inside and outside of the mainstream (e.g., Loewald, 1980; Fogel, 1991; Symposium, 1994; Panel, 1996).

In contrast to Loewald's more preservational approach to classical ideas, Kohut went out on a limb and kept on going, inventing a new language for his revolutionary theory. Kohut developed a highly organized system of thought, which included a new and overarching *psychic structure* and a new psychoanalytic phenomenology. He identified a new class of transferences, offered a new narrative of individual development, and suggested what he believed to be a new mode of observation. It was, therefore, Kohut, of the two men, who attracted an organized group of colleagues during his lifetime and arrived at a new depth psychology that ultimately broke with central tenets of classical psychoanalytic theory. For these and other reasons, Kohut's work, far more than Loewald's, has been the subject of extensive and passionate criticism.

Common Themes in Kohut's and Loewald's Work

There is no public record of a meeting or direct dialogue between Kohut and Loewald. Over the decade of the 1970s, however, they each made some reference to the other's ideas with respect and appreciation (Kohut, 1971, 1978a; Loewald, 1973). In 1973, Loewald wrote a favorable review of Kohut's 1971 book *The Analysis of the Self.* In that monograph, Kohut had begun to create a new language through which to think about many of the ideas that Loewald (1960) had expressed in his much earlier article on the therapeutic action of psychoanalysis. In his review of Kohut's book, there is something of gratitude in Loewald's tone for having found a kindred spirit on the importance of humanizing the analytic situation and perhaps also amazement that Kohut had dared to be as explicit and thoroughgoing as he had about certain ideas with clearly anticlassical implications. In particular, Loewald underscored his appreciation of Kohut's idea of the self–selfobject relationship and its structure-building function. Several years later, Kohut (1977a) expressed appreciation of Loewald's "valuable contributions" (p. 254n) to the elucidation (and humanization) of the therapeutic attitude; and, in 1984, he included Loewald in a short list of analysts who had done work that "perfected" psychoanalytic treatment (p. 107) from Freud's original contributions onwards. Also in common, the two men recognized a similarity of processes between primary development and later change through psychoanalytic treatment.

Although Loewald still spoke in terms of Freud's tripartite structure, while Kohut spoke of *self,* both analysts saw internalization processes as being at the center of psychic development. Kohut (1971) referred appreciatively to Loewald's (1962, 1973b) work on internalization. Kohut shared with Loewald a conviction that, although healthy and mature internalizations result in relatively impersonalized and autonomous structures internally, external object ties continue to be important along with the ongoing internalization processes. For both Loewald and Kohut, then, structure-building internalizations transformed, but did not replace, object relations. In this view, Kohut and Loewald differed from Freud, (e.g., 1923a), who suggested that internalizations (i.e., oedipal identifications) replaced earlier object ties. Both Kohut and Loewald emphasized the importance of the actual functioning of the external object and the quality of the primary relationship for individual growth and change.

Kohut and Loewald further departed from Freudian theory in their shared recognition of certain basic developmental and psychological needs, which were not derivatives of instinctual life (Teicholz, 1996). These needs had to be met, either in the primary relationships of childhood or in the psychoanalytic situation in order for normal development or curative processes to occur (see also Winnicott, 1958). Both men argued for an experiential and relational curative effect in treatment, beyond the insight that evolves through the interpretive process (Kohut, 1971, 1977a, 1984; Loewald, 1960, 1973). Today, many of these ideas have been seamlessly absorbed into the communal analytic mind. But in the 1960s and 70s, they constituted near-heresy for many mainstream American psychoanalysts.

Kohut and Loewald as Early Forecasters of the Postmodern

It seems as if there was barely a moment in history between the time when Kohut and Loewald were hailed as revolutionary and the present time, when aspects of their writings are seen as outdated under the glare of an unflattering postmodern spotlight. And yet both Kohut and Loewald still inspire loyalty and generativity in a multitude of psychoanalytic followers. One way of understanding these apparently contradictory phenomena is through the recognition that the writings of Kohut and Loewald may have represented a way station between the essentialist, positivist, objectivist, or deterministic theories that preceded them and the relational-perspectivist (Aron, 1991), social-constructivist (Hoffman, 1992, Stern, 1996), or postmodern-historicist (Protter, 1996) theories that proliferate today. I propose that these newer theories not only followed upon Kohut and Loewald's work, but that Kohut and Loewald themselves forecast and paved the way for them.

Of course, there were many ways in which Kohut and Loewald were distinctly not postmodern. For instance, they were deterministic in positing a cause-and-effect relationship between early experience and later psychopathology. They were positivist or essentialist in proposing universals of human development and experience, such as Kohut's concept of universal selfobject needs or Loewald's recognition of universal oedipal conflict (quite different, however, from Freud's version of oedipal conflict, to be discussed in a later section of the book). Although both Kohut and Loewald made dramatic departures from Freud's instinct theory, they were nevertheless positivist in offering an idiosyncratic but highly articulated theory of intrapsychic structural development.

At the same time, however, Kohut and Loewald both approached the postmodern in the emphasis that they placed on relational factors and on the phenomenological or experiential in their theories. Both men addressed the ways in which psychoanalysis was as much an art as a science. Loewald (1975) claimed "that science and art are not as far apart from one another as Freud and his scientific age liked to assume" (p. 352). Kohut (1978a), for his part, identified creative artists, performers, and their appreciative audiences as demonstrating the "precursors of that ability to enjoy the pursuit of internalized interests" which he believed would be necessary for the human race to survive in our troubled world (p. 543). Kohut hoped that psychoanalysis could further humanity on the road to developing these interests through "an intensification of . . . inner life" (p. 543), which, in turn, would deflect from more libidinous and aggressive pursuits in the external world. He was concerned that if such a shift were not made at the psychological level, increasing overpopulation and dwindling resources could lead only to widespread frustration and further aggression. Kohut (1978) spoke of psychoanalysis as leading to greater "psychological openness, perhaps even a spark of that playful creativeness which turns toward new situations with joyful interest and responds to them with life-affirming initiative" (p. 545). Here, Kohut seems to have presaged a postmodern emphasis on openness, creativity, and playfulness.

Loewald (1979a) also sounded postmodern in speaking of "an uncommon quality and degree of spontaneity and freedom" (p. 373) required of the analyst in the psychoanalytic situation, a situation in which "the analyst must relive, create the action of the play" (Loewald, 1975, p. 354). On the basis of certain passages from his writing, it can be argued that Loewald, by raising early questions concerning the possibility for discovering or knowing an external reality, was influential in heralding the scientific-hermeneutic debate in mainstream psychoanalysis. Twenty years ago, sounding very much in tune with such contemporary writers as Hoffman and Aron, Loewald (1979a) asked:

> Is the psychoanalytic process one of objective investigation of psychological facts, or is it interpretation of meanings? If the latter, are the meanings there, to be uncovered by us as analysts, or are we, although not arbitrarily, providing the meanings, or the

psychological facts, as a function of our active receptivity as analysts? Are "meanings" something that arise in the interactions between analysand and analyst? [p. 374].

There are also passages in the writings of both Kohut and Loewald that, in their recogntion of the analyst's subjectivity and in their perspectivist outlook, sound eerily similar to the postmoderns. For example, Loewald (1979a) wrote the following: "Objectivity, rationality, and reality . . . are not what we thought them to be, not absolute states of mind or world that would be independent of . . . the generative process-structures of mind" (p. 773). He went on to say, "Objective reality . . . appears to be more circumscribed . . . than we assumed, analogous to Newtonian physics" (p. 774).

Kohut as well noted the impact on psychoanalysis brought about by the shift in physics from Newtonian to quantum theory (see also Sucharov, 1994; Mayer, 1996b). As early as 1977, he drew our attention to the "fundamental claim of modern physics that the means of observation and the target of observation constitute a unit that . . . is in principle indivisible" (p. 31). And, going on to link the revolution in physics to his own revolution, he writes that, in psychoanalysis, "the presence of an empathic . . . observer defines . . . the psychological field" (p. 32). Kohut thus wrote of "a scientific objectivity which includes the subjective," and he acknowledged the unknowability of objective reality (Kohut, 1982, p. 400). In spite of these comments, postmodern analysts often fail to credit Kohut and Loewald as originators of their own, late 20th-century focus on the subjectivity of the analyst and the indissoluble intersubjectivity of the analytic situation.

Kohut (1980) continued to forecast the postmodern emphasis on the perspectivist nature of theory when he wrote: "We, too, are children of our time, just as Breuer and Freud were children of theirs. Thus our sensitivity to certain aspects of the human condition that are characteristic of our era is sharpened and we respond to them" (p. 518). Kohut was referring to a sensitivity that he saw as unique to his time, a sensitivity that translated into the need for a coherent sense of self. In his view, this need had priority over the need to discharge formerly repressed sexual and aggressive impulses. The need for a coherent sense of self went hand-in-hand with a need for participation in an affectively resonant human environment, which need took precedence over strivings for autonomy. Following Kohut's belief that each era accentuates unique aspects of the human condition to which its psychoanalytic theorists become differentially sensitized, what might be the "aspects of the human condition . . . characteristic of *our* era," aspects to which the sensitivities of the *postmoderns* now seem to be sharpened?

Kohut, Loewald, and the Postmodern Turn in Psychoanalysis

Throughout our culture, the postmodern has emerged from the modern and is its own commentary on the modern experience. To distinguish more clearly the postmodern from the modern, I will begin by identifying postmodern trends in their most extreme or radical form. In all subsequent discussions, however, I will try to convey the gradations of postmodern thought that are more representative of the analysts I have chosen to illustrate the "moderate" expression of these trends.

Although both Kohut and Loewald had a strong sense of history, the contemporary historicist view in psychoanalysis (Eagle, 1987; Protter, 1996) expresses an even greater sensitivity to historical perspective than did previous analysts. This sensitivity may derive from that aspect of the human condition exacerbated by a technology-driven, ever-faster pace of communication and change on a global scale, which makes ordinary individuals and theorists alike increasingly doubt that there can be any truths that will stand as truths for all time. From the historicist framework, any theoretical emphasis is seen as a reflection of its own time and place and also as a reaction to some previous swing of the theoretical pendulum.

Also prominent in contemporary psychoanalytic literature is a relational-perspectivist (Aron, 1991) or social-constructivist (Hoffman, 1992) view of reality. The relational-perspectivist view in psychoanalysis emphasizes that my reality and yours are equally valid and that they mutually influence each other. Each, in turn, is influenced by its place in a wider culture and by a specific moment in history. The radical social-constructivist view says that, for the purposes of the analytic relationship, there is no reality between us that you and I did not together construct and that any meaning assigned to that reality must result from a collaborative effort.

This insistence on a plurality of perspectives and on a social construction of reality invalidates Freud's model of the analyst's unilaterally making interpretations of the patient's material. It also leads to a rejection of common ground rules and of universals (Elliott and Spezzano, 1996). There is in postmodern thought a suspicious attitude toward *any* "grand narrative" (p. 57), regardless of content. This means that Kohut's (1982) offering of the story of Odysseus and Telemachus as a paradigm for human development is just as unacceptable as Freud's earlier myth of Oedipus. But while rejecting *grand* narrative, the postmodern has embraced *individual* narrative by turning to a search, at least, for narrative truth now that belief in the possibility of knowing historical truth is lost (Spence, 1982; Schafer, 1976, 1978, 1993).

Outside of psychoanalysis, the postmodern sensibility seems to be enamored of style and surface (Elliott and Spezzano, 1996). Inside psychoanalysis, this trend, in its most radical manifestations, is expressed in a focus on conscious experience in the patient–analyst interaction. This focus is maintained not because the unconscious has been devalued, but because there is increasing recognition that the analyst is not always a better judge of the patient's unconscious experience than is the patient herself and that, additionally, the analyst is as likely as is the patient to be unaware of his own unconscious motivations (Hoffman, 1983, 1994; Aron, 1992, 1996). The analyst's search for universally occurring motivations in his patient has thus tended to recede in contemporary relational theories, making Kohut's concept of disavowed grandiosity as suspect as Freud's concept of repressed sexuality. Postmodern thought further emphasizes the multidirectional, the random, and the chaotic nature of events (Elliott and Spezzano, 1996), including the events of individual psychic development. This emphasis calls into question older notions of linear stages of development as well as the possibility of an organized and coherent self as the goal of this developmental process.

With a diminishing faith in the possibility of order and predictability, there is a general weakening of interest in metapsychology; theories of intrapsychic structure, therefore, take a back seat to more purely clinical theories. The work of George Klein (1964) and Roy Schafer (1976, 1978) is a precursor of this trend. This shift goes hand in hand with a trend toward understanding both development and psychoanalysis in more purely relational terms (Mitchell, 1988). Within the relational viewpoint, there is a focus on the present rather than on the past, with strong emphasis on the here-and-now of relationship between patient and analyst. For some analysts, this emphasis serves to diminish even further the role that the analyst's interpretation is understood to play in the therapeutic action (Russell, 1990, personal communication, 1996; Renik, 1993; Mitchell, 1996a). Also within the relational viewpoint is an emphasis on subjectivity (Aron, 1992; Renik, 1993) as opposed to objectivity; on a fluid and open-ended subjectivity as opposed to a solid and completed self (Stolorow and Atwood, 1993); and on the intersubjective field between two persons (Stolorow, et al., 1987) as opposed to the earlier focus on the inner experience of just one party to the analytic dyad.

The current emphasis on the intersubjective, along with an increasing awareness of the unknowability of either outer or inner realities, tends to blur earlier hierarchical divisions between patient and analyst and places transference and countertransference on a more even plane. Each member of the analytic dyad is seen as contributing importantly to the analytic experience of the other, with both patient and analyst developing transferences and countertransferences in relation to one another (McLaughlin, 1981; Loewald, 1986). The analyst is no longer seen as observing and interpreting from *outside* the psychodynamic or interpersonal field, but is viewed as a participant in cocreating it. Interpretation is recognized as being a mental activity in which either analyst or patient might engage. Analysts can no longer hold on to the "naive patient fallacy" nor cling to "the notion that the patient . . . takes the analyst's behavior at face value even while his own is continually scrutinized for the most subtle indications of unspoken or unconscious meanings" (Hoffman, 1983, p. 395). The analyst is therefore encouraged to facilitate the analysand's articulation of her observations and interpretations concerning the analyst, rather than having them go unspoken and unexplored (Hoffman, 1983, 1994; Aron, 1992, 1996). Together, patient and analyst construct a shared reality (Hoffman, 1994) and consensually, create its meaning.

Contemporary analysts struggle with issues of hierarchy, symmetry, equality, mutuality, and authority, but the old "givens" are no longer taken for granted. The analyst's loss of his former claim to knowledge and authority has led the postmoderns and others to struggle productively with ambiguity (Adler, 1984), dialectic (Hoffman, 1994), and paradox (Winnicott, 1971; Pizer, 1992, 1996): these preoccupations may represent an attempt to make a virtue or an aesthetic out of the increasing recognition of complexities in the analytic situation and out of the sometimes bewildering aspects of postmodern life.

The postmodern embrace of ambiguity and paradox has a number of implications. A recognition that development does not proceed in a linear fashion; a mistrust of the neatness of earlier established categories and causal relationships; an appreciation of the staggering complexity, the multifacetedness, the unpredictability, and the mutual influence of countless variables in human experience and relationships; the acknowledgement that unconscious organizing principles and the subjectivity of the analyst or scientist contribute to choices about what is studied, observed, and perceived; the increasing emphasis on affective and relational experience over cognitive processes and insight in the analytic process; and the awareness that cultural and historical factors have an impact on what is deemed rational or irrational—all these trends have tended to diminish the value that psychoanalysts have placed on logic and reason, as traditionally understood, in the analytic enterprise.

Kohut (1977a, 1982, 1984) and Loewald (1960, 1975) anticipated the postmoderns in their attempts to highlight the value of the nonrational. They placed clear limitations on the importance that Freud had earlier given to reason and insight in psychoanalytic cure. Loewald (1979b), for instance, spoke of "a psychotic core" as "an active constituent of normal psychic life" (p. 774). He suggested that insofar as we might succeed in eliminating transference, with its roots in infantile, or prerational, experience, "human life becomes sterile and an empty shell" (Loewald, 1960, p. 250). In 1975, he wrote that, in a healthy individual, fantasy life is "in communication with" or "linked up with" actuality and "reinserted within the stream of total mental life," without which "reality" becomes meaningless (pp. 362–363). Loewald seemed to be everywhere cognizant of a tension between rational and nonrational forces and values in human experience and to take a balanced view of their respective contributions to mental health and its absence. He expressed this position as follows:

> While it has been . . . [the] intent [of psychoanalysis] to penetrate unconscious mentality with the light of rational understanding, it also has been and is its intent to uncover the irrational unconscious sources and forces motivating and organizing conscious and rational mental processes. In the course of these explorations unconscious processes became accessible to rational understanding, and *at the same time rational thought itself and our rational experience of the world as an "object world" became problematic* [Loewald, 1979b, p. 772, italics added].

Kohut (1978a) likewise placed limitations on the value of the rational in human experience. While focused on the problems of man's untamed aggression, he nevertheless recognized the dangers of pure reason as a basis for human life and relationships. And, while arguing for self-understanding as a path toward greater control of destructive feelings and behavior, he nevertheless warned against the inhumanity of "man as a thinking machine" (p. 537) and reminded us that "*[h]umanness comprises not only reason and equanimity but also irrationality and passion*" (p. 537). Thus both Kohut and Loewald strove for a balanced recognition of the relative value of rationality and the nonrational in human affairs; neither subscribed in full to Freud's (1923a) oft-quoted, "where id was, there ego shall be." But at its radical edge postmodern psychoanalytic thought goes beyond simply valuing the nonrational: it sometimes casts doubt on the possiblility of finding any genuine order or shared meaning in human experience (Barratt, 1993). This doubt cuts to the theoretical core of psychoanalysis as Freud, Kohut, Loewald, and most other analysts have historically construed it.

The particular group of analysts that I am designating postmodern are all keenly attuned to the multifaceted postmodern phenomena summarized earlier and are currently doing much to further the revolution in their respective ways. In spite of their significant differences, what they have in common is their success in negotiating the treacherous shoals between an extremely productive and creative kind of postmodern psychoanalytic self-consciousness, on one hand, and the chaos or nihilism that such thorough-going questioning of the old order can potentially bring, on the other.

Two Overlapping Revolutions: Kohut's and Loewald's Roles

I earlier referred to Mitchell's (1993) identification of a two-tiered revolution within psychoanalysis: one at the theoretical level and one at the metatheoretical. Building on Mitchell's observations, we may look at Kohut and Loewald's revolution as one that, although pointing to the future metatheoretical revolution, was mostly at a theoretical level. Although Kohut and Loewald repeatedly raised epistemological issues, their major contributions can be seen as lying in shifts of emphasis in the *content* of our theory: shifts from Freud's primary emphasis on the instincts and drives to their own emphases on self and relationship. This is what I have called a part-revolution and what Mitchell has called a revolution at the theoretical level.

But, alternatively, we may argue that, especially in Kohut's work, there was the germ of a metatheoretical revolution as well. In Kohut's (1977a) insistence on the indivisibility of observer and observed (p. 31), expressed through the empathic mode of observation (Kohut, 1982), is the seed of much of the contemporary focus on the analyst's subjectivity (through his loss of objectivity), the analyst's loss of access to (objective) knowledge, and the analyst's loss of absolute authority as a direct consequence of these first two losses.

Kohut's (1984) insistence on the indivisibility of observer and observed has led as well to our multiple theories of intersubjectivity. To be sure, this assertion is debatable, as Kohut is often interpeted as having recommended the use of empathy as an *objective method* for gaining access to the patient's subjectivity; in this interpretation, the "disciplined" use of empathy is intended to help the analyst to transcend his own subjectivity (Stepansky, 1997, personal communication). In his 1959 paper on empathy, Kohut indeed emphasized the objective potential of empathy as an observational instrument. By 1982, however, he had come down on the side of the subjective aspects of empathy, underscoring its potential for creating and sustaining a bond of connectedness between and among individuals. He spoke explicitly of the inappropriateness of an objective, scientific stance in the analytic endeavor. Thus, by 1982, in proffering the empathic mode of observation, Kohut was postulating two subjectivities in the analytic situation: the analyst, through her own subjectivity, would try to divine the subjectivity of the patient. She was to do this by looking into herself (introspecting) and searching her own experience in order to find a way to understand (vicariously) the patient's affect and perspective: this is my understanding of what Kohut meant by *vicarious introspection*, and it is in this way that Kohut lay the groundwork for our late 20th century theories of intersubjectivity.

Kohut's concept of selfobject has frequently been misunderstood as implying that the caretaker or analyst does not fully experience her own subjectivity. *This (mis)interpretation of Kohut's selfobject concept fails to recognize the distinction between the patient's inability to perceive the analyst's separate subjectivity, on one hand, and the analyst's robust experience of her own subjectivity, on the other.* In my view, Kohut fully recognized the subjectivity of the analyst or caretaker in his concept of selfobject even though the developing individual does not experience the selfobject's subjectivity as separate from her own. Kohut did not, however, spell out, as the postmoderns do, the contribution made by the analyst's subjectivity to the construction of meaning between patient and analyst. Going beyond Kohut's recognition of the analyst's subjectivity as the basis for her understanding of the patient and as the wellspring of empathy, the post moderns recognize the analyst's subjectivity as shaping both method and meaning in psychoanalysis.

Kohut did not commonly use the term subjectivity, but he did place the analyst's introspection at the center of the psychoanalytic process (Kohut, 1982). Introspection is, by definition, directed toward one's own thoughts and feelings, or toward one's subjective experience. Since Kohut (1978a) defined empathy as "vicarious introspection" (pp. 205–232; see also Kohut, 1984, p. 82), in his view, *the analyst's introspection, and therefore her contact with her own subjectivity, was the source of her empathy with her patient's experience.* For Kohut, the analyst's awareness of her own subjectivity was quite independent of the degree to which it was recognized or not recognized by the patient; and, regardless of how the patient saw the analyst's subjectivity, it would remain a source of the analyst's empathic responsiveness to the analysand as well as the wellspring of the analyst's overall functioning within and outside of any given analysis.

In 1982, Kohut clearly rejected classical psychoanalysis and its claim to objectivity, while explicitly offering in its place a subjective mode of participation for the analyst. He no longer saw empathy's potential as an observational method as its most important contribution to psychoanalysis; instead he underscored empathy's potential for creating an affective bond between two individuals on the basis of their shared experience. Therefore, although we might say that, for Kohut, therapeutic empathy involved the *selective* use of the analyst's subjectivity in the service of highlighting the experiential commonality between herself and her patient, true empathy could never bypass or transcend the subjectivity of its author. In fact, by 1982, it was this very characteristic of empathy—its subjective rather than its objective basis—that made it, for Kohut, the only acceptable mode of observation in the psychoanalytic endeavor. It was only through his own subjective experience, accessed through vicarious introspection, that the analyst could hope to understand the subjective experience of the analysand (see also Kohut, 1984, pp. 36–39). Although postmodern analysts may have legitimate concerns about what they see as this *limitation* on the use and expression of the analyst's subjectivity in Kohut's self psychology, they often seem not to recognize at all Kohut's insistence on the analyst's ongoing contact with, and use of, his subjectivity on the patient's behalf. They seem not to recognize that Kohut's shift from objective observation to empathic observation was precisely a shift from the analyst's objectivity to his subjectivity as a mode of observation and participation in the work. This essential step prepared the way for the postmodern attention to the far-reaching implications of the analyst's subjectivity, now recognized as affecting every act in the execution of the analyst's professional role.

Understood from this vantage point, Kohut can be seen as having contributed to the launching of two overlapping and interconnected revolutions: a modern and partial revolution, carried out at a theoretical level, by replacing Freud's drives with self and relational motivations and by shifting the focus of the psychoanalytic exchange from the intrapsychic to the relational; and also a postmodern and more complete revolution, which Mitchell (1993) has called the revolution at a metatheoretical level. It is possible to argue, therefore, that Kohut's work contains the seeds of much of the creative ferment in psychoanalysis today.

Looking at Loewald in terms of his influence on the metatheoretical revolution, we find many of his ideas as well have led to an unraveling of the tapestry of psychoanalysis's original theoretical fabric. I earlier noted the value he placed on the ongoing positive role of fantasy and a measure of irrationality in human life. In common with Winnicott and many postmodern analysts, he emphasized the necessity for "an uncommon quality and degree of spontaneity and freedom . . . from both partners" to the psychoanalytic endeavor (Loewald, 1979b, p. 373). Loewald's (1960) insistence on the analytic relationship and the actual interactions between parent and child, as well as between patient and analyst, as the basis of internalizations that would result in psychic structure, departed dramatically from the classical view that interpretation and insight alone could lead to the structural changes that were the goal of psychoanalysis. Loewald (1960), more than Kohut, however, maintained a view of the analyst as having something to offer the analysand through the analyst's higher level of ego functioning and organization.

In opposition to this residual, hierarchical thinking in Loewald's work, Kohut's work did more to lay the groundwork for the postmodern trend toward egalitarianism. Kohut's notion of the analyst's empathic immersion in the patient's experience, and his identification of vicarious introspection as the primary analytic activity, more radically placed analyst and analysand in the same experiential position vis-à-vis one another and more irrevocably turned psychoanalysis toward a postmodern future in which the hierarchical divisions, or perhaps all divisions, between patient and analyst could easily dissolve. I earlier suggested that it is Kohut's suggestion of an indivisibility of observer and observed, or of analyst and analysand, that tends to break down the boundaries between theory and metatheory, or between content and epistemology in our theory making.

There are other ways as well that we might understand the relationship between the theoretical and metatheoretical revolutions. For instance, the metatheoretical revolution seems to have evolved naturally out of the theoretical changes that Kohut and Loewald fought for, even though on some points it becomes increasingly difficult to discern what is theory and what metatheory. If we look at the changes from this vantage point, it seems that we would inevitably have moved from a focus on the self or subjectivity of the patient to the self or subjectivity of the analyst; that we would naturally have moved from a recognition of the (curative) power of the relationship to a dawning recognition that there may really be little else we can do in the analytic situation but participate in it, little else we can comment on but our own participation and the patient's. And following on the new recognition of the analyst's subjectivity, it was surely inevitable that we would go on to recognize the analyst's loss of privileged access to knowledge, along with the loss of authority that belief in such access once brought. Thus we could say that most of the metatheoretical shifts seem to have evolved naturally both from the revolutionary content of Kohut's and Loewald's writings at a theoretical level and from Kohut's insistence on the indivisibility between observer and observed, which I would classify as a metatheoretical assumption.

In spite of my earlier comment that it is not always clear what is theoretical and what metatheoretical, nor in which direction the influences flow most powerfully between theory and metatheory, there also seems to be a sense in which the epistemological revolution seems to be totally independent of the content of any one theory or paradigm. *Once we start questioning what the analyst can know, we can no longer have faith in the validity of any theory.* We used to see our theories as constituting what the analyst could know about all patients, or about all psychoanalytic processes, before she met with an individual analysand. *But through our recognition that there is no absolute knowledge, our theories teeter on the brink of losing whatever validity we formerly attributed to them. This situation seems simultaneously to close down previous options and to open up new possibilities. In either case, it impels us to search for new ways to carry out our analytic and curative intentions.* I have suggested that the group of analysts whom I have designated postmodern exemplify the constructive aspects of this search.

THE INTELLECTUAL CLIMATE OF
KOHUT'S TIME AND THE
MODERN–POSTMODERN DUALITY
OF SELF PSYCHOLOGY

There are periods in philosophy when a general consensus becomes apparent. As our century draws to a close, we seem to be agreed that modernity has ended. A sign of this is the change in our sense of what it means to be a self.

—James R. Mensch

The end of the 20th century has seen a change in both the philosophical and the psychological senses of what it means to be a "self." Certainly within psychoanalysis, Kohut has contributed to this change; but also in the short time since his death, the concept of self has progressed in ways that he perhaps could not have foreseen. In later chapters I examine some of the ways that the psychoanalytic self is now seen as we near the end of the century. I note the permutations it has undergone from its version in Kohut's theory to the shape it seems to take under postmodern scrutiny.

In this chapter, however, I try to place Kohut's concept of self in historical perspective and to identify modern and postmodern aspects of his self theory. In so doing, I will necessarily be presenting Kohut's idea of the self through the filter of my own personal/cultural/historical subjectivity, one that has already been irrevocably changed by exposure to late 20th-century life and thought. I cannot even assess the degree to which my current reading of Kohut and Loewald has been filtered through a different lens, and been unconsciously revised, by my having read the works of the analysts I have selected as representative of the postmodern critique. Although I was originally attracted to Kohut's theory because of his dual emphasis on self and relationship, now more than ever I have difficulty addressing his concept of self independently of his concept of selfobject. Could this be how Kohut himself wanted it? In this chapter, you will see undeniable evidence of my struggle to stay with the topic of self, without simultaneously addressing the concept of the self–selfobject matrix, within which, in Kohut's view, the self originated, developed, and was maintained.

Historical Preludes to Kohut's Concept of Self

I noted earlier that the postmodern sensibility gives us a heightened sense of the place in history and in the larger culture that our theories seem to occupy. In attempting to place the discourse concerning self in historical perspective, I will be examining Kohut's concept of self in the light of certain ideas that were afloat in the early and mid-20th-century intellectual climate. In some cases I explore certain relationships between Kohut's and others' ideas even where we have little evidence that Kohut actually was influenced by the authors of the ideas in question. Kohut himself remained somewhat elusive about the sources of his own inspiration. In his preface to *The Restoration of the Self* (Kohut, 1977a), he listed several authors in whose work *others* had seen similarities with some of his own ideas. These authors included Hartmann, Winnicott, Aichhorn, Sartre, Adler, Rogers, Rank, and the general field of Indian philosophy. Kohut singled out the works of Aichhorn (1936) concerning narcissistic transference phenomena, Hartmann (1950) concerning the adaptive qualities of the ego, and Winnicott (1960) concerning true and false self, as having had particular meaning for him, and he did not deny the influence of any of those writers. In fact, he seemed implicitly to acknowledge the imputed links between their works and his own. Addressing the attribution of similarities between his own ideas and these others, Kohut (1977a) wrote the following:

> I know this list is incomplete, and, what is even more important, I know there is yet another group of investigators whose

names should be added to those already given. I am thinking here of those—such as Balint (1968), Erikson (1956), Jacobson (1964), Kernberg (1975), Lacan (1953), Lampl-de Groot (1965), Lichtenstein (1961), Mahler (1968), Sander et al. (1963), Schafer (1968), and others—whose investigation, even if not their methods of approach or their conclusions, overlap the subject matter of my own investigations to varying degrees [pp. xix–xx].

Loewald is noticeably absent from both lists, but others (Hoffman, 1983; Friedman, 1991, 1996; Greenberg, 1996) have identified links between Kohut's and Loewald's ideas, and we earlier noted contexts in which Kohut himself identified Loewald as a writer with whom he shared certain important ideas. Referring both to the writers he named and the writers that others had identified as having ideas similar to his, Kohut (1977a) went on to say that he had "great admiration for most of them" but that he had been unable to integrate their ideas with his own due to a "struggle toward greater clarity" in which he found himself "floundering in a morass of conflicting, poorly based, and often vague theoretical speculation" (p. xx). This experience led him to give up aspirations to "scholarly completeness" and instead to restrict himself "to the direct observation of clinical phenomena and the construction of new formulations that would accommodate {his} observations" (pp. xx–xxi).

With this kind of scant reference to the role that the ideas of others played in the development of his work, we might be tempted to say that the field is open for speculation concerning sources that may have contributed directly or indirectly to the evolution of Kohut's thought. Yet the openness of our speculative field is limited to the extent that Kohut explicitly set out to base his conclusions as much as possible on direct clinical observation. In what follows, therefore, I simply play with possibilities concerning how his ideas might relate to certain aspects of the intellectual climate of his time. I make no claim that Kohut was substantively influenced by any of the ideas to which I make reference except where I explicitly articulate such a connection.

With these caveats in place, we may envision Kohut's concept of the self as, in part, a provisional solution to certain problems presented by the Enlightenment vision of humankind, to problems in the Existentialist formulation of self, and, of course, to problems that he experienced in relation to Freud's and the interpersonalists' visions of the individual. In what follows I offer several conjectures as to events and ideas of Kohut's time that may have become fertile ground for the development of his particular self theory.

The Enlightenment view of humanity emphasized the power of reason and the individual's capacity for autonomy through scientific objectivity. It has been said that the Enlightenment envisioned the individual as living in "a negative space hollowed out by the will to autonomy and self-reflexivity" (Santner, 1996). Kohut's notion of the self in its *selfobject matrix* directly countered the Enlightenment emphasis on autonomy and self-reflexivity. *Kohut's selfobject concept expressed an insistence on a lifelong, mutual interpenetration of selves, rather than on autonomy*; it expressed an insistence on mutual reflection (mirroring) between self and other, rather than on self-reflexivity alone. Although Kohut's psychology has been labeled a self psychology, it could just as properly have been called a psychology of selfobject or a psychology of self-and-other. Some of the disagreement, misunderstanding, and confusion concerning whether Kohut's is a psychology of self or a psychology of self-and-other may derive from his focus on what gives each individual a sustainable sense of self. But his answers to that question had to do with the individual's embeddedness in particular kinds of relationships from birth to death.

Although the Enlightenment vision of humankind celebrated autonomy, reason, and self-reflexivity, the newly autonomous individual would come to threaten the social order by undermining large-scale acceptance of external authority. At the political level, this threat often led to government-sponsored coercion and enforced submission to power (Santner, 1996). At the level of personal experience, individuals might well strive for authenticity and self-authorship; but questions remained as to who would be responsible for the larger community and how competing individual and communal interests could be balanced and resolved. Long before Kohut, the Enlightenment emphasis on autonomy and individual reason was countered by alternative world views such as the restorationist sociologies and Romanticism of the first half of the 19th century. By the end of the 19th century, German and French existentialists had come to see humankind afloat in foundationless suspension, at sea in a world without ultimate value or meaning: this is one aspect of what Nietzsche meant when he proclaimed, "God is dead."

For Sartre, the Nothingness of a godless world was matched by the

Nothingness residing in the individual psyche. One way out of this void was for the individual to create his or her own meaning. Thus Sartre, upon confronting Nothingness, took action to write about his existential nausea. He unexpectedly and tentatively arrived at a way of beginning to live with it, perhaps even live through it. In Sartre's (1968) view, it was man's capacity for consciousness that presented a gap in his being:

> The being of consciousness qua consciousness is to exist at a distance from itself as presence to itself, and this empty distance which being carries in its being is Nothingness. Thus, in order for a self to exist, it is necessary that the unity of this own being include its own nothingness as the nihilation of identity" [p. 125].

Here Sartre articulated what sounds like a postmodern paradox of the self in which "unity of being" and "nihilation of identity" coexist.

Although Sartre was more narrowly focused than Kohut on the internal, cognitive experience of the singular individual, Sartre's proposal for a coexistence of opposites seems to have anticipated Kohut's concept of a self that both achieves and repeatedly dissolves its autonomy through immersion in a self–selfobject matrix. In Sartre's schema, the nothingness, or gap, between the self that simply is and the self that splits off from pure being to become conscious of its experience is filled with projects and goals that arise out of human contingency and freedom and thereby imply creative choices. One's goals represent the "not yet" and thus expand the possibilities open to the self; such goals add a future dimension to the contingencies or limitations dictated by the past (Sartre, 1968; Mensch, 1996).

Others have identified similarities between Sartre's and Kohut's ideas (Heinz, 1976, cited by Kohut, 1977a), but Kohut himself did not directly discuss Sartre's ideas in a public forum. Hence, what follows is only my observation of overlapping areas of interest in their respective writings, as well as a notation of some outstanding differences. Sharing with Sartre an interest in a phenomenology of the self, but constructing a self from the viewpoint of psychic development and healing rather than from a purely philosophical standpoint, Kohut focused not on Sartre's gap between being and consciousness, but on a *tension arc* between ambitions and ideals. Nevertheless, in synchrony with Sartre's ideas, Kohut suggested that the development of goals and the carrying out of plans (projects) in accordance with one's ambitions served the purpose of easing this tension (or filling the gap).

For Kohut, individuals who were unable to develop ambitions and goals would indeed suffer a gap or *deficit* in the self; or, more accurately, those with developmental self deficits would be unable to evolve attainable ambitions and goals. But, for Kohut, this deficit (gap or nothingness) did not inevitably originate within the individual as an existential aspect of the human condition. Rather, whether one went through life with a gap or deficit or whether the deficit was prevented or redressed depended on the availability of adequate selfobject responsiveness from the human environment. Thus Kohut held out the possiblility that what Sartre saw as a universal aspect of the human condition (the Nothingness that is inevitably confronted in the space between pure being, on one hand, and self-consciousness, on the other) could be resolved through adequate selfobject provision in early development. For Sartre, the individual stood alone and struggled with the paradoxes of freedom and determination. For Kohut, the capacity to use one's talents creatively and to construct a meaningful life was not an individual achievement in the face of a universal existential dilemma, but one that hinged on "an average expectable psychological environment" (Hartmann, 1939; Tolpin, 1977) meeting "a normal endowment" at least halfway (Tolpin, 1977, p. 172); in Kohut's (1971, 1977a, 1982, 1984) own language, it depended on the empathic responsiveness of the selfobject milieu.

Even though we have no evidence that Kohut himself wrestled with notions of "existential nothingness," his concept of the bipolar self, with its (meaning-giving) ambitions, goals, and ideals, as well as his notion of selfobject relatedness throughout the life cycle, may be understood as offering a way out of the existential nothingness that grew out of critiques of enlightenment ideas. Kohut's theory may in part be seen as an attempt to deal with an emergent dilemma of the 20th century: on what basis do we create a world, a life, a self, if no such basis can be taken as an absolute given? These questions represented not just intellectual debates; they reflected individual struggles about how to live as old orders broke down. Philosophically, the possibility of a *choice of meanings* for a single life went hand-in-hand with the allowance of a panoply of principles of interpretation for a given text. The recognition of multiple meanings led to a rebirth in the field of hermeneutics and its application to fields of knowledge outside its original application to the reading of biblical writings.

The hermeneutic viewpoint was making inroads in psychoanalytic discourse in the same years that Kohut was writing and publishing his first two books (e.g., Rycroft, 1966; Gadamer, 1975; Ricoeur, 1970; Habermas, 1971). But Kohut was at least as concerned with how a *personal* sense of meaning could be facilitated developmentally as he was with the epistemological issues surrounding the concept of meaning in psychoanalysis. His interest in empathy "in an epistemological context" (Kohut, 1959, 1982)—empathy as a way of knowing—eventually was matched by his interest in empathy "as a powerful emotional bond between people" and "as an informer of . . . therapeutic and psychoanalytic action" (Kohut, 1982, p. 397). Similarly, it seems that he was at least as concerned with world problems created by the psychological difficulties of mankind (Kohut, 1978a) as he was with philosophical fine points. Kohut (1982) spoke of having studied what he referred to as the "classical" philosophers, from Plato to Kant (p. 400), but he did not discuss their ideas. And, as noted, he made scant reference to Sartre or any other 20th century philosopher. Nevertheless, Kohut's self theory did share with the writings of French existentialists a concern for individual meaning-making and self-expression. What Kohut added to these shared concerns, thereby making his contribution unique and original, was *the central notion of self–selfobject relating*.

The Existential movement had widespread reverberations inside as well as outside of psychoanalysis, sometimes seeming to glorify mental illness with an emphasis on the universality of psychotic experience. At the outer reaches of this movement, R. D. Laing (1970) may unwittingly have contributed to the phenomenon by poeticizing the excruciatingly painful experience of profound and severe splits in the psyche. In contrast to this emphasis on fragmentation, Kohut emphasized coherence. And yet, Kohut's emphasis on the importance of a coherent and continuous sense of self was not without recognition of a vulnerability to fragmentation as one of the leading forms of self-pathology (Kohut, 1978c, p. 738). Because contemporary analysts underscore the multiplicity of selves and the ubiquitousness of fragmentation experiences within the range of "normal" functioning (Barratt, 1993; Mitchell, 1993; Aron, 1996), there is an implicit judgment that Kohut overstated the linkage between mental health and self-coherence. But Kohut (1978c) recognized a broad range of fragmentation experiences and even saw in the fragmented adult self a reflection of an earlier, normal stage of development; at this stage, "unstable, prepsychological fragments of the mind-body-self and its functions" predominate experience (p. 740). In Kohut's view, such modes of experiencing were the norm prior to "the birth of the nuclear self" (p. 741), a "birth" that he saw as a later developmental achievement evolving out of interaction with the selfobject milieu.

In spite of Kohut's recognition of a normative, early phase of fragmentation, he saw coherence as an indicator of adult health. At the same time, his emphasis on coherence in health may have expressed his appreciation of the tragic "fissility of personality" in vulnerable adults and his recognition that "the work of relating the bits to one another waited to be done" (Dinnage, 1996, p. 31). This integrative task obtained at the level of individual psychology as well as at the level of theory. And in the third quarter of the 20th century Kohut seems to have carried out that work of relating the bits to one another so effectively that the late 1980s and 90s inevitably brought us to the next set of problems or tasks. In the eyes of many, this new set of tasks importantly involves a breaking down, a destablizing, or a deconstruction of the seemingly too well put together Kohutian self (Barratt, 1993, 1995; Jacobson, 1997).

Like the Existential movement in philosophy, the Interpersonal school of psychoanalysis offered its own amendments to Freud's theory by emphasizing the exogenous, or relational, contribution to psychopathology. Rather than welcoming this apparent similarity to an aspect of his own thinking, however, Kohut (1971) contrasted his own ideas with Sullivan's, using the original American interpersonalist as an example of analysts with "a single-axis approach," who "give a prominent or even exclusive place in neurogenesis to the earliest developmental stages and to primitive mental organizations" (p. 281). Kohut's own approach was different in that he posited original self-development as spanning the years from birth through the oedipal period, with further essential consolidations during latency and adolescence. Therefore, for Kohut, differing qualities and degrees of psychopathogenesis could be set in motion at any stage of infancy or childhood.

Kohut further differentiated his thinking from Sullivan's by pointing to Sullivan's tendency to "understand . . . the various forms and varieties of psychopathology as degrees and nuances of psychosis or as defenses against it" (p. 281). We have already noted a similar emphasis on psychosis in some of the existential psychoanalytic writings. In contrast to the view ascribed to Sullivan, Kohut (1971, 1977a) clearly identified conditions in need of treatment that not only did not fall within the category of the psychoses, but also failed to fit the established diagnostic categories of borderline or neurotic psychopathologies. These were what Kohut at first labeled narcissistic personality disorders but were later and more broadly termed disorders of the self. Furthermore, rather than joining Sullivan in recognizing ubiquitous defenses against psychosis, Kohut (1977, 1984) focused on the *adaptive* aspects of phenomena that both classical and interpersonal analysts were more likely to perceive as defensive. In 1980, Kohut distanced himself even more explicitly from Sullivan's work. Replying to a query from Michael Ferguson concerning similarities between Sullivan's and Kohut's ideas, Kohut (1980) wrote that he had long before read something of Sullivan's (1947) and remembered it as "interesting but undisciplined: [m]ore the expansion of a gifted but pathological mind than a scientific contribution" (Cocks, 1994, p. 411). For further enlightenment, Kohut referred Ferguson to his (Kohut, 1978, pp. 150–166) discussion of "The Function of the Analyst" *The Search for the Self, Vol. 1*, but added that he doubted that Ferguson would be able to "discern (any)thing Sullivanian there" (Cocks, 1994, p. 411).

Thus, in spite of the fact that a "self-system" was central in Sullivan's (1953) work, any link between Sullivan's and Kohut's ideas are clearly incidental to Kohut's own intentions. What Sullivan called the interpersonal field, Kohut termed the self–selfobject matrix; and although their two different terms referred to something that an outside observer might see as one and the same phenomenon, the psychological meaning and function of the self–selfobject matrix in Kohut's understanding of experience was far different from Sullivan's interpersonal field. For instance, Sullivan's concept of self did not share with Kohut's a central importance in health: whereas Kohut elaborated the "poles" of the self and their functions in normal development, Sullivan (1953) saw the self primarily as a defensive structure that interfered with psychic development and normal relatedness (see also Mitchell, 1993). Unlike Sullivan and other interpersonalists, Kohut went to great lengths to articulate the elements of a *healthy* self, which efforts culminated in his exposition concerning the origins of ambitions, goals, and ideals in the self–selfobject matrix. Going far beyond Sullivan's acknowledgment of global interpersonal effects on individual development, Kohut identified particular, universally occurring self needs that had to be met in the interpersonal field, such as needs for omnipotent merger, mirroring, twinship, and idealization. He emphasized as well a particular quality of environmental input needed by the developing self, namely, a quality of empathic resonance or responsiveness. For Kohut, self–self-object relating was an essential and specific kind of interaction in the interpersonal field that was necessary to the development and maintenance of the self.

To move even further into conjecture: in a brief historical review of possible influences on Kohut's self psychology, we may also ask whether his emphasis on selfobject relating and on empathy, as essential ingredients for psychic survival and the self, might have grown out his exposure to, and meditations on, the horrors of the world wars, fascism, and the Holocaust. In 1938, when Kohut was 25 years old and still in medical school, Nazi Germany annexed Austria, where Kohut had been born and had lived up to that time (Cocks, 1994). Three months later, Kohut witnessed Freud's departure from Vienna, and early the following year he himself left Vienna for England, where he spent several months in a refugee camp awaiting papers that would enable him to emigrate to the United States (Kohut, 1939, cited in Cocks, 1994).

This intersection of world events and personal history must have left its mark both on Kohut's psyche and on his later theories, as he continued a lifelong struggle to come to terms with his experience. In a 1970 address given at the Free University in Berlin, Kohut (1978a) expressed a profound concern with humanity's aggression and directed the attention of his audience to the potential of psychoanalysis to influence society toward more harmonious pursuits through the deepening of the inner life of the individual. In two later lectures Kohut, (1978a, b) continued to see empathy as an essential bond between individuals and groups that could serve to diminish aggression.

Further corroboration of the notion that Kohut's particular self psychology might have reflected a preoccupation with the problem of mankind's aggression comes from Strozier (1980), who has drawn our attention to Kohut's (1971, 1972) insights into Hitler's early development and to Kohut's psychological explorations of the frightening readiness—and willingness—of Hitler's followers to execute his plans. Kohut understood all these phenomena in the context of his evolving psychology of the self, in which he saw the empathic surround as essential for healthy human development and sustenance. From this standpoint, one way of looking at the lives of Hitler and his henchmen was in terms of the dire consequences for the individual and the world when this essential ingredient from the environment is lacking in individual development. Kohut (1982) also suggested that beyond all the material horrors endured by Holocaust survivors, their exposure to the "impersonal, dehumanized" system of extermination, constituting "the total absence of empathy," added significantly to the already devastating psychological destructiveness of concentration camp experience (pp. 397–398).

Although the historical conjectures, the philosophical world views, and the psychoanalytic theories taken up thus far address ideas that overlap with elements of Kohut's self psychology, most of them were not directly or extensively discussed in Kohut's writings. In relation to Freud's thought, however, throughout his career, Kohut struggled explicitly to identify and communicate areas of agreement and disagreement. Freud's understanding of human motivation and development in terms of his theory of dual instincts and his tripartite structural theory became increasingly unsatisfactory to Kohut (1977a, 1978) as he tried to understand and work with his own analysands. Kohut (1971) also suggested that the development of his new theory took some of its impetus from his sense that something essential was not being addressed in his own analysis.

One might say, then, that, above all, Kohut's self psychology was an answer to what he felt were the limitations of Freud's drive theory. Where Freud saw sexual and aggressive instincts as the driving force of development, Kohut saw the need for a coherent and continuous sense of self. Freud (1916) postulated the capacity for love and work as the primary achievements of mental health, but these capacities developed only through sublimation, as derivatives of the instincts. For Kohut, the capacities for both love and work evolved directly from nondrive aspects of self, depending for their "unfolding" on the selective responsiveness of the child's human environment to her innate potentialities for affectionate attachment and for productive and creative self-expression. Kohut preferred to think of humanity as being pulled forward by ideals that were a subtle blend of inner and outer phenomena rather than being driven by purely internal, psychologically experienced biological forces.

Another difference in the theories of Freud and Kohut concerns their respective emphases on psychological wholeness versus discrete psychic agencies and mechanisms. In spite of Freud's having posited a synthesizing role for the ego, his elucidation of a tripartite psychic structure led to a classical analytic focus on discrete and mechanistic functions of the mind. Partially in response to this phenomenon, Kohut emphasized psychic experience rather than mechanisms and wholeness rather than parts. He gave the self a supraordinate, or transcendent, position in the psyche. This supraordinate structure, in health, contributed to synthesis (or coherence and continuity), but was also an experiencing (phenomenological) self and an initiating self (self as agent); these latter two aspects of human development had received little attention in much of Freud's theorizing.

Kohut himself drew our attention to other ways in which he was offering an alternative to Freud's view of the human individual. For instance, in his 1974 letter to Dr. L, Kohut (1978a, p. 137) noted that Freud tended to see humankind as primarily guilty, whereas Kohut (1974) saw it as primarily tragic. Tragic Man, wrote Kohut, "does not fear death as a symbolic punishment (castration) for forbidden pleasure aims (as does Guilty Man); he fears premature death, a death which prevents the realization of the aims of his nuclear self" (p. 757). Because in this passage Kohut was addressing himself only to the question of whether mankind is better characterized as guilty or tragic, he credited neither himself nor Freud with suggesting that individuals might also fear dying with a sense of unconnectedness to others. Nevertheless, it seems to be inconsistent with Kohut's writings in general that he spoke here of self-realization apart from selfobject relatedness, which surely would also be on the mind of his hypothetical Tragic Man as he confronted the prospect of his death. And, in 1982, Kohut actually wrote of the fear of death as "in many instances, the expression of the fear of the loss of the empathic milieu that in responding to the self keeps it *psychologically* alive" (p. 397).

By way of multiple pathways, then, Kohut's unique engagement with intellectual, political, and psychoanalytic history may have predisposed him to argue for an empathically sustained, coherent, and continuous sense of self as being at the center of the psychological universe, a universe that in health and good fortune would be populated by similar individuals in selfobject relatedness to one another. But, just as Kohut's theory may have been intended to "correct" certain problems of earlier intellectual positions, current theorists are now similarly making valiant attempts to resolve difficulties that they find in Kohut's body of thought. Kohut's theory is now sometimes thought of as containing too much self and not enough relationship; too much selfobject and not enough object; too much one-person subjectivity and not enough intersubjectivity; or too much coherence and continuity and not enough multiplicity, fragmentation, and discontinuity. We are now well into the era of the "problematization" of the self (Ricoeur, 1992; Protter, 1996), with many substantive issues still to be elucidated. But quite often contemporary discussions concerning the problems of the self seem to be addressed to a concept of self far removed from Kohut's as I understand it. Or, alternatively, we may ask, how many theoretical selves did Kohut have and express, such that we can find and critique within his writing such a multiplicity of meanings?

The Modern and Postmodern in Kohut's Writings on the Self

My thesis is that Kohut's ideas, in their different aspects, express both a modern and a postmodern sensibility, making it possible for different readers to find or critique the elements of his thought that represent either of these two trends. For instance, moving toward the postmodern, Kohut threw out the psychoanalytic foundations of the drives and the Oedipus complex as the cornerstones of personality and psychopathology. But, in line with the modern, Kohut offered an alternative system of meanings and givens centered on the development and maintenance of a sense of self. Again on the postmodern side, Kohut's theory anticipated the contemporary emphasis on fluidity and mutual influence among subjects: it was more experience near than Freud's theory; it saw the individual, in her selfobject relatedness, as more open and porous than did Freud's closed-system theory of the individual; and it saw the subject and object as fused (indivisible) in the empathic mode of observation, explicitly leaving behind Freud's claim for psychoanalysis as an objective science (Kohut, 1977a, 1982, 1984).

Despite the somewhat tendentious quality of his writing style, Kohut (1977a, 1984) often returned to a questioning of his own theories and made regular reminders to himself and his readers of the inevitable cultural and historical limitations of his own viewpoint, which he fully and explicitly expected to be amended across time and place (Kohut, 1977a, p. 308; see also Stepansky, 1989, p. 68). To the extent that Kohut preferred to leave things somewhat open and slightly unsettled, and to the extent that he refused to offer definitions, he was anticipating an aspect of postmodern theorizing.

For an example of such postmodern nonclosure, consider Kohut's response to countless requests to provide a definition of his concept of the self. He seemed to take great care that his answers to such questions would be at least as elusive as they were enlightening. In one context he replied as follows:

> "The self" is not a concept of an abstract science, but a generalization derived from . . . the set of introspectively or empathically perceived inner experiences to which we later refer as "I."
> . . . [W]e can observe certain characteristic vicissitudes of this experience. We can describe the various cohesive forms in which the self appears, can demonstrate the several constituents that make up the self . . . We can do all that, but *we will still not know the essence of the self* as differentiated from its manifestations [Kohut, 1977a, pp. 310–311; italics added].

In this not atypical rendering, Kohut speaks as much about what the self is not as about what it is. It is not synonymous with its various forms of appearance, it is not synonymous with its several constituents, it is not synonymous with its manifestations. Rather, Kohut uses the term self to refer only to a *generalization* derived from the set of introspectively and empathically perceived inner experiences to which I later refer as "I." This avoidance of pinning things down seemed to express Kohut's own postmodern sensibility, a sensibility that alternated with and interpenetrated the more modern (foundational and structured) aspects of his thinking. Again, the postmodern seemed to prevail when he raised questions concerning the origins of the self:

> The crucial question concerns, of course, the point in time when, within the matrix of mutual empathy between the infant and his self-object, the baby's innate potentialities and the self-object's expectations with regard to the baby converge. *Is it permissible to consider this juncture the point of origin of the infant's primal, rudimentary self?* [Kohut, 1977a, p. 99; italics added].

Although even to search for a "point in time" suggests a linear, and therefore modern, developmental viewpoint, we also see Kohut here giving his answer in the form of a question and making it impossible to say whether he would place the point of origin of the self at the moment of conception, at the moment of birth, or at some later moment in the early months of life. While refusing to assign the birth of the self a precise temporal moment, Kohut did suggest that the origins and the substance of self reside in the convergence between the baby's potentialities and the selfobject's expectations. His emphasis on this convergence seems to counter certain relational critiques of self psychology that fault it for being a "one-person" rather than a "two-person" psychology: the two persons in this instance being a baby who has potentialities and a parent who has expectations. There is much more to this debate than I can appropriately address in the context of a chapter on the self; further aspects of the "one-person" critique are taken up in chapters that address intersubjectivity and other relational issues.

Alongside these postmodern leanings, Kohut did much to elucidate his concept of self in a traditionally modern mode. He imputed universal status to the self and described in exquisite detail the quality of its experience and its constituents. Taken on its surface only, and outside of the context of his own qualifying commentary, Kohut's argument for a nuclear, bipolar self, the primary function of which was to give its "owner" a sense of coherence and continuity, was anything but deconstructionist. Even within his own apparently delimited, experiential/ structural theory, however, Kohut's self entailed fluidity, motion, direction, richness, worth, growth, and enhancement. Not all these qualities of experience conferred by a "robust" self were spelled out explicitly in Kohut's writings, but each one of them was at least strongly implied. The healthy and robust self provides experiences of affective fluidity and motion (through empathic openness to others); it can yield an experience of directedness (through ambitions and goals); it has a quality of richness (through the integration and expression of the broadest and deepest array of self experiences from birth to death, and as opposed to impoverishment, which Kohut equated with self pathology); it contributes to feelings of worth (through the exercise of one's skills and talents and through working toward the accomplishment of one's goals); it is constantly undergoing expansion and growth (through efforts to resolve the inevitable tension between one's actual and ideal selves); and it is capable of enhancement (through relationships with admired others and through a lifelong process of internalizing ideals).

In Kohut's view, all these experiences of self depended on the availability of responsive selfobjects throughout the life cycle. Of course, there is a difference in the degree of need, as well as in the quality of responsiveness needed, based on the individual's level of self development. Therefore, Kohut (1984) distinguished between archaic selfobject need, pertaining to the "beginnings," or original development, of the self, and more mature selfobject need, which pertained to the maintenance or enhancement of a more fully developed and cohesive self (p. 49). Consistent with this distinction between archaic and more mature selfobject experiences, selfobject needs never disappeared but rather were transformed as psychological development proceeded toward greater maturity. Mature relationships, for Kohut, involved a mutual giving and receiving in the self–selfobject realm.

Kohut (1977a) was explicit about mutuality, even in early development, when he spoke of "the matrix of mutual empathy between the infant and his self-object" (p. 99). He also wrote of "the mutual selfobject functions that the partners in a good marriage provide for each other," and defined a good marriage as "one in which one or the other partner rises to the challenge of providing the selfobject functions that the other's temporarily impaired self needs at a particular moment" (Kohut, 1984, p. 220n). Although in this context Kohut referred to a "quip" that in a good marriage "only one partner is crazy at any given time," the weight of his more serious remarks comes down on the side of mutual involvement in a good marriage and the role flexibility of both partners in providing temporarily needed selfobject functions for each other.

In addition to these explicit references to the mutuality of selfobject functioning in mother–child and marital relationships, the mutuality of selfobject relating was also implied in Kohut's conviction that healthy development (and successful analytic treatment) lead to greater capacities for humor, wisdom, and empathy. All such qualities facilitate one's ability to provide selfobject functioning for others. I suggest that Kohut did not emphasize this mutuality of selfobject relating in healthy or mature adulthood because he was more intent on addressing the critical question of how an individual, in the beginning, is able to develop and maintain "a self." But, since each individual develops and maintains a self only through selfobject relatedness, Kohut must have assumed that every healthy or mature self is necessarily engaged with others in the mutual fulfilment of selfobject needs. If not, who would the fulfilling selfobjects be in friendships, marriages, collegial interactions, and parent–offspring relationships into old age? Especially in optimal peer relationships (i.e., with spouses, lovers, friends, and colleagues), selfobject functioning must be reciprocal, even if not always simultaneous.

The potential for reading into Kohut's writings a multifaceted and relational view of the self should not minimize appreciation of the traditionally modern tendencies in his theory. My point, once more, is that his self psychology plays out the modern even as it anticipates the postmodern. Although the concept of the self has been criticized in postmodern literature for its singular emphasis on coherence and continuity, a thorough reading of Kohut's work allows for a broader and richer interpretation of these terms than the postmodern theorists tend to make. For instance, often criticism argues against a unity of self, but unity is a term that Kohut did not use and did not intend to convey by his emphasis on coherence and continuity. These latter notions were far removed from any sense of self characterized by unidimensionality, rigidity, or "thingness." In point of fact, Kohut implied and placed a value on psychological fluidity, openness, and motion through his concept of mature selfobject relating and by his insistence on internalized ideals and goals as an ongoing source of tension moving the individual toward the future. Although Kohut (1977a) spoke of the origins of ambitions and ideals as being "laid down" in the earliest interactions between parents and children, he also suggested that in health these aspects of the self remain open to change and continue to evolve throughout adult life in ongoing and lifelong interactions with others within the selfobject milieu.

PART II

KOHUT'S AND LOEWALD'S
IDEAS AND THE
POSTMODERN RESPONSE

THE SELF IN KOHUT'S WORK AND IN
POSTMODERN DISCOURSE

There are long stretches of time in a normal infant's life in which a baby does not mind whether he is many bits or one whole being . . . provided that from time to time he comes together and feels something.

—D. W. Winnicott

Analysis gives me confidence that I can express all the parts of my being.

—Julia Kristeva

Kohut's self psychology is a theory of how, through certain dimensions of relationships with significant others, the individual "comes together and feels something," a theory of how the individual develops a sense of self that enables an optimal expression of "all the parts of [her] being." Some of the commonalities between Kohut's ideas and those of others' may be obfuscated by differences in language, style, and formality of presentation. There are, however, substantive differences, as well, between Kohut's thought and that of the postmoderns, differences that have real implications for how an analysis might be conducted. Since in Loewald's work the self was largely implicit, his thought does not figure importantly in this discussion. I will come back to Loewald in later explorations of the selfobject concept, intergenerational conflict, and the analytic relationship, through which his ideas of the analyst's role in relation to developmental needs and his notions concerning autonomy of the self are elaborated.

In this chapter I present and discuss the postmodern critiques of Kohut's ideas, particularly his concept of self. Besides looking at work that explicitly grapples with concepts from Kohut's self psychology, I include writings that have not directly named Kohut as a target of criticism but that raise questions about the notion of self and thereby constitute an implicit critique of his work. Indeed, there is a growing literature in philosophy and psychoanalysis that addresses what has been labeled the "problematization of the self" (Ricoeur, 1992; Jacobson, 1997; Protter, 1996).

Is the self unitary or multiple, coherent or fragmented, continuous or discontinuous, bounded or permeable, completed or in process? Is it biologically or interpersonally constituted, autonomous or embedded, separate from or connected to others, known or unknowable, real or illusory? If it should turn out to be multiple, fragmented, discontinuous, permeable, in process, interpersonally constituted, relationally embedded, irrevocably connected to others, unknowable to self or other, and illusory, is it any longer a self? These are some of the questions that contribute to the problematization of the self.

Postmodern Critiques of Kohut's Self: Coherence, Continuity, Unity, Autonomy

Kohut (1984), was not unaware of problems with his self concept, and it is his sensitivity to these problems that contributes to the tension in his writings between the modern and the postmodern: between establishing fundamentals or universals, on one hand, and recognizing the idiosyncracy and immediacy of individual experience, on the other; between itemizing the "constituents" of a bounded self and acknowledging the fluidity among subjects; between establishing cause and effect from early childhood experience to psychopathology in adulthood and insisting on the open-ended creative potential of the individual. Nevertheless, in contemporary analytic discourse, Kohut's theory of self has been identified almost exclusively with concepts of unity, autonomy, boundedness, and fixedness. Thus, by the mid-1980s, newer theories began to place much more emphasis on the *process quality of self*. As an influential representative of this shift, Kristeva (1987) writes: "[W]e are subjects *in process*, ceaselessly losing our identity, destablized by fluctuations in our relations to the other" (p. 9). Commenting on the continuation of this trend in Barratt's (1993) book on the postmodern impulse, Sass (1995) writes:

> For Barratt, human existence consists in the aleatory freedom of a wandering, ever-transmuting kind of *nonself*. He opposes any attempt to achieve "ideological stasis," any attempt to reduce the fundamental ambiguity and mobility, what he calls the vital "contradictoriousness" and "incessant transmutation" of the "subject-in-process" [p. 127; italics added].

Not just Kristeva and Barratt, well known for their radical postmodern viewpoints, but also a more moderate voice such as Mitchell's (1993) has recognized that "consciousness itself is fragmentary, discontinuous, . . . complex and inaccessible" (p. 54). And for me, I have only to catch one moment of my own fleeting reveries, listen to two analytic patients, or read three pages of James Joyce's *Ulysses*, to be reminded of these special qualities of consciousness. But must this recognition of the fragmentary and discontinuous nature of consciousness lead us to reject Kohut's emphasis on a healthy sense of coherence and continuity (a rejection, be it noted, in which Mitchell himself does not participate)? I think not.

Kohut (1977a) spoke of the "sense of continuity despite change" (p. 312), and by analogy we may assume that he also postulated a need for a sense of coherence despite or because of inevitable transient experiences of disintegration and fragmentation. I think that Kohut may have meant that we need a sense of continuity *because* of the discontinuities in modern living and in development; and that we need a sense of coherence exactly *because* of the complexity and multifaceted nature of our lives and our psyches, *because* of the multiplicity of our roles and relationships. As Mitchell (1993), even in the midst of presenting the contemporary argument for multiple selves, reminds us, "[t]he experience of self as singular and constant serves an important adaptive, psychological purpose" (p. 110). With the postmodern emphasis on multiple selves and the discontinuities of experience, Mitchell's (and Kohut's) point about the adaptive functionality or necessity of coherence and continuity often gets lost.

To say that we need a *sense* of coherence and continuity denies neither the experience of multiplicity, the human potentiality for fragmentation and discontinuity, nor that this "sense" may even in part be based on an illusion (Mitchell, 1993). In Kohut's theory, our needs for *feelings* of coherence and continuity are directly related to our very potentialities for all those opposite kinds of experiencing; small and reversible disruptions in these feelings (i.e., mild and short-lived fragmentation experiences and discontinuities) are within the range of normal functioning. In fact, Kohut (1984) described a continuum of mental health in which he placed the greatest vulnerability to fragmentation at the most pathological end (pp. 8–9). But in his schema, "brittle" defenses and other psychic rigidities tended to accompany or alternate with fragmentation at the more severely psychopathological end of the continuum (p. 9). The implied corollary of his recognition of brittleness and rigidity as related to pathology is that greater openness and flexibility would denote health in a context allowing for the broadest possible array of choices for self-expression. I am suggesting that the fullness, richness, and flexibility associated with Kohut's notion of the "robust self" might be close to what moderate postmodern analysts refer to as "a multiplicity of selves" (Mitchell, 1993; Aron, 1996). But this latter notion does not connote the degree of formlessness and fluidity implied by the more radical concept of "self as process" (Kristeva, 1987; Barratt, 1993).

Some of the confusion in the debates about multiple versus coherent selves can perhaps be clarified by asking what some of the differences might be between those who are diagnosed with "multiple personality disorder" and those who simply live out and express multiple aspects of a more healthy self from one relationship or situation to the next. One difference is that the individual with a so-called sense of coherence can often bring to mind many different aspects of self, can prioritize them at a given moment or within a particular context, can feel the incompatibilities and discontinuities as well as some sense of sameness, continuity, or connection running through them all. Conversely, the healthy individual can also surrender her sense of coherence in the pursuit of artistic creation or pleasure and reengage it as needed. In the patient suffering from what might be called multiple personality disorder, however, the multiple selves cannot be recognized or acknowledged and cannot at any time or for any purpose be brought together. Mitchell (1993) has made a similar point, acknowledging psychopathology when "there is no sense of continuity from one self-organization to the next" (p. 108). In multiple personality disorders, each of these isolated self fragments is more vulnerable to further breakdown than are transient fragmentation products in other individuals and thus frequently render ordinary functioning out of reach.

It is in contrast to these severely dysfunctional phenomena and their milder versions that Kohut spoke of a sense of coherence as an experience to strive for in health: an experiential quality that comes into being through relationships and that is furthered by the development and lived expression of talents and skills in a vitalizing selfobject milieu. This sense of coherence, argued Kohut, in turn makes possible greater mutuality in relationships, as well as the setting of goals, the pursuit of ambitions, and the striving toward ideals: what we might call love, work, and transcendence. All these "achievements" Kohut attributed to a coherent and continuous sense of selfhood and its structural coordinate, "the self."

It is understandable that Kohut's emphasis on coherence and continuity should lead many contemporary readers to misinterpret him as suggesting a unidimensionality, a boundedness, and a rigid fixity of self. Much of the current discourse concerning the self centers on whether one needs to have—indeed, whether one can have—a coherent and continuous sense of self in the face of the undeniable complexity, richness, and multifaceted nature of lived experience. Those analysts who lean more toward the postmodern tend to view any such sense as based primarily on illusion (Lacan, 1977; see also discussions by Mitchell, 1993, and Mitchell and Black, 1995), or on arbitrary foreclosure of multiple alternative selves (Barratt, 1993, 1995). The ontological issue, however, is whether we can go about the business of living without a subjective sense of cohesion (Stepansky, 1997, personal communication). Although Lacan (1977), Barratt (1993), and others seem to insist that we can and must give up this illusory sense of self, it is difficult for me to imagine that Barratt himself, for instance, without the sense of self or identity that he theoretically rejects as a foreclosure, could have decided on a project of value and interest to him, such as a book on the postmodern impulse, carried out the sustained research necessary to implement it, and motivated and organized himself to do the writing. In other words, without such concepts as ambitions, goals, and ideals in the Kohutian sense, how can we understand the processes through which any personally meaningful project is chosen, sustained, and implemented?

Is Barratt engaging in a level of discourse that I have failed to grasp when he seems to deny that a subjective sense of self as coherent and continuous is, at the very least, a functional necessity for the business of living a life in the western world as we know it today? Or is he, having made the judgment that such organizations as have evolved thus far seem to have led us to destroy one another and our planet, perhaps making a plea for a thoroughgoing change in how our psyches (and societies) have been organized in recent centuries? If the latter interpretation comes closer to Barratt's meaning and intent, then his proposals for change emanate from admirable concerns. But how could such changes, were we to agree on their desirability, be facilitated? And how would we deal with the inevitable collapse of persons and societies in the wake of such a seemingly unimaginable transformation?

Barratt (1993, 1995) seems to deconstruct the self as we have known it but offers nothing in its place beyond the flux of consciousness and the unconscious. As noted earlier, Kohut (1970) certainly shared some of Barratt's concerns about the direction in which mankind was going and suggested that a greater emphasis on shared cultural values, artistic/creative self-expression, and the inner life might ease rising tensions. I believe that Kohut's concept of selfobject relating may offer a further solution to the problem of aggression and destructiveness in human societies to the extent that how we theorize about the self can have an impact on how we live our individual and communal lives.

The views of self put forth respectively by Kohut and Barratt offer stark contrasts. There are, however, postmodern analysts proffering ideas more compatible with Kohut's concept of self, in particular his notion of a self that emerges out of selfobject relationships and is sustained by them. Outstanding among these is Kristeva (1987), who writes: "The analyst looks forward to the ultimate dissolution of desire . . . to be replaced by relationship with another, from which meaning derives" (p. 63). Kristeva believes that Freud's focus on man's desire represented "the culmination of the nihilist program" (p. 60), and she approvingly suggests that, in contrast to the self of desire, the postmodern "self has . . . subordinated itself to the other for the sake of a necessary, if temporary, tie" (p. 62). In her radical departure from Freud's drive theory, Kristeva seems to have moved beyond even Kohut by envisioning a psychic world in which desire is not only peripheral, but is entirely dissolved: *a world in which the self prevails only through its bonds with others.* Though Kristeva identifies herself as a French intellectual, an analyst, and a feminist philosopher, her position is in fascinating contrast to such American feminist analysts as Benjamin, whose ideas are introduced later in this chapter.

For Kristeva (1987), the dissolution of desire is equated with the dissolution of subjectivity (p. 62), and these valued dissolutions are achieved through the individual's (transient but repeated) "subordination" of herself to the other. This self-subordination calls to mind Kohut's concept of an analytic selfobject relationship, in which the individual strives for a sustained immersion in the other's experience, and a life-long search for what is ideal in the other. According to Kristeva, when this self-subordination is reciprocal, there is no danger of exploitation or domination of one individual over another, no danger of one person's desire or subjectivity being forced upon another. In fact, it is this very capacity for self-subordination and the human bonds that it makes possible that serve to preserve the larger society and to create the moral basis for human life. Both Kristeva and Kohut thus recognize that, on one hand, we need a relatively coherent sense of self in order to create our lives and live them but that, on the other hand, too much attachment to our own individual self-coherence can make us insensitive to the needs of others (our "fellow subjectivities") and to the world around us. Kohut's notion of selfobject relating, I submit, allows for interactions that affirm individual self-coherence and at the same time create or consolidate necessary bonds between individuals.

Again, we can conclude that Kohut's dual concepts of self and self-object represent a dialectic, unnamed as such in his own theorizing, that predates the postmoderns and is compatible with their world views. I have already noted that Mitchell (1993) explicitly acknowledges both the illusory quality and the adaptive utility of a sense of coherence. Aron (1996), resonating with Mitchell on this point, suggests that one goal of psychoanalysis is to help patients "achieve a cohesive self, a solid identity . . . {while} another goal is to give them access to their multiplicities" (p. 154). In further enumerating the desired outcomes of psychoanalysis, Aron includes as one goal the achievement of viewing oneself "as autonomous agent, center of one's own experience, having *a core and cohesive self,* and as a center of subjectivity" (p. 153). Interestingly, Aron, whose book is full of generous and meticulous references to other writers, does not here cite Kohut as an influential proponent of these ideas. Could it be that, in spite of the ongoing critique of Kohut's work, some of his ideas have become so commonly accepted that they are completely integrated into contemporary theorists' basic assumptions?

At the same time that Aron includes the achievement of a cohesive self as being among the goals of psychoanalysis, he also invokes the ability "to recognize oneself as an object among other objects, including [recognizing oneself as] the object of the other's desire." And he adds still another capability, that of being able "to view the other as both an autonomous subject and (as) the object of one's (own) desires." Aron concludes: "Achieving these capabilities and maintaining the tension between them may be viewed as a principal goal of psychoanalysis" (p. 153). Aron's view of psychoanalysis resonates with themes earlier taken up by Benjamin (1988) and makes a unique contribution by going beyond Kohut's emphasis on the cohesive and unfolding self. These different, relational aspects of self are taken up in later sections of the book when we turn to the feminist critique and contemporary writings on relationship, subjectivity, and intersubjectivity.

Since Kohut consistently avoided attributing a "thingness" or a "location" to the self, and since he consistently spoke of the *sense* of coherence and continuity rather than of coherence and continuity per se, I think it might be accurate to say that coherence and continuity were for him primarily experiential phenomena, regularly associated with psychic health; therefore he set up both as developmental achievements and treatment goals. The intrapsychic and structural aspects of Kohut's theory were simply an extension of his empathically derived observation that reliable external or interactional phenomena (i.e., adequate parental selfobject functioning) contribute to more or less stable patterns of internal experience (an adequate "structuring" of the self) in the developing individual. Once established through (optimal) relational experience, these relatively stable internal phenomena or psychic structures enable individuals to weather the storms of external fortune or misfortune in more intact states than might otherwise be possible. Thus, although Kohut did postulate (self) structure, the phenomenological and the structural aspects of his theory were never very far apart. Kohut's self was, above all, an experiential self, and his notion of self structure was always directly linked to its experiential base and experiential consequences.

Kohut's "Grand Narrative" and the Postmodern Response

For Kohut, to have normal self structure meant simply to have reliable-*enough* patterns of self experience: with such patterns, an individual would be able to experience a sense of well-being and to harness inborn potential into a richly expressive life in relationships and personal achievement. The alternative to richness of self was the impoverished or depleted self presented for treatment. The impoverished self for Kohut was fragile and fragmentation prone owing to its disavowal and the exclusion of large tracts of early experience related to fantasies of grandiosity, fantasies required for psychic survival at a particular stage of early development. With too much of the individual's early fantasy life and experience excluded from its organization, the self became impoverished and therefore fragile. In Kohut's view, grandiose fantasies were based on developmentally normal feelings of vigor and perfection (Kohut and Wolf, 1978). These early self experiences required an optimal responsiveness from the human environment in order to be, first, mirrored or affirmed and then "tamed" and integrated through inevitable but minor disappointments in one's own and the caregiver's capacities. These titrated disappointments went hand in hand with increasing recognition of growing skills and real achievements.

Parents who erred by either failing to modulate their offspring's grandiosity at the appropriate stage (by a gradually more accurate mirroring process), or by squashing the child's stage-appropiate grandiosity (through a refusal to mirror), set the stage for an impoverishment of self in their developing child. Without the parents' optimal responsiveness to the child's grandiosity, overwhelmingly intense self experiences would either destablize the child or would constrict the child by being split off and disavowed. If such overwhelming experiences were split off, the child (and later the adult) would tend to be unduly inhibited and without affect in relation to ambitions and goals; if not split off, ambitions and goals would tend to be overreaching and infused with an unmodulated excitement that would interfere with their achievement. The relational corollary to these states of self involved an individual who was either radically cut off from, or overwhelmingly needy of, affirming responses from the environment or who tended to experience dramatic oscillations between these two states. Kohut undertook to spell out the route by which an adult in psychoanalysis might retrieve or integrate (or both) these lost riches of the self, which involved the analyst's acceptance of, optimal responsiveness to, and eventual interpretation of, the patient's reawakened grandiosities, often expressed in the form of overreaching ambitions, goals, or ideals as they began to emerge in treatment.

This Kohutian grand narrative of how impoverishment of self is avoided and self potential realized is a modern and not postmodern phenomenon. Contemporary relationists tend to focus on present psychoanalytic interactions and avoid universal historical narratives. Cause-and-effect hypotheses between early experience and current suffering also tend to be minimized in postmodern theorizing. These theoretical and clinical trends present a challenge when contemporary relational theorists discuss how psychoanalytic treatment can make a difference in what sometimes begins to look like a here-and-now vacuum chamber.

Kohut's attention to issues concerning impoverishment versus richness of self are echoed in Mitchell's (1993) work, where Mitchell repeatedly suggests that increased "richness of experience" is a primary goal of psychoanalysis. This richness resists definition because it refers to the broadest array and texture of human experience. Mitchell tells us, however, that "[s]atisfaction and the relative richness of life have a great deal to do with the dialectic between multiplicity and integrity in the experience of self, the balance between discontinuity and continuity" (p. 116). And he adds that "[w]here there is too much discontinuity, there is a dread of fragmentation, splitting, dislocation, or dissolution [and where] there is too much continuity, there is a dread of paralysis and stagnation" (p. 116).

Kohut (1977a) explicitly recognized the chaos and terror of too little psychic integrity and continuity but did not often address the potential for "too much continuity." He did, however, emphasize ongoing needs for idealizable (self)objects, which suggests, in health, a life-long openness to transformative internalizations (Kohut, 1977a; 1984). Kohut (1971, 1977a, 1978a, 1984) also described analytic treaments in which the analysand arrived at creative solutions to old problems, and he emphasized playfulness and creativity in general as outcomes of healthy development and successful analytic treatments. Empathy, humor, and wisdom, which Kohut (1971) saw as further hallmarks of mental health and maturity, all seem to be qualities that entail psychological movement and openness rather than paralysis and stagnation. Thus Kohut would hardly have taken exception to Mitchell's characterization of the dialectic between multiplicity and integrity in the experience of self.

Still, Mitchell (1993) and other contemporary analysts feel constrained by Kohut's construction of richness or impoverishment in terms of the integration of early grandiose fantasies and idealizations or of later ambitions, goals, and ongoing selfobject relatedness. Many of Kohut's critics seem not to recognize just how much of human experience he intended to encompass within these concepts, as indicated by a complete reading of his published case presentations (Kohut, 1971, 1977a, b, 1984), his discussion of historical events (1977a; 1978), public figures (1977, 1978a), creativity (1977a, 1984), and the arts (1978a). Furthermore, the major psychoanalytic theme that is omitted or underemphasized in Kohut's theory (i.e., instinctual experience, understood as constitutionally determined and as the primary motivator in human life) tends to be omitted or underemphasized in most of the relational theories as well. But, although Kohut did not subscribe to Freud's drive theory and did not assign to instinctual life a central place in personality development or psychopathology, he still recognized a "body–mind–self" and the importance for the self of experiences that originate in the body (Kohut, 1971, p. 152; pp. 214–218). Be that as it may, relational theorists such as Mitchell feel they are pursuing a non-self-psychological agenda as they strive to broaden and deepen the basis for richness to include the widest array of bodily, intrapsychic, and interpersonal experience. And yet it was Kohut who consistently directed analysts to resonate empathically to *all* the different kinds of experience that analysands might bring. On this and other points, the differences between Kohut's self theory and Mitchell's relational/conflict theory may be more apparent than real.

In fact, in my view, the similarities between the theories are at least as compelling as the differences. Both Kohut and Mitchell speak to the goal of richness and authenticity of self, and both believe that the self emerges through an individual's relational experiences. The differences between their viewpoints lie primarily in divergent conceptualizations of what contributes to richness and authenticity and of what is essential and curative in relationships.

In particular, Mitchell and other postmoderns see an important role for the analyst in mobilizing the patient's relational patterns in the transference and helping him or her move beyond them. To this end, they tend to emphasize direct, interpersonal engagement and authentic self-expression on the part of the analyst, in contrast to Kohut's greater emphasis on the analyst's affective resonance with, and communication of, empathic understanding of the patient's experience. Up to a point, Kohut seemed to suggest that, once the analyst, through understanding and explaining, had "restored" the patient's self development, the patient's object relationships would spontaneously take care of themselves. He seemed to believe that the once-impoverished self, having over sustained periods of time received affective responsiveness coupled with cognitive understanding and explanation concerning early development, would gradually become robust. With robustness thus restored, the individual would be able to express creatively her richness and authenticity; to wrestle with, resolve, or tolerate conflict; and to find "objects" with whom she can forge maturely gratifying relationships. In contrast, the relational theorists try to elaborate the qualities of relationship beyond selfobject responsiveness and functioning that might foster richness and authenticity of self. They place their emphasis on the analyst experienced as a separate and different other, rather than on the analyst experienced as an extension of the analysand's self. This emphasis on the relationship between two separate and different others tends to lead to a new postmodern interest in conflict, especially interpersonal conflict, which is absent in Kohut's theory. In Mitchell's and in Slavin and Kriegman's (1992, 1998) writings particularly, we see once again a central role for conflict in human experience, but a role that does not follow Freud's formulation of intrapsychic conflict.

Further discussion of these differences between Kohut and the postmodern analysts is reserved for chapters focusing on relationship and conflict. For now I am simply observing that there is a paradox at the heart of Kohut's and Mitchell's perspectives alike. Mitchell (1993) may have unwittingly touched on it by observing: "In contemporary analysis, . . . the most important question to be asked has shifted to: How meaningful and authentic is a person's experience and expression of herself?" (pp. 132–133, italics added). Although we tend to think that relational theories have burgeoned at this moment in history at least partly in response to what was perceived as an excessive emphasis on the self in Kohut's theory, Mitchell clearly believes that *at the heart of most relational theories, there is still an essential concern with the experience and expression of an individual self.* Mitchell's focus on self in his relational theory presents us with the mirror image of the paradox at the center of Kohut's theory, *because at the heart of self psychology, there is always an essential concern with the experience of relationship.*

As noted, one significant way of understanding the contemporary emergence of relational theories is in terms of a perception that Kohut's view of relationship was too narrowly focused on the construction, maintenance, and enhancement of self, to the exclusion of other dimensions of human interaction. The postmoderns (Hoffman, 1983, 1994, 1996; Benjamin, 1988; Aron, 1992, 1996; Mitchell, 1993, 1996a; Renik, 1993, 1996) therefore emphasize the subjectivity, authenticity, and self-expression of the analyst (or parent) in explicit or implicit protest against what they feel to be Kohut's constricted emphasis on the self-object function of the analyst (or parent). These theorists want to broaden our understanding of the kinds of interactions that go into a relationship and the kinds of interactions that go into constructing a self; they also want to expand the range of meanings imputed to these diverse kinds of interactions by the developing individual. Near the end of his life, Kohut (1984) himself spoke of wanting to widen his lens and focus on aspects of relationship beyond the provision of selfobject function (p. 53). He hoped that such a broadened focus would become the next step in the development of self psychology and suggested that his own original narrower focus on selfobject aspects of relating had been necessary as a corrective to Freud's almost exclusive attention to the drive-discharge dimension of relatonships in classical theory.

The Postmodern Analysts On Kohut's Ideas: Dimensions of Self and Relationship

Among the postmodern analysts, Mitchell (1993, 1996; Mitchell and Black, 1995) stands out as one who has given a most careful reading to Kohut's work; he explicitly recognizes and credits his contribution while offering a thoughtful critique. As an indication of how seriously Mitchell (1993) explores the concept of self, we note first that he devotes three chapters of *Hope and Dread* to discussing it. Aron (1996) has also given a fair-minded appraisal of Kohut's ideas, while other postmoderns have tended to present his work more summarily than either Aron or Mitchell has and with less consistency. For example, Hoffman (1983) criticizes an incomplete rendering of Kohut's selfobject concept and questions Kohut's self-psychological focus on empathy (Hoffman, 1994); Benjamin (1988, 1990), acknowledging some areas of overlap between Kohut's and her own ideas, at the same time arrives at a close convergence with certain other of his ideas with no apparent recognition of Kohut as their source; Stolorow and Atwood (1992) emphasize and extend the intersubjective aspects of Kohut's theory but go on to criticize what seems to be a significant misrepresentation of his thought in what they call the "myth of the isolated mind"; and Renik (1993) criticizes certain ideas that seem to derive from Kohut's self psychology but without citing his work as the object of the critical analysis.

While offering his own radical critique of Freud's blank screen metaphor, Hoffman (1983) has identified Kohut, Loewald, Strachey, and Stone as "conservative" critics of Freud's notion. Hoffman credits these authors with "some kind of amplification of the realistically benign and facilitating aspects of the therapsit's influence" (p. 396); but he faulted Kohut, in particular, for conveying "the impression that a friendly, naturally responsive attitude on the part of the analyst will promote the unfolding of transference . . . without specific reference to other aspects of the analyst's personality" (p. 400). Although Hoffman was perhaps expressing a legitimate concern with the narrowness of Kohut's (selfobject) relational focus, his 1983 representation of Kohut's ideas seems to reduce the entire selfobject concept to a "friendly, naturally responsive attitude." In 1994, Hoffman again lumped Kohut with another theorist, this time with fellow "deficit" theorist Winnicott. Hoffman suggests that, while Kohut and Winnicott "legitimized certain kinds of gratification as an intrinsic part of the psychoanalytic process," they "introduced a new kind of institutionalized disguise for personal, countertransferential tendencies" (p. 196). But since postmodern analysts emphasize that *all* theorizing expresses the subjectivity (and therefore presumably the "countertransferential tendencies") of its authors, it is not clear why Kohut and Winnicott should be singled out in this regard. Do their theories express countertransferential tendencies to a greater degree than do, for instance, those of the postmodern analysts, whose theories are concerned with issues of the analyst's self-expression, authenticity, and self-disclosure?

Hoffman (1994) also expresses concern that the self psychologist's "conformity" to the " 'benign' principle" of sustained empathic inquiry could "cast the shadow of the bad object on the analyst" (p. 191). Citing Slavin and Kriegman (1992) to support this viewpoint, he quotes a passage in which they refer to empathy practiced "as a technique, rather than as [a] general intimate act and sign of mutuality." Slavin and Kriegman further describe the self psychologist as one "whose only substantial utterances take the form of validating affirmations of the patient's own subjective world and developmental strivings" (pp. 252–253);

they add that such an analyst is necessarily engaged in one or another kind of self-deception (p. 253).

In citing Slavin and Kriegman's comments, Hoffman joins those authors in a caricature of the self psychologist that portrays her more as an *empathy machine* (an oxymoron, I suggest) than as an individual struggling to find an empathic *connection* between her own experience and that of the analysand. An equivalent critique of the postmodern analytic stance would be to suggest that every analyst writing about the analyst's subjectivity or self-expression is a veiled narcissist, unable to focus attention on anyone outside himself; or that those contemporary analysts arguing for negotiation as an aspect of the analytic relationship (i.e., Slavin and Kriegman, 1992) are aggressive egotists exploiting the vulnerability of their patients in dealings that are rigged from the start owing to the analyst's relative position of power. Such assertions are sustainable only by removal of the authors' words from their original contexts and an almost willful distortion of their authors' intent; they involve a ludicrous exaggeration of an author's central point through the portrayal of a mindless and perseverative execution of a recommended stance. In spite of this transient lapse, Hoffman's (1994) rendering of Kohut's concept of empathy is not typical of his usual dealings with others' ideas. Least of all can such exaggerations accurately be applied to Hoffman (1983, 1994, 1996) himself, who despite his sometimes less than optimal treatment of self psychology, has moved toward ever-increasing richness, complexity, and balance in the presentation of his own ideas. This movement is evident particularly in his portrayal of the analyst's tension and struggle to remain true to the multiple dialectics of the analytic situation.

Aron (1992) credits Kohut, Winnicott, and Loewald with having made significant contributions to changes in how contemporary analysts view interpetation in the analytic process. He sees Kohut as having "shifted the focus of our interpretive efforts from explanation to understanding and [as having] proposed that new experience with the analyst as selfobject is as important as explanation" (p. 491). Aron (1996) offers an excellent précis of self psychology and its areas of difference and overlap with other relational theories:

> Self psychology makes an important contribution to clinical psychoanalysis in its emphasis on the need for the analyst to be responsive and empathic; in recognizing the vital experience of emotional attunement . . . ; and in its rich description of self-

object transferences. Self psychology, however . . . in the work of its more conservative practitioners, maintains an emphasis both on a one-person psychology, by placing the self in a supraordinate position, and on the individual's talents and ideals. More important, however, self psychology in its conservative form maintains the classical view that who the analyst is as a unique character is irrelevant to the process of the analysis [p. 53].

Aron's comments cut to the heart of critiques of ("conservative") self psychology. In fact, much of the postmodern movement is engaged in "rounding out" the relational field, which was placed in center stage by self psychology but with the spotlight focused almost exclusively on the selfobject aspects of relating. I argue, however, that, although Kohut was far less adept than Benjamin, Hoffman, Aron, and Mitchell at pointing out the dialectics of his own theory, his theory nevertheless embodies significant tensions between a "one-person" and a "two-person" psychology. Aron (1992) suggests that Kohut's supraordinate self was one of the features of self psychology that rendered it a one-person, as opposed to a two-person, psychology. Even in Kohut's broadest rendering of the self, however, he never made a claim for its supraordinance in the *relational* field: it was supraordinate only in the intrapsychic realm (in its relationship to ego, id, or superego). It was a self that always needed the second person, the other, for its development and sustenance.

Furthermore, Kohut's (1977a) emphasis on his patients' selfobject transferences, defined by "preanalytically established internal factors in the analysand's personality structure" (p. 217), was balanced by his simultaneous emphasis on the analyst's contribution to selfobject failures and the importance of the analyst's acknowledgment of such. I have earlier noted my understanding of empathy and vicarious introspection as concepts that, in spite of the focus on the patient's viewpoint, keep the analyst's own person and his affective experience and expression, at the center of the therapeutic action. The analyst's empathy is made possible only through her open and imaginative reference to her own subjectivity. Therefore, although the postmoderns tend to interpret Kohut's concept of empathy as a method of inquiry that transcends the analyst's subjectivity, it can also be understood as a mode of interaction in which the analyst selectively uses her subjectivity in the service of her affective resonance with and understanding of the patient. But this very selectivity is a problem for the postmoderns. They tend to see it as limiting and also as constituting a denial of the analyst's contribution to the meanings that are constructed within the analyst dyad. Perhaps there is a chronic tension in Kohut's self psychology between one- and two-person phenomena, which accounts for a diversity of interpretation and practice in the application of his writings to the clinical situation.

Aron (1996), finally, makes the point that in Kohut's theory, "who the analyst is as a unique character is irrelevant to the analytic process" (p. 53). This central criticism of self psychology is in some form repeated in every postmodern discussion of Kohut's ideas. I have begun to address it in my explications of empathy and vicarious introspection and will return to it in later chapters.

Benjamin pays brief tribute to Kohut's contribution while emphasizing its limitations for relational psychoanalytic theory. In several contexts, Benjamin (1988, 1995a) offers only one-sentence summaries of his contribution; in another context Benjamin (1991) uses one of his case vignettes to illustrate a child's turn from a disappointing, hurtful, and mentally ill mother to a more emotionally responsive father. Benjamin, offering her own addendum to Kohut's case discussion, suggests that his vignette also reflects the "developmentally appropriate wish [of a child] to be seen by the father . . . as *like him*" (pp. 291–292, italics added). Benjamin does not acknowledge that the wish to be recognized in one's similarity to one's parents is subsumed in Kohut's twinship concept. I also see Benjamin's (1988, 1990) central concept of *recognition* as conceptually and experientially related to Kohut's *mirroring*; throughout her work there are both acknowledged and unacknowledged resonances with this and other self-psychological ideas.

As an example of her simultaneous appreciation and frustration in relation to self psychology, Benjamin (1990) writes:

> Even self psychology, which has placed such emphasis on attunement and empathy, which has focused on the intersubjectivity of the analytic encounter, has been tacitly one-sided in its understanding of the parent–child relationship. Perhaps in reaction against the oedipal reality principal, Kohut (1977, 1984) defined the necessary confrontation with the others' needs or with limits in a self-referential way—optimal failures in empathy . . .—as if there were nothing for children to learn about the others' rights or feelings. Although the goal was to enable indi-

viduals to open "new channels of empathy" (p. 27) and "in-
tuneness between self and selfobject" (1984, p. 66), the self was
always the recipient, never the giver of empathy. The responsiveness of the selfobject, by definition, serves the function of
"shoring up the self" throughout life, but at what point does it
become the responsiveness of the outside other whom we love?
[pp. 36–37, italics added].

In this passage, Benjamin explicitly recognizes the intersubjective
thrust of Kohut's self psychology at the same time as she criticizes its
failure to go far enough in this dimension of relating. I have earlier
argued that there is a greater allowance for mutuality and intersubjectivity in Kohut's selfobject concept than is usually granted by postmodern authors; this is so in his concept of archaic selfobject experience but
especially in the notion of mature selfobject relating. The selfobject is an
"outside other whom we love," even when the child does not experience
her as such. In other words, although not recognized as such, *an actual
outside other is required in order for the child to have a selfobject experience.*
The child's experience is broadened by virtue of participating in this outside other's capacities *as if* they were the child's own. And the "shoring
up" of self involved in selfobject experience results in the child's moving
toward the experience and acceptance of the outside other as separate
and different. It also leads the child toward increasing mutual participation in the selfobject dimension of relationships. Kohut believed that it
is only through the parental affirmation of, and resonance with, the
child's "rights or feelings" that the child comes to know and accept the
rights and feelings of "outside others"; whereas the postmoderns seem
to expect the child to achieve recognition of the parents' subjectivity simply by virtue of the parents' insistence on it. Current preoccupation with
the analyst's subjectivity and self-disclosure is based on this commonly
held conviction that development is generally facilitated by the encounter
with the separate and different other.

Benjamin (1988) is concerned that a child whose (m)other consistently defers to the child's rights and feelings may grow up to be an
adult who fails to recognize and accept the rights and feelings (i.e., the
subjectivity) of others. In Benjamin's view, girls tend to grow up identifying with their mothers' abdication of their subjectivity and desire,
whereas boys, in rejecting such identification, continue to expect
(m)others to subordinate their subjectivity to the boys' own. Adult rela-

tionships between the sexes therefore remain complementary, in subject–object patterns, rather than developing into subject–subject connections, the mark of true intersubjectivity. Benjamin sees these subject–object, complementary relationships as being at the root of sadomasochism in men and women.

Through her description of parent–child relationships in complementary terms—with the mother (actually) subordinating her subjectivity to the infant's needs—Benjamin suggests a link between Kohut's concept of archaic selfobject relating and later complementary power relationships between men and women. How has it come about that Kohut's concept of the selfobject, initially intended to challenge the dichotomy and complementarity of subject and object, is now seen as having been instrumental in perpetuating this complementarity? Benjamin, in her dual loyalties to object relations and feminist theory, is understandably alert to any formulation that undermines societal recognition of the mother's autonomy and desire. In her view, such undermining has led women to become the object of men's desire at the expense of becoming the subjects of their own desire.

Does Kohut's concept of selfobject functioning necessarily entail the giving up of subjectivity and the negation of desire by the parent or analyst? On a transient and discrete interactional basis, perhaps yes. But neither the mother nor the analyst need restrict her life or her relationships entirely to those in which she performs a selfobject role; furthermore, not all parent–child or patient–analyst interactions are experienced primarily in the selfobject realm by child or patient. In Kohut's view, archaic selfobject experience optimally evolves into mature selfobject experience, which involves the recognition of the other's subjectivity through mutual empathy and vicarious introspection. Ultimately, the selfobject/mother can joyfully recognize her daughter's autonomy and desire only by reference to her own subjective experience. This is implied, if not spelled out, in Kohut's notion of vicarious introspection. Nevertheless, Benjamin has responded to the real tension and duality in Kohut's theory by pointing out the *limits* of its intersubjective dimension. And it is through her elaboration of this dimension of relationships that she has made her very significant contribution to psychoanalysis.

Renik (1993, 1996) does not cite Kohut, but his writings on the analyst's subjectivity nonetheless constitute an implicit commentary on Kohut's selfobject concept. For instance, Renik (1993) writes that "the

problem with an analyst believing that he or she can transcend subjectivity and focus on the patient's inner reality is that it can promote idealization of the analyst" (p. 568). Renik joins other postmoderns here
in equating the focus on the patient's inner reality with the analyst's
attempt to transcend his own subjectivity. In Kohut's empathy as vicarious introspection, however, the analyst does not transcend, but rather
taps into, his subjective experience in order to understand the experience of his patient.

Renik speaks also of the patient's autonomy as being "coopted in the
name of empathy" (p. 568). He asserts that "an analyst is much more
disposed to being inadvertently coercive toward agreement with his or
her underlying assumptions when the analyst believes that he or she
has been successful in putting aside subjectivity and allowing the
patient's inner reality to determine the investigation" (p. 568). He sees
this belief as being "mistaken" (p. 568) and the analyst as "self-deceived"
(p. 564). I agree with Renik to the extent that aspects of the analyst's
subjectivity and countertransference are always operating outside of
awareness and inevitably affect the analytic process in ways that the
analyst cannot know. But Kohut (1984) himself acknowledged this
problem, and it should be no more true for the self-psychologically oriented analyst than it is for the various postmoderns. Whether we
undertake to resonate affectively with our patients or to confront them
with what we take to be our unique subjectivities, we are similarly limited in our capacities to know ourselves and the other.

Renik believes that the analyst's attempts to "put aside" or transcend
her subjectivity will have negative effects on the analyst's functioning
and on the patient's autonomy; Benjamin is concerned that the child's
or the patient's capacity to recognize the other's subjectivity will be compromised by an absence of confrontation with the other's separateness
and difference. These different concerns reflect varying difficulties that
all postmodern analysts have with Kohut's selfobject concept, which by
definition involves the child's or the analysand's transient failure to recognize the other's subjectivity. Some contemporary analysts join Kohut
in the recognition of the other's subjectivity as a developmental achievement, whereas others assume it to be a capacity present from birth. Even
those who join Kohut in seeing it as an achievement (Benjamin, 1988;
Aron, 1996) do not share his view of how this achievement is most likely
to come about. Aron and Benjamin both argue that it is the analyst's
very confrontation of the patient with her separateness and difference

that facilitates the patient's growing capacity to recognize the other's subjectivity, whereas self psychologists are more likely to argue that it is the analyst's success in transiently *protecting* the patient from this confrontation that contributes to the patient's eventual recognition and acceptance of the analyst's "otherness."

One question for later discussion is whether the selfobject functioning of the analyst (or mother) precludes her own experience of her subjectivity and whether it precludes the full expression of her subjectivity in other contexts (Benjamin, 1988). Another is whether the patient's or the child's repeated experiences of the analyst or the mother in the selfobject dimension, as an extension of self, will ultimately *contribute* to the developing individual's greater capacity for recognition and acceptance of the separateness and subjectivity of others, as Kohut argues, or whether these repeated experiences are more likely, in the long run, to constrict and *interfere* with the developing individual's capacity to recognize and accept the subjectivity of others, as all the postmoderns seem to suggest. The postmoderns are concerned with the analyst's expression of his own subjectivity within the analytic relationship because they see in the analyst's selfobject functioning a constriction of self-expression, and they believe that a fuller and more explicit expression of the analyst's separate subjectivity will contribute more effectively to the patient's essential recognition of others, as well as to the patient's unique development of self (Benjamin, 1988; Mitchell, 1996a).

Renik (1993), as noted, has spoken out against what he sees as the mistaken belief that the analyst can transcend his subjectivity (p. 568). But in Kohut's (1982, 1984) later writings, he moved beyond his earlier suggestion of transcendence in this regard (Kohut, 1959). Although many self psychologists still might argue that the analyst transiently puts aside his needs, interests, and value judgments in the service of imaginatively entering the patient's inner world, Kohut (1982, 1984) explicitly rendered psychoanalysis a *subjective* undertaking by the analyst and did not ultimately aspire to transcendance. I suggest that a father who feeds his infant before feeding himself is not transcending his subjectivity; he is simply temporarily putting aside his own need for food to take care of his baby first. Similarly, mothers and analysts may temporarily put aside varying psychological needs of their own in the interests of carrying out their maternal or analytic functions, but they do so without necessarily compromising their own subjective sense of self.

Most contemporary discussions of the analyst's subjectivity and its expression in the analytic encounter either explicitly or implicitly contrast such expression with selfobject functioning in general, or with the analyst's expression of empathy in particular. The postmoderns only inconsistently recognize that they share with Kohut a concern for the goal of mutual human recognition and only inconsistently realize that Kohut's selfobject concept expressed his attempt to deal with the very problems of humanity that have come about because of the failure of such recognition.

Mitchell and Black (1995) provide careful, balanced, and appreciative descriptions of important post-Freudian theorists, and their treatment of Kohut's ideas is one of the best available expositions of his work. Two years earlier, in presenting his new relational/conflict paradigm, Mitchell (1993) raised several questions about the concept of self. He elucidated his new ideas and extensively cited other important writers within and outside the field of psychoanalysis. He began by asking where we can locate the "core self" in a relational paradigm (p. 112; pp. 124–131) and suggested that in classical theory the drives and other bodily experiences played a central role in "locating" the core self. Since most relational theories no longer see the drives as centrally expressive of individuality, however, the core self can neither derive from, nor be located in, the drives. Having lost the drives as determinative of personal experience and intrapsychic structure, Mitchell sees the question of a core self and its location in theory as "a real problem" (p. 124).

Not only have we given up the drives as determinative of the self's "location" in theory but, as Mitchell (1993) points out, in relational theories the core self cannot even be attributed to, or "located" in, an isolated individual. Relational theories tend to see "the meanings generated by the self [as] all interactive products" (p. 125). Finally, in his critique of the concept of a core self, Mitchell observes that such a concept tends to evoke spatial imagery (i.e., the "core" of an apple is at its physical center and is its innermost part). He suggests that our theoretical and clinical understanding and communication might be enhanced by adding temporal metaphors to our spatial ones or perhaps even by substituting temporal language for the spatial in our elucidation of the self.

The word core can mean either "the innermost" or "the most important" part of something (*American Heritage Dictionary*). To the extent that the concept of a core self represents a spatial metaphor denoting an innermost self, then that is a concept which Kohut did not try to address. If, on the other hand, by core Mitchell means the most important aspect of the self, then Kohut may well have conceived of the self as having a core in the form of what he termed a nuclear self. In spite of the spatial imagery and meaning easily evoked by Kohut's term nuclear, the nuclear self was not intended as a spatial metaphor, and he never spoke of its "location." It was simply the term he used to refer to "the basic ambitions and ideals" of the individual (Kohut, 1974, p. 757n). Kohut's emphasis on the *sense* of coherence serves to remind us that he was referring to individual *experience* rather than to "places" in the mind. And his emphasis on the sense of continuity reminds us of the central temporal dimension of the self. Thus Kohut (1982) wrote of "that joyful awareness of the human self of being temporal" (p. 404). He would not have disagreed either with Mitchell regarding the applicability of temporal metaphors to the self or with the contemporary philosopher Ricoeur (1992), who observed that "a primary trait of the self [is] its temporality" (p. 2).

In fact, Kohut, who was the founder of self psychology, and Mitchell, who is the principal architect of a new relational/conflict paradigm, sound surprisingly resonant themes in their respective discussions. Whether it is a matter of the origins or the content of the self, these two theorists sing in considerable harmony and counterpoint, with fewer significant discordancies than one would expect. Much in the spirit of Kohut's self psychology, Mitchell (1993) wrestles with the loss of drives as primary motivators and organizers of the self. He asks, "[H]ow do we understand the *meaning* that body parts and experiences take on for the individual" when we no longer see drives as providing that meaning? And he answers: "They [the meanings] must derive to a significant degree from the mutually regulatory, interpersonal, linguistic, and cultural matrix into which the individual is born" (p. 126). Similarly Kohut (1977a) discussing the origins of the nuclear self, wrote:

> At the moment when the mother sees her baby for the first time and is also in contact with him (through tactile, olfactory, and proprioceptive channels as she feeds, carries, bathes him), a process that lays down a person's self has its virtual beginning. I have in mind *the specific interactions* . . . through which, in countless repetitions, the self-objects empathically respond to certain potentialities of the child . . . but not to others. . . . The nuclear

self . . . is . . . formed . . . by the deeply anchored responsiveness of the self-objects [p. 100, italics added].

Thus both Mitchell and Kohut address the question of the origins of a core or nuclear self in terms of *interactions* between the developing individual and the human environment. So where is the disagreement between these two paradigms? At particular points in his writings, Mitchell (1993), like Stolorow and Atwood (1992), seems to have misunderstood Kohut's *nuclear self* to be a preexperiential, inborn phenomenon. But Kohut (1978a) made it clear that his notion of the nuclear self was a developmental achievement that had its "birth" *following* specific interactions between the infant and the selfobject milieu (p. 741). Thus the inborn versus socially constructed self does not really hold up as a battle line between self psychology and more purely relational theories. In later chapters, we will see that real differences between Kohut and Mitchell's renderings of self and relationship have to do with the nature of the growing individual's experience and use of the (self)object, not with whether the self is an inborn given or a relationally determined achievement. The differences hinge on our interpretation of "how phenomenologically and dynamically rich {Kohut's} notion of selfobject responsiveness" is and whether or not his concept of selfobject milieu "can really account for and address the cultural, interpersonal, and linguistic dynamics of individual experience and relationships" (Stepansky, 1997, personal communication).

Mitchell (1993) generally offers a thoughtful and balanced rendering of Kohut's work. Nonetheless, he is intent on highlighting particular differences between Kohut's self psychology and other psychoanalytic theories; in my reading, some of the differences on which he focuses seem minimal or even nonexistent. For instance, Mitchell at one point, contrasting Kohut with Sullivan, states that Sullivan "believes that our commonality with others, not our distinctness, holds the key to a richer life" (p. 108). Yet we need to remember that, early in the development of self psychology, Kohut (1971) identified twinship needs as a regularly occurring feature of development. These needs had to do with a sense, required for optimal development, that a young child was similar to the others by whom he was surrounded. This sense of similarity consisted of mutual recognition of experiences and qualities in common (i.e., of commonalities), between the child and her caretakers. Although Kohut originally saw these as a subclass of mirroring needs, he ultimately placed *twinship* on a par with mirroring and idealization (1984) as one of three major classes of selfobject need. Explaining what he meant by twinship needs, Kohut (1984) wrote:

> {T}he young child, even the baby, obtains a vague but intense and pervasive sense of security as he feels himself to be a human among humans. . . . The mere presence of people in a child's surroundings—their voices and body odors, the emotions they express, the noises they produce as they engage in human activities, the specific aromas of the foods they prepare and eat—creates a security in the child, a sense of belonging and participating. . . . These feelings derive from confirmation of the feeling that one is a human being among other human beings [p. 200].

To be sure, not every reader of Kohut will see in his specific concept of twinship, or in his general concept of selfobject relating, an appreciation of commonality among individuals that approximates his appreciation of individuality and uniqueness; in my reading of Kohut, however, this is a plausible interpretation of his intent. For what could speak more clearly to Kohut's recognition of our need for commonality with others than his having designated a sense of twinship, or likeness with others, as one of three basic and universal needs of the individual? Since Kohut (1971) described twinship phenomena early in his career but did not designate it as a selfobject function in its own right until the end of his life (Kohut, 1984), we may reasonably infer that he would have attended further to this aspect of commonality had he lived longer (Stepansky, 1997, personal communication).

In Kohut's (1984) clinical examples, he described normative strivings in children for experiences in which their feelings of commonality with their parents are confirmed: commonalities of affect, interest, abilities, and shared pleasure in activities. I wonder if Kohut didn't finally place equal emphasis on the individual's uniqueness (expressed through her ambitions and goals) and the individual's commonality with others (through her sense of twinship and through her idealizations and ideals). Insofar as Kohut saw all these experiences, including the achievement of uniqueness, as mediated through essential self–selfobject relationships, perhaps we may even claim that Kohut ultimately weighted the "commonality" aspects of the self a little more heavily than the "singularity" aspects. It may be part of the genius of his work, however, that it does not seem to be entirely clear, one way or the other, whether the singularities of selves or the commonalities among them are more essential to their being.

In a further effort to differentiate relational theories from self psychology, Mitchell (1993) claims that, according to self psychology, "it is not possible to connect with others in a way that is vital and alive without first being centered in and deeply connected with one's own distinctive subjectivity" (p. 108). And yet, in Kohut's (1971, 1977a, 1982, 1984) portrayal of the infant–mother relationship there is certainly the potential of a vital and alive connection from birth onward. Even though an infant has only primitive or archaic ways of experiencing, there is room for joy in relating from the start (Kohut, 1971), joy being an expression of vitality and aliveness. Mitchell may have in mind Kohut's (1984) description of more mature forms of love and object relations, in which a capacity develops to provide selfobject functioning for others while simultaneously experiencing others in their selfobject functioning toward oneself. In other words, it is true that for Kohut *mature* forms of connectedness required a relatively coherent sense of self, but it does not follow that, for Kohut, a vital and alive connection with another was possible only when one was "centered in and deeply connected with one's own distinctive subjectivity."

What I think Mitchell has left out here (although he has recognized it in other contexts) is that, for Kohut, "distinctive subjectivities," or the ongoing sense of self, come about through the vital and alive connection with others. Kohut (1975) defined empathy as a "psychological bond between individuals" and spoke about "*mutual* empathy" between mother and infant (Kohut, 1977a, p. 99), strongly implying a vital and alive connection before a "distinctive" subjectivity has developed in the infant. Throughout his writings, Kohut referred to joyful exchanges between parents and their infants, well before the children could have been expected to develop very much in the way of "distinctive subjectivities." As I read Mitchell and Kohut, both claim that it is, at least in part, the repeated experience of the parents' "vital and alive" responsiveness to the growing child's potentialities, and to her spontaneous gestures, that contributes to the child's ongoing development, confidence, and pleasure in her own "distinctive subjectivity." After all, it was Mitchell (1996) who, in another context, spoke charmingly of the impossibility of pulling oneself up by one's own bootstraps, from which I extrapolate that he would also agree to the impossiblity of creating one's own "distinctive subjectivity" without the necessary "platform"

(p. 176) of (selfobject) relationship underneath one's feet (or self). Can Mitchell doubt that he and Kohut would be in basic agreement about this?

I have singled out select passages in Mitchell's writing to draw attention to what I see as a tendency, even among the most astute readers of Kohut's work, subtly to transform Kohut's ideas and then to claim a difference from self psychology on the basis of these slightly altered conceptualizations. In another example of this tendency, Mitchell (1993) represents Kohut's view of the analytic process as a situation in which the analyst, " 'in her empathic attitude,' finds and mirrors [the patient's] core subjectivity." Mitchell suggests that this core subjectivity, for Kohut, represents just "one thread or one voice" (p. 108).

The contrast seems to be between a multifaceted "unraveling" of the self, which Mitchell sees in his own work, and what he mistakenly imputes to Kohut: a process in which the analyst identifies and empathically responds to just a single thread or voice of the analysand, one that exists independently of relationship. But for Kohut (1971, 1977a, 1984), the process of the unfolding of the self in psychoanalytic treatment allowed for a broad and diverse elaboration of self-experience from all periods of development and in relation to the full spectrum of early objects. The attribution to Kohut of a concept of the patient's "core" subjectivity, in the sense of a single thread or voice seems to fly in the face of what Kohut explicated about his clinical work and the theory that he derived from it.

In my reading of Kohut, then, I find throughout his work multifaceted, rich, and textured pictures of the self, a self that is supposed to be able to unfold in all its multiple aspects through the analytic process. For Kohut (1974), "Body parts and single physical and mental functions are not only the foci of intense pleasure strivings . . . they are the leading narcissistic zones of the body–mind self" (p. 763). And he went on to speak of pleasure aims, self-preservative aims, ambitions, and ideals, all contributing to a richness of experience within a milieu of mutual selfobject empathy. In much of Kohut's writing, the schematization of the concept of self and its delimitation in terms of a few universal basic needs masks this richness. Yet, despite his penchant for schematization, the view of the self as comprising multiple woven threads can be found throughout his work. In one such passage he likened the analytic process to the experience of reading great works of literature, such as those by Tolstoy: "The deep reverberations of our nuclear selves as we participate in the works of great novelists and dramatists intensifies our reactions to the world and thus heightens our self-awareness ... [enabling] us to experience our existence more fully" (Kohut, 1974, p. 761). Kohut's (1971, 1977a, 1984) concern with more intensified reactions, more heightened self-awareness, and a fuller experience of our existence gains expression in his extensive consideration of joy, creativity, transformation, wisdom, and humor. None of these concepts is compatible with a view of the self as unidimensional or as represented by a single thread or voice. I conclude that Kohut's ideas about the self are much more resonant with Mitchell's own concern for the multiplicity, texture, and richness of experience than Mitchell himself grants.

Is There a Private Self?

If Kohut's view of the self cannot be represented by one thread or one voice, it is not surprising that his self can also be neither a self of separateness nor a self of privacy. One might have expected that a Kohutian perspective on these questions of separate and private selves would line up on the side of modernity, with its emphasis on the bounded individual, rather than on the side of postmodernity, with its breaking down of boundaries. But Kohut never seemed to express an interest in the privacy of the self, and he did not address the topic in his writings.

Perhaps his discussion of *lying* comes closest to giving us insight into his notion of a private self. Here Kohut (1984) differentiated between childhood and adult lies and attributed to some childhood lies an attempt to test the omniscience of selfobjects and discover whether or not the parents "can penetrate into his mind" (p. 72). In my reading of this discussion, however, it seems that Kohut equivocated about the possible consequences of the child's lie in such a way that the lying child cannot lose: if the child's lie goes undetected, the experience is likely to constitute an *optimal* frustration through the manageable and growth-promoting loss of an omnipotent view of the parent as all-knowing; this occurs along with the child's sense of success in Kohut's assertion of "the rights of an individual self" to construe and present his experience as he chooses (p. 72). The manageable disappointment, and the new self-experieince it entails, can lead to a miniscule step in the accretion of psychic function for the child. But even if the lie is detected, the child still achieves a growth-promoting confrontation with the reality of the other and an accurate mirroring of his own knowledge of the falsehood. Thus, regardless of its immediate inter-personal consequence, the lie yields the potential for a constructive developmental outcome. In this as in other elaborations, Kohut strad-dled the fence between a bounded individual for whom secrets, privacy, and lies are understood as one-person phenomena in the service of a separate self and a permeable or unbounded individual for whom these activities are understood primarily as relational events with relational consequences.

Winnicott (1963) who, like Kohut, seemed to give equal weight to self and relationship, assigned a role to the analyst's interpretation sim-ilar to that which Kohut assigned to the undetected lie: it establishes "the limits of the analyst's understanding" (p. 189) and thereby aids the analysand in his "discovery that his own understanding of his mental states and attitudes is at times better than that of the analyst" (Kohut, 1984, p. 72). To the extent that people have secrets and undetected lies, to the extent that their analysts are unable to understand them accu-rately, to that degree they may feel themselves to be separate individu-als with bounded selves. To the extent that the responses of an individual's selfobjects or facilitating environment are constitutive of self-feeling and development, on the other hand, the individual is inex-tricably entwined in relationships with others. Both Winnicott and Kohut seem to have made sure that we can never accuse them of stand-ing permanently on one side of these questions or the other.

In spite of Kohut's intentional straddling of these issues of self-and-other, he often elicited criticism for the concept of a bounded self. Yet, it is theorists like Winnicott (1963), Khan (1974), and Modell (1993) who address far more fully the notion of a private self capable of remaining isolated from relational pressures that impinge or interper-sonal rewards that seduce. Modell, for instance, argues that "the need to protect the private self from intrusions by others is universal" (p. 75). And in Winnicott's (1963) words:

> I am putting forward and stressing the importance of the idea of the *permanent isolation of the individual* and claiming that at the core of the individual there is no communication with the not-me world. . . . This preservation of isolation is part of the search for identity, and for the establishment of a personal

technique for communicating which does not lead to violation of the central self [pp. 189–190].

This seems to be a statement on behalf of the individual as "an isolate" that Kohut would never have accepted in so unequivocal a form. With these words, we might say, Winnicott established himself as more of a *self* psychologist than Kohut, in spite of Winnicott's customary emphasis on the facilitating environment.

Despite this portrayal of the individual as an isolate, Winnicott seems to have been one of a small handful of analysts who rival Kohut in a seamless embrace of self and relationship in development and treatment. Many of Winnicott's relational comments have achieved the status of analytic aphorisms, such as "there is no such thing as an infant" (Winnicott, 1960b, p. 39*n*). But as we have just seen, Winnicott occasionally made statements on the *self* side of the equation that went far beyond anything Kohut ever wrote. As for a final example of this tendency, consider Winnicott's (1945) remark: "In the earliest, theoretical primitive state, the self has its own environment, self-created" (p. 155*n*). But Winnicott then went on to make a very Kohutian point concerning the necessity for the external human environment to meet the child's self-created world in a way that provides the child with an essential experience of omnipotence. In Winnicott's view, when the caretaker is able to "meet" the child's omnipotence, the child is allowed the fantasy that she has created the means of her own fulfilment. Winnicott's concept of omnipotence comes close to what Kohut (1977a) labeled the fantasy of omnipotent merger, a necessary precursor of the later selfobject experiences of mirroring, twinship, and idealization. Kohut's omnipotent merger allows the child a fantasy of sharing in the adult's capacities that are inevitably exaggerated in the small child's eyes.

One important difference between Winnicott's and Kohut's notions of childhood omnipotence was expressed in Winnicott's suggestion that, through the adult's meeting of the infant's needs, the infant will have a fantasy of her own (separate) omnipotence; whereas, for Kohut, the infant's fantasy is of sharing in or merging with the adult's fantasized omnipotence. Here again Winnicott seems more of a pure "self psychologist" than Kohut. Another difference between Winnicott's and Kohut's notions of developmental omnipotence is that, in Winnicott's (1963) depiction of omnipotence, he explicitly included an element pertaining to the child's early experience of creativity, an element that Kohut did not directly address in relation to this particular concept. For both Winnicott and Kohut, however, these experiences of fantasized omnipotence were needed to protect the infant from what would otherwise have been a terrifying awareness of actual helplessness and vulnerability in the face of basic needs. With these concepts, Winnicott and Kohut set themselves apart from Freud and other classical theorists who emphasized renunciation of infantile fantasies of omnipotence; both theorists clearly stressed the normal and essential function of such fantasies. Whatever Kohut's and Winnicott's further divergences, their respective concepts of omnipotence speak to a shared insistence on the necessity of the selfobject matrix or the facilitating environment for the development of self.

The discussion of how much "self" lies outside the "self–other matrix" continues as we head toward the millenium, perhaps because the complexities of the subject matter, including its paradoxical treatment by both Winnicott and Kohut, require each serious theorist to go through her own private struggle with the elements of this seeming duality. Thus Benjamin (1988), like other contemporary relational theorists, tries to balance within herself the opposing views. Sounding eerily like Kohut, but apparently not aware of retracing his ground, she writes:

> Of course not all actions are underaken in direct relation to a recognizing other. The child . . . feels . . . pleasure in mastery as well as self-expression. Yet we know that such pleasure in one's own assertion requires and is associated with a supportive social context. We know that serious impairment of the sense of mastery and the capacity for pleasure results when the self-other matrix is disrupted, when the life-giving exchange with others is blocked [p. 22].

Bollas (1992), like Benjamin, starts out by addressing what might be intrinisic to the individual, but then goes on to invoke an essential environmental ingredient. He writes that "the infant has his own intrinsic 'form,' given the design of his inherent disposition" (p. 32) and goes on to say that "the true self is the historical kernel of the infant's instinctual and ego dispositions" (p. 51). In spite of these tributes to the self's unique and inherent dispositions, however, Bollas also significantly brings in the environment. Sounding very close not only to Winnicott but also to Mitchell and Kohut, he adds that the ego is structured through the "interplay of the inherited (true self) and the environment" (p. 59). Ultimately, then, Winnicott, Bollas,

Benjamin, Kohut, and Mitchell all seem to agree that some central psychological aspect of experiencing, whether it is called ego, self, or distinctive subjectivity, is based on the "convergence" (Kohut), the "interactions" (Kohut), the "mutually regulatory matrix" (Mitchell), the "self–other matrix" (Benjamin), or the "interplay" (Bollas) between certain inborn potentialities of the individual and his or her human (facilitating) environment.

Although not directly addressing issues of early development, Modell (1992, 1993) sings in a different key, suggesting that, for some people, the pleasures in functional capacities and personal well-being may outweigh the value placed on the responses of others. Modell, be it noted, is one of very few voices today arguing for the possibility of an uncompromised and nonpathological separateness of self. In so doing, he stands apart from the many contemporary voices joining the intersubjective and relational choruses. Aron (1996), for instance, at first seems to join Winnicott, Khan, and Modell in insisting that the individual has "a preexperiential motivational push" to remain hidden, unfound, untouched by others. But for Aron this push clearly goes hand in hand with a counterbalancing push to know and be known, achieving what he calls an essential "meeting of minds" (p. 80). In discussing problems of treatment, Jacobson (1997) joins the colloquy. He struggles to find a theoretical place for the self between what he sees as its "temporally flattened" form in the here-and-now relational world (p. 83), where it becomes a self with no past and no substance outside of the current context; and the self as "a deep isolate," cut off from impingements from others, but carrying deep reservoirs of experience within, which are never shared or communicated.

There are indeed new developments in the many contemporary relational and intersubjective theories that challenge aspects of Kohut's thinking, and these ideas are addressed on their own terms in the chapters to follow. For now, what is intriguing is that many voices in the postmodern chorus think that they are striking a discordant note with Kohut concerning the self, whereas, in certain significant ways, they seem to be adding verses, counterpoint, harmonies, and improvisations while substantively continuing his tune.

Kohut's Concept of the Selfobject

I am an other.

—Rimbaud

Kohut's selfobject concept, from the start, held within it the seeds of a deconstruction of the self. Because of the self–selfobject milieu in which the self developed and was sustained, the self was never seen as an entity that could or should be able to stand on its own. Many theorists who have explicitly expressed their appreciation of Kohut's contribution to psychoanalysis nevertheless seem to have underestimated the implications of Kohut's selfobject concept for his theory of self as a whole. They tend to see the Kohutian self as far more autonomous and bounded than a careful and complete reading of Kohut's work should allow. The unhyphenated, compound noun *selfobject* denotes a process of self-development in which equal weight is given to the inseparable contributions of self and object. I suggest that, together with his insistence on the empathic mode of observation in psychoanalysis, Kohut's selfobject concept has rendered self psychology a postmodern, more than a modern, theory of self. In its breaking down of boundaries, both within and among selves, the selfobject concept very much anticipated, and perhaps even precipitated, current psychoanalytic preoccupations with issues of subjectivity, objectivity, and intersubjectivity.

Kohut, Loewald, and the Selfobject Concept

Kohut (1971) challenged Freud's oedipal model when he identified organized transferences, which he came to believe were expressive of his patients' unmet early developmental needs. These needs centered on what Kohut (1966) saw as normal narcissism, subject to transformation as the individual matured. Such transformation required parental responsiveness to the child's stage-appropriate grandiosity, as well as reliable manifestations of parental qualities that the young child could admire and idealize (Kohut, 1971). These qualities included strength, calmness, and emotional responsiveness. Although Kohut began with a relatively narrow focus on narcissistic phenomena prevalent in patients with particular diagnostic features (1959; 1966; 1971), he eventually developed a comprehensive theory of a supraordinate self for which he claimed universal status (Kohut, 1977a; 1982; 1984). Throughout his writings, he worked backwards from clinical observation to hypotheses about early development. Ultimately he saw the narcissistic transferences as an adult expression of the unmet selfobject needs of childhood. Initially identifying primary selfobject needs for mirroring, idealization (1971), and omnipotent merger (1977a), he later moved twinship experiences from their original status as a subclass of mirroring needs (1971) to being a selfobject need in their own right (1984).

Although the term selfobject was Kohut's alone, both Kohut (1971, 1977a, 1982, 1984) and Loewald (1960, 1962, 1977, 1979b) believed that the analyst is able to *function psychologically* for the patient (and the mother for the infant) in ways that the patient (and infant) cannot function for themselves. Such functioning can contribute to psychic growth in the developing individual. This contribution is the essence of Kohut's selfobject concept and is centrally important in Loewald's theory of development and therapeutic action as well. For an example of how closely Kohut's ideas were anticipated by Loewald (1960), consider this passage from Loewald's paper on the therapeutic action of psychoanalysis:

> The bodily handling of and concern with the child, the manner in which the child is fed, touched, cleaned, the way it is looked at, talked to, called by name, recognized and *re-recognized*—all these and many other ways of communicating with the child, and communicating to him his identity, sameness, unity, and

individuality, shape and mould him so that he can begin to identify himself, *to feel and recognize himself as one and as separate from others yet with others. The child begins to experience himself as a centered unit by being centered upon* [p. 230, italics added].

Loewald went on to say, "In psychoanalysis, if it is to be a process leading to structural changes, interactions of a comparable nature have to take place" (p. 230).

What Kohut and Loewald clearly share is an emphasis on the psychological functioning of the parent or analyst, as it is spontaneously used by the developing individual for structural growth and change. When the structural growth or change involves the self, the child has had, in Kohut's language, a selfobject experience. Close adherence to the principles of self psychology does not allow for a definition from the standpoint of an outside observer; but, if it did, we might say that a *selfobject function* is any psychological process, action, or communication carried out by one person that contributes to the construction, maintenance, or enhancement of self-experience in an other. And I might add that, once such functioning has been adequately provided by the caretaking environment of a developing child, the child gradually takes over basic aspects of such functioning, so that the earlier dependence on others for self-maintenance and enhancement is modified. As the developing individual increasingly achieves self-sustaining functions and structure in this way, she gradually gains in the capacity to engage in mutually sustaining selfobject relationships with significant others. Thus, as development progresses, the need for selfobject sustenance is less absolute and less relentless (less *archaic*, in Kohut's language) and is replaced by more mature and more reciprocal selfobject exchanges (Kohut, 1977a; 1984).

Kohut eventually extrapolated from his identification of *narcissistic transferences in treatment* (1971) to a notion of *developmental selfobject needs* and corresponding parental functions (1977). In an *archaic* selfobject transference, the patient, outside of her awareness, turns to the analyst for provision of self-bolstering or self-maintaining functions not yet consolidated internally. To the extent that the analyst does nothing to interfere with the patient's selfobject experience, it holds the potential for reinstating normal developmental processes in the patient and thus results in accrual of structure and function. In Kohut's (1971) view, interferences come mostly in the form of the analyst's premature interpretations and failures of affective responsiveness.

Over the course of his writings, Kohut identified four self-constructive or self-maintaining functions, related to four corresponding selfobject needs. They include: 1) soothing, containing, and modulation of affect (for Kohut, these functions were part of the *omnipotent merger* experience; for Winnicott, they constituted the *holding environment*); 2) twinship experiences in which basic similarities to significant others are felt and accepted; 3) the mirroring or affirming of all dimensions of experience, physiological and psychological; and 4) the idealization of the "parental imagos" (Kohut, 1971; 1977a; 1984). All selfobject experiences involve relational interactions filtered through the subjectivity of the developing individual (child or analysand). Although Kohut identified these four specific functions as experiences essential to the "beginnings" of a sense of self, he also insisted that the need for such experiences continues, optimally transformed, throughout the life cycle.

The names that Kohut gave to these selfobject functions have become so familiar to us that it is easy to forget the important developmental experiences to which they refer. For Kohut (1977a), the *omnipotent merger* experience, in the first year of life, warded off primal feelings of prestructural chaos and terror and contributed to the early self-regulation of affect. The *mirroring function* (Kohut, 1971) affirmed the individual's affective experience and his sense of having a unique and valued identity, consisting of the full range of developmental experience in relation to important others. For Kohut, adequate developmental mirroring, together with twinship experiences, contributed to the selective development of talents and skills around which ambitions and goals could eventually be constructed. The *twinship function* (Kohut, 1984) affirmed the individual's sense of being accepted as a human among other humans, with similar affective experiences and sharable interests and activities. The *idealizing function* (Kohut, 1971) required the availability and suitability of the object for unquestioned admiration. These admirable, hence idealizable, qualities of the early parental images—the parents' perceived competence, strength, warmth, and caring—became the basis for later (internalized and transformed) values and ideals that would guide the individual's actions. In addition to guiding life choices, ideals and values become the standards against which the mature adult is able to measure her own worthiness or admirability.

Although Loewald (1960) used more familiar language when presenting his own ideas, in his review of Kohut's 1971 book, he seemed admiringly to embrace Kohut's selfobject concept. Presenting Kohut's recommendations on how the analyst should respond to the patient's selfobject transferences, Loewald (1973) wrote:

> That the analyst provides these favorable circumstances means that his general empathic attitude and understanding of the patient's narcissistic needs, demands, and defenses prevent his interventions from interfering with their activation in the transference, for instance, by premature or ill-timed demonstration of their unrealistic nature, by judgmental statements, or hostile withdrawal. *These are pitfalls in the treatment of such disorders to which most analysts are susceptible, since we ourselves have to struggle often enough with unresolved or recurring problems of similar vintage* [p. 346, italics added].

Although Loewald began this passage with a straightforward attempt to paraphrase one of Kohut's central ideas, he showed his identification with Kohut's position by stepping back to make his own observations concerning universal narcissistic struggles, clearly including not just patients but also the community of psychoanalysts among those who are subject to narcissistic vicissitudes. In this way, Loewald seems to have welcomed Kohut's emphasis on allowing a fuller flowering of the narcissistic transference before subjecting it to analytic scrutiny.

In many later papers, as well, Loewald showed his appreciation of Kohut's contribution by referring to Kohut's concept of the selfobject. Struggling to differentiate "objectifying cathexes" from narcissistic or identificatory cathexes, Loewald (1978a) wrote: "There are all kinds of gradations, intermediate states, and interminglings of these two {kinds of} cathexes. Winnicott's transitional objects . . . and Kohut's selfobject would be examples of such" (p. 195). Loewald went on to say:

> According to this interpretation of cathexis, there is not a given structure—object or object representation—that is invested with a charge of psychic energy. Instead these structures come into being, are maintained and restructured by virtue of objectifying cathexis. Similarly, such "psychic structures" as ego or superego come into being, are maintained and modified by virtue of narcisssistic cathexes. Winnicott (1967, p. 371) and Kohut (1971, pp. 26, 39n. 1) I believe, think about cathexis along similar lines [p. 195].

In that passage, Loewald continued to use the language of instincts while completely redefining the term "cathexis" to parallel Kohut's (1971) meaning in his description of the structure-building potential of the self–selfobject bond.

Writing of his analytic work in another context, Loewald (1978b) described a ruptured "empathic bond" (p. 212) that produced an immediate "deadening" of the sense of self in one of his patients (p. 213). The patient's reaction was in response to Loewald's having come to an analytic session with his arm in a sling following a weekend accident. Surmising that the patient had been reminded of early experiences in relation to a sick mother, Loewald made an interpretation of the patient's deadness in terms of the lost connection with a needed other. The patient was immediately enlivened, which led Loewald to surmise that his interpetive and "meaning-giving activity" had reactivated "the patient's organizing potential so that *we could reconstitute the selfobject as a live psychic structure*" (p. 214, italics added). Loewald spoke of this "structure" as straddling the internal and external worlds. In the same paper, he spoke of *narcissistic transferences*, "following Kohut (1971) . . . or selfobject transferences (Kohut, 1977), insofar as there is a relatedness, a rapport between patient and analyst . . . an archaic form of relatedness" (p. 217). These references suggest that Loewald had by 1978 integrated important aspects of Kohut's thinking into his working model of psychoanalysis and was using ideas and language that derived not only from Kohut's first book (1971), but from his 1977(a) book as well.

Where Loewald (1973) questioned Kohut's ideas, he did so in a circumscribed manner. Each time he presented a challenge to one of Kohut's ideas, he seemed to offer an affirmation of some other aspect of Kohut's thinking in the same context. For instance, he suggested that, counter to Kohut's concept of the coherent self, the individual exhibits a "powerful resistance against . . . integration . . . not merely due to technical errors or countertransference reactions, although the importance of the latter is beyond doubt" (p. 348). In a similar vein, Loewald wrote:

> To my mind a not inconsiderable share of the analytic work consists in more or less actively confronting these freed narcissistic needs and narcissistic transferences with what Kohut calls the mature aspects of the reality ego of the patient. Granted that

such confrontations too often are ill-timed or judgmentally tinged, there are also good times for them and a balanced attitude may be maintained [p. 348].

Still mixing praise with criticism, Loewald suggested that Kohut's "passion and superior ability for comprehensive and precise formulations tends to interfere with his presentation of the case material and to preempt the reader's own judgment" (p. 347–348).

Perhaps the most damning criticism Loewald proffered in relation to Kohut's work is the suggestion that "a subtle kind of seduction of the patient may be at play in his work," in his failure to confront patients with "an affirmation of the positive and enriching aspects of limitations . . . in particular . . . in the expansion of object love and true object relations" (p. 349). In these concerns, Loewald was foreshadowing the postmodern critique of Kohut's self psychology.

Nevertheless, Loewald (1973) spoke of the "pertinence and usefulness" of Kohut's work and stated that "every analyst will be stimulated and enabled to review and deepen his understanding of his own case material, particularly in relation to transference–countertransference problems" (p. 347). Loewald closed his review by identifying Kohut's first book as an "outstanding contribution" (p. 351).

It is not surprising that Loewald found much to appreciate in Kohut's first book. Both men seemed to see the functioning of the parental figure or analyst as a "precursor of psychic structure" in the child or analysand (Loewald, 1973, p. 344). In fact, even more explicitly than Kohut, Loewald (1960) spelled out a cluster of personal qualities that must reside in the analyst to facilitate the therapeutic action, the very qualities that must reside in the mother to foster the child's original psychic development.

In contrast to Loewald's overt focus on the caretaker's or analyst's qualities, Kohut generally avoided spelling out those qualities because he intended the selfobject concept to refer to an aspect of the developing individual's experience. He was afraid that, if he articulated the qualities and behaviors "required" of the caretaker or the analyst, the selfobject concept as an aspect of the developing individual's experience would become reified, concretized, externalized, or "socialized," and thereby its essence as a (depth) psychological experience would be lost. Very often, however, Kohut (1982, 1984) departed from this position and spoke of the analyst's or the mother's stance, attitude, responsiveness, empathy, or actions.

Kohut (1984) also experienced epistemological tensions that led him to struggle against hierarchical aspects of his theory. Loewald (1960), seemingly freer of such concerns, articulated a process by which the analyst's *higher level of ego functioning* could be internalized by the patient through the quality of their interactions. Clearly foreshadowing Kohut's concept of mirroring, Loewald (1960) emphasized that in these interactions the patient became the center of the analyst's sustained, focused attention and that this experience contributed to the formation or strengthening of self-structure in the patient: to the sense of being "a centered unit" and to the achievement of "identity, sameness, unity, and individuality" (p. 230). In this and other passages, Loewald described structural development as taking place through a specific quality of relationship. Loewald's emphasis on the structure-building aspects of relationship preceded by more than 10 years Kohut's (1971) description of the parental mirroring function that contributed to the child's sense of self or of the analytic mirroring function's "shoring up" the fragile self of the analysand. For Kohut, if an interaction served the function of contributing to self-structure in one party to the relationship, then that relationship contained a selfobject component. Thus, *both Kohut and Loewald were concerned with the patient's accretion of psychological function and structure through relational interactions, and Kohut eventually characterized these interactions as self–selfobject relationships.*

In his earlier works, Kohut (1971, 1977a, b) spelled the term self-object with a hyphen but later made it an unhyphenated compound noun (1984). In either form, the term has been mystifying and troubling for many readers because it refers to a multiplicity of ideas and processes. True to its component elements of self and object, the term selfobject refers to contributions to development that originate in both a subject and an object. Central to the concept is the subject's (unconscious) use of the object's psychological functioning for the development, maintenance, or enhancement of self-structure. In *archaic* forms of selfobject experience, the subject experiences certain self-maintaining aspects of the object's psychological functioning as if they belonged to, or originated in, the subject and not in the object.

In his 1971 work, Kohut posited a developmental continuum, from a lesser to a greater capacity for awareness of the other as a source of selfobject functioning (pp. 115–116). For instance, an infant feels soothed by his father's presence but does not recognize that his sense of well-being derives from that presence and is unaware that his father could leave, with the result that the child would become anxious or agitated. Similarly, a two-year-old girl who is dancing to music on the radio while her rapt parents laugh and clap their pleasure is not aware that her parents' joyful attention is "firming up" her sense of self, or that this nascent self might collapse and wither in the absence of such loving attention. In mature selfobject relating, however, the "recipient" of another's selfobject functioning can recognize the sources of self-enhancing experiences at the same time as benefiting from their availability.

For example, during the final year of a four-year analysis with me, a business executive was flying twice a month to a distant city in order to visit his recently widowed mother who had a life-threatening illness. Ordinarily this man spent his weekends gardening, playing tennis, participating in outings with his children, and attending social and cultural events with his wife. During an analytic hour, he reported that a friend had said to him, "I admire you for the sacrifices you're making. I don't know how you can go on for so many months giving up your usual sources of relaxation and pleasure. I hope that what you're doing at least gives you the satisfaction of knowing that you're a wonderful son." The man felt grateful to his friend for affirming an aspect of his sense of self and for supporting his inner, self-affirming processes. By amplifying the man's own self-regulating processes, this small interaction helped to carry him through the strain of a difficult period in his life. In all the foregoing examples of selfobject experience, archaic or mature, what was experienced by the individual in need, and what the external object actually felt, did, and said, were in intricate relationship but not necessarily in direct or predictable correspondence with one another.

Considerable confusion persists concerning the intrapsychic and interpersonal referents for the term selfobject. Although in the use of the term, Kohut (1984) understandably emphasized the inner experience of the subject (as I also did in my examples of the children and the man with an ailing mother), he recognized that the subject's experience was also importantly affected by the content and quality of the object's behavior and attitudes within the relationship. He illustrated his recognition of this point with the example of a friend's placing his hand on the shoulder of a grief-stricken person. Kohut seemed to be suggesting that such a gesture could serve a twinship function through its implicit communication of the message, "I feel with you, my friend, as a fellow member of the human race. I know that, like you, I am vulnerable to the blows of fate and would feel something of what you now feel if I were called on to deal with a similar loss or challenge."

In other contexts as well, Kohut manifested his recognition of the importance in selfobject experiences of both the subject's experience and the object's actual functioning. For instance, Kohut (1982) insisted that it was the mother's actions, guided by empathy, that constituted the selfobject experience for her child and thereby contributed to the child's optimal development. Because of this duality and tension in the concept between how the subject experiences the selfobject and how the external object actually behaves interpersonally, a certain degree of confusion has reigned since Kohut first coined the term selfobject. This confusion has left Kohut's concept open to criticism from opposing theoretical viewpoints, such that it has been criticized both for too much and for too little emphasis on the actual behavior of external objects in the selfobject experience, as well as for too little articulation of the *subjectivity* of the (self)object.

It seems to be inarguable that the growing child's experiences of the primary caretaker, and the patient's experiences of the analyst, are necessarily affected by both the emergent subjectivity of the child or patient and by the content and quality of the behavior and attitude of the external mother or analyst. Throughout the history of psychoanalysis, their abhorence of being seen as a social psychologist has occasionally led analytic theorists to avoid acknowledging the impact of the actual behavior and attitudes of external objects on the internal or psychic experience of subjects. In spite of these concerns, to differing degrees both Loewald and Kohut did spell out a range of particular behaviors and attitudes on the part of the mothering figure or the analyst which they believed contributed to optimal psychic development in the child or analysand.

While the critiques of Kohut's selfobject concept are many, Kohut and his postmodern critics would agree that there is not an invariable or predictable correspondence among: 1) the actual functioning of an object as it might be seen by relatively disinterested observers; 2) what that "object" (as a subject in her own right) believes she is doing and intends to accomplish; and 3) the way that the (self)object's functioning might be perceived and experienced by a developing individual who is in need of the other for the development or maintenance of self. Beyond this baseline agreement, however, postmodern theorists are often uncomfortable with Kohut's theory because it suggests that the analyst might "know" in advance what the patient will need and because it proposes that the analyst might come to the analytic encounter expecting to provide the patient with certain, preordained experiences, such as mirroring, twinship, or idealization. For the postmodern analyst, such expectations simply take us from the (classical/oedipal) frying pan, to the (self-psychological/selfobject) fire. In addition to insisting that the analyst should not arrive with a repertoire of responses prepared in advance for preestablished needs of the patient, some postmodern analysts have spoken of feeling constrained by Kohut's having limited the identified selfobject functions to a finite number. Rather, these postmodernists believe that there might be a universe of additional behaviors and attitudes on the part of parents and analysts that could contribute to psychic growth in children and analysands. Thus, the critiques of the selfobject concept have ranged from suggestions that it is flawed on epistemological grounds and should be dropped to the idea that it is useful but should not be limited to the four selfobject needs identified by Kohut.

Both Kohut and Loewald, then, pointed to caretaker behaviors and attitudes thought to be important for optimal development in childhood and in analysis. But Kohut, more than Loewald, seemed to be troubled by the implications of making recommendations that were directed toward parents or analysts, and he tried to highlight the inner experiences of children and patients themselves. Throughout Kohut's writings, we see him attempting to offset his discussions of the analyst's and the mother's optimal stance—their responsiveness, their empathy, their actions—with an insistence that the selfobject concept should refer primarily to the psychological experience of the developing child or patient and not directly to the actual functioning of any "outside object."

Not only do Kohut's writings seem to reveal this ubiquitous tension concerning the respective contributions of self and object to selfobject experience, but his entire theory embodies a tension between the two pivotal concepts of self and selfobject. Although Kohut did not gravitate toward the resolution of intellectual tensions through an invocation of paradox, in his theory there is an abiding dialectic between the concept of self and the concept of selfobject, with neither concept having meaning except in relation to the other.

The dialectical tension in Kohut's theory may be understood to express his view that self and selfobject are two coexisting, interacting, and inseparable aspects of self-experience. They refer, respectively, to the for-and-within-oneself aspect of experience, in which individual ambitions, goals, and ideals are developed and expressed; and the for-and-through-the-other aspect of experience, in which the self is developed and sustained only through the individual's experience of interactions with others. Kohut repeatedly (1984) expressed his belief that these two aspects of experience were in psychic reality inseparable through the somewhat awkward phrases, "self–selfobject matrix" and "self–selfobject relationship" (pp. 49–63). Kohut's idea of the self–selfobject relationship has recently been amended and extended in the theory of intersubjectivity put forth by Stolorow and his colleagues (Stolorow et al., 1987; Stolorow and Atwood, 1992; Stolorow et al., 1994). This extension and elaboration is presented briefly in a later section of this chapter and then discussed more fully in a chapter devoted to the topic of intersubjectivity.

Historical Intimations of Kohut's Selfobject Concept

Kohut (1980) argued against *premature* (p. 476) integration of his ideas with other psychoanalytic viewpoints, but he did acknowledge that scholarly comparisons, objective comparisons, and integrations "should be undertaken by others," simply awaiting "a later, more consolidated stage in the development of self psychology" (p. 476). In the 1960s, Kohut had written to Margaret Mahler, suggesting that he and Mahler were simply "digging tunnels from different directions into the same area of the mountain" (p. 477). By 1980, however, Kohut saw an "unbridgeable obstacle [in] the basically different outlook regarding the scientific evaluation of the nature of man and the significance of his unrolling life" (p. 478). This unbridgeable obstacle had to do with the "maturational morality" (p. 480) that Kohut saw in all child analytic work and research (with the possible exception of Sander's, 1975, work). This morality, attributed by Kohut to Spitz, Mahler, Winnicott, and others, posited a normal developmental path that moved "from dependence to independence, from merger to autonomy, or even . . . from no-self to self" (p. 478). Kohut contrasted this view of development to self psychology's, in which a lifelong need for selfobject responsiveness is recognized, rendering autonomy an impossible goal. Furthermore, although Kohut acknowledged "the greater physical distance" between individuals as development proceeded, he saw no corresponding "lessening of the {the need for an} empathic bond" throughout the life cycle (p. 478). Closely related to his insistence on a primary and lifelong need for selfobjects was Kohut's rejection of the notions of primary aggression and lust, which he understood to be central to Winnicott's and Mahler's theories. For Kohut, these were merely secondary phenomena, deriving from "disturbances in the self–selfobject unit" (p. 478). In spite of these important differences noted by Kohut himself, I see several areas of overlap between Kohut's concept of selfobject and pivotal ideas proffered by several earlier analytic authors. Furthermore, I suggest that some of these earlier analytic authors explicitly shared with Kohut an emphasis on lifelong attachment (Bowlby) and relational needs of the individual (Ferenczi, the Balints, Fairbairn, Guntrip). Thus, in discussing early analytic intimations of Kohut's later selfobject concept, I must acknowledge that Kohut (1980) himself might have been less likely than I to make accommodations and disregard inconsistencies (p. 477), even at this further historical remove.

Although Kohut coined a new term for his concept of selfobject, the phenomena to which his term referred were not at all new as a focus of interest in psychoanalysis. In particular, several British and Hungarian object relations theorists seem to have prepared the way for Kohut's selfobject concept to a significant extent. For instance, there seems to be overlap between Kohut's concept of selfobject experience and Winnicott's concept of transitional relationship. Kohut (1971) himself used the term "transitional" at one point in describing the archaic or earliest selfobject experiences (p. 37), and he referred to the analyst as a transitional object in his selfobject function for the patient in at least one context (p. 275). Although Kohut did not directly discuss Winnicott's ideas, Winnicott's (1951) seminal article on transitional phenomena was listed as a reference in Kohut's (1971, 1977a) first and second books; and Winnicott's (1965) entire book on the maturational processes and facilitating environment was listed among the references of Kohut's (1984) posthumously published book on analytic cure. Kohut's reference to Winnicott's work suggests that at no time was Kohut using the term transitional naively, in ignorance of Winnicott's construction of the concept.

What Kohut's selfobject concept and Winnicott's concept of the transitional object have in common is the reference to a *realm of experience* somewhere between self and object, somewhere between intrapsychic and interpersonal, somewhere between internal and external. Furthermore, both concepts refer to normal and necessary developmental experiences that in health undergo a transformation, infusing adult life with meaningfulness, relatedness, and creative potential. In health, neither the selfobject mode of relating nor the experience of transitional space is ever renounced or outgrown.

As with the concept of self, so with the concept of the selfobject: Winnicott sometimes outdid Kohut in carrying their similar ideas to ultimate conclusions. For instance, we have already cited Kohut's (1971) notion of archaic selfobject experience in which the child is not aware of the selfobject as a separate and independent entity. In discussing the transitional object, Winnicott (1951) seems to have made an even more radical statement of this idea: "There is no interchange between the mother and the infant. Psychologically the infant takes from a breast that is part of the infant, and the mother gives milk to an infant that is part of herself. *In psychology, the idea of interchange is based on an illusion*" (p. 239, italics added).

In fact, the concept of illusion is at the heart of Winnicott's concept of transitional experience, with Winnicott more likely than Kohut to use the word illusion in discussing early mother–child interactions. Kohut (1984), however, did speak of the "fantasy" aspect of omnipotent merger experiences as the earliest (pre)selfobject function and of the centrality of early grandiose *fantasies* in contributing to the development of the self, with its ambitions and goals. I see a parallel between Winnicott's notion that the caretaker promotes growth in the developing individual by allowing the infant the *illusion* that she has created the fulfilment of her own need, and Kohut's notion that the parent fosters development by allowing the small child to maintain *fantasies* of grandiosity and of merger with omnipotent others. Both Winnicott and Kohut recognized phase-appropriate experiences that laid the groundwork for further psychological development in which illusions of self-sufficiency or fantasies of grandiosity and omnipotence were gradually transformed into more mature (and more reality-based) forms of relating to self and other.

Along with these similarities, there are important differences between Winnicott's concept of the transitional object and Kohut's concept of the selfobject. These lie primarily in Winnicott's emphasis on the role of the spontaneous gesture and the creative impulse in transitional experiencing. For Winnicott, the child at least partly *creates* the transitional object, whereas for Kohut the child simply *experiences* the selfobject. Nevertheless, Kohut's selfobject experiences do provide the foundations for all that will become creative and productive in the individual's life. Thus, I believe it would be accurate to say that both Winnicott's transitional experience and Kohut's archaic selfobject experience function as *wellsprings* of creativity in later life.

Winnicott (1954) used the term "pre-ruth" to signify his understanding that children who act without concern for their significant others cannot be deemed ruthless, since their lack of concern reflects neither callousness nor a hardened heart, but rather a still-to-be-completed developmental process of cognitive/affective recognition of the other. Only after the developmental achievement of recognition of the mother as a separate person, with a subjectivity of her own, can the child experience real concern for her and her experience; and only then can an expressed lack of consideration for the mother's well-being be considered "ruthless." We, therefore, might say that, in Winnicott's stage of pre-ruth, certain psychic incapacities, rather than either illusion or aggression, prevail.

Winnicott's *pre-ruth* and Kohut's *archaic selfobject relating* have in common the child's developmental inability to recognize the caretaker's environmental provision as coming from the outside. To underscore his notion that the child lacked awareness of self as separate from the caretaking object, Winnicott (1954) proposed that we speak of an "environment–individual set-up" rather than of an individual alone (p. 266). The meaning of this phrase resonates with Kohut's (1984) later use of the verbal concoction "self–selfobject matrix." We earlier noted that Winnicott (1960) equated *good enough mothering* with meeting the baby's omnipotence, which involved protecting the child from traumatic confrontation with his helplessness. This protective function is carried out through the mother's active ministrations and facilitates the baby's necessary illusion that he is sufficient unto himself.

Both Winnicott (1954) and Kohut (1971; 1977a; 1984) argued for the necessity of early environmental provision and for the child's early inability to identify her caretakers as the source of this provision. It seems that the mother's holding in the first year of life in Winnicott's theory, and the parental twinship, mirroring, and idealizability during the second and third years of life in Kohut's theory, form a developmental continuum of such environmental provision (Teicholz, 1996).

Winnicott's discussion of the infant's pre-ruth stage, and the developmental process through which the child achieves concern for the object, is in part a critique of Melanie Klein's theory of the paranoid/schizoid and depressive positions. For Klein, the depressive position is achieved after the child develops the capacity to integrate her experience of part-objects into whole-object experiences. This developmental achievement results in guilt toward the object, now recognized as a whole person, for the destructive impulses and fantasies of the earlier paranoid/schizoid position. With the introduction of his pre-ruth concept, Winnicott was countering Klein's interpretation of the infant's "destructiveness" in the paranoid/schizoid position as expressive of inborn aggression or of rage reactive to the drive-determined fantasy of a bad and frustrating object. Winnicott was suggesting that what Klein saw as the child's destructive aggression against the breast might be nothing more than a vigorous pursuit of the child's own goals and desires, in the absence of awareness of the other as a whole and separate being. In contradistinction to Klein, Winnicott believed that the infant, in the first months of life, is not intending to destroy the object (or part-object), but simply is trying to get what he needs without awareness that there are distinct others who could get hurt in the process (see Bacal, 1989, on Winnicott and self psychology).

Because Melanie Klein embraced Freud's death instinct and the notion of inborn aggression, she and Kohut are usually seen as being diametrically opposed in their theoretical assumptions and technical approaches. Therefore it is somewhat surprising that Kohut's quarrel with Klein was only a partial one. Comparing Klein with Freud, Kohut (1984) held up Klein as a preferred model for understanding a patient's early dyadic needs as they emerge in the transference (pp. 97–98). Kohut suggested that a patient suffering from a disorder of the self might find a Kleinian, as compared with a Freudian, analyst, more "in tune with the state of her self" (p. 98). In Kohut's view, this relative attunement would compensate somewhat for the *inaccuracy* of Kleinian interpretations in terms of the patient's destructive instincts!

In spite of Kohut's modest tolerance of Klein's psychoanalytic approach, readers do not usually turn to Melanie Klein's writings in search of support for Kohut's self psychology. Nevertheless, I believe that there are occasional moments in Klein's writing that suggest a possible compatibility with Kohut's much later concept of archaic selfobject experience. These flashes of resonance with Kohut's ideas emerged primarily in Klein's writing on love, which in her work was not often elaborated outside of a discussion of guilt and reparation for destructive impulses and fantasies. Very occasionally, however, her writings took on a quite "Kohutian" ring, for instance in the following passage:

(F)eelings of love and gratitude arise directly and spontaneously in the baby in response to the love and care of his mother . . . In the unconscious mind both of the child and of the adult, there exists a profound urge to make sacrifices, . . . the urge to make people happy, . . . a strong feeling of responsibility and concern for them, which manifests itself in genuine sympathy with other people and in the ability to understand them, as they are and as they feel [Klein, 1937, p. 311].

Although the *child* in Kohut's framework was more likely to experience identificatory admiration and idealization of the parent than love and gratitude for an object perceived as separate, this passage nevertheless resonates with much of what Kohut wrote about *parental* love, empathy, and understanding. Furthermore, Klein's unusual passage is compatible with self psychology's focus on mutual love and understanding and stands in contrast with the more familiar Kleinian emphasis on death instinct derivatives, such as hatred, envy, and greed. In most Kleinian writings, gratitude is understood primarily as an act of reparation for prior fantasies of destruction.

Parallel to Klein's unusual comments concerning the infant's inborn capacity for love are her relatively rare invocations of the importance of the mother's loving attitude in providing for her child. Again in the context of her discussion of love, Klein speaks of "the child's helplessness and its great need for its mother's care." She writes of a maternal attitude in which "the mother's first concern will be for the baby's good, and her own gratification will become bound up with his welfare" (p. 318). In these atypical passages, Klein seems to share with Winnicott and Kohut certain ideas: first, the allowance for a period in the infant's development when it is recognized that the infant's level of need and degree of dependence on the human environment calls for putting aside of the caretaker's other goals in the service of caring for the child and, second, an acknowledgment that, during this early period, the child cannot recognize the separate subjectivity of the other.

In chapter 3 we noted that Michael Balint has also been identified as important for the development of self psychology (Kohut, 1971,

1977a). Specifically, Balint's (1937) idea of *primary love* and Kohut's concept of *archaic selfobject* have much in common. Balint's primary love pertains to the earliest stage of extrauterine mental life and entails a passive aim: "*I shall be loved and satisfied, without being under any obligation to give anything in return*" (pp. 98–99). Like Kohut's archaic selfobject-relating, Balint's primary love represents, at first, "a necessary stage of mental development . . . not linked to any of the erotogenic zones . . . [but being] something of its own" (pp. 101–102). For both Kohut and Balint, this "archaic" (Kohut, 1984, p. 49) or "primitive" (Balint, 1953, p. 151) form of relating goes through transformations to more mature forms of relating under optimal developmental or treatment conditions. Both Kohut and Balint implied a developmental thrust that nevertheless requires a certain quality of environmental responsiveness in order to be optimally expressed. Speaking of the transformation of relationships from their primitive to their more mature forms, Balint (1953) wrote: "Our work as analysts consists above all in providing well-aimed and well-controlled external influences for the release and maintenance of such evolutionary processes" (p. 151). I suggest that Kohut's notion of empathic attunement and his recommendation that we conduct our analytic work in such a way that the patient is able to sustain (or repair) the disrupted selfobject bond is compatible with the spirit of Balint's "well-aimed and well-controlled external influences."

Kohut (1980, 1984), speaking of the need for the archaic selfobject, and Balint (1951), speaking of the need for the primary love object, both used the analogy of the lungs' need for air. Balint wrote:

> In my view in this peculiar (primary) form of love, proper and timely satisfaction of all needs is crucially important, because of the infant's (or the patient's) almost absolute dependence on the object . . . We find a very instructive example of this kind of object-relation in the adult's attitude to the supply of air . . . {I}f the need for air is gratified we can see hardly any signs of satisfaction; on the other hand, if it is not and suffocation threatens, very noisy, dramatic and vehement symptoms develop. Moreover, the supply of air is taken for granted by all of us and we do not stop to consider whether the air does or does not like to be used by us for our own ends. Our attitude is simply: we need it and therefore it must be there for us all the time [p. 145].

Besides adding his own "oxygen" analogy to the literature, (1980, 1984), Kohut (1971) offered an additional comparison to illuminate the extent and intensity of need, and expectation of response, in the growing child (or the narcissistically vulnerable patient) as she approaches the archaic selfobject. Kohut wrote that the archaic selfobject is likely to be experienced as an extension of one's own self, such that when the selfobject behaves contrary to need and expectation, the developing individual feels the way a healthy adult would be likely to feel should her arm not carry out an intended action. The respective contributions of Kohut and Balint on this subject read as if the two analysts were engaged in a contemporaneous dialogue across a table from each other, rather than writing independently of one another across decades and continents. In Balint's (1953) ongoing exposition of what is entailed in primary object love, he wrote:

> "Proper" analytic help—from the point of view of the analyst. . . . means . . . an ever-present alertness to respond in the 'right' way to any need or demand of the patient . . . [T]he other partner of this primitive two-person relation, the analyst, agrees in every respect with the "object" of the primary object love, both in his actual behavior in the analytic situation and in the roles he has to play in the patient's phantasies [p. 152].

Balint (1937) had earlier written that, in the primitive form of love, the subject "does not recognize any difference between one's own interests and the interests of the object; it assumes as a matter of fact that the partner's desires are identical with one's own" (p. 100). It seems that Kohut took this idea one small step further when he said that in the realm of selfobject experience the subject simply does not recognize the object as a separate being. Thus, both Balint and Kohut argued for a silent and unacknowledged provision of psychological responsiveness on the part of the caretaking environment, which facilitates the normal transformation from archaic or primitive forms of relating to more mature forms of relationships. For both Balint and Kohut, in the course of normal development, the early demand for, or expectation of, immediate response and perfect attunement gives way to a tolerance for a greater degree of give and take, more mutuality in the provision of psychic sustenance, and an increased acceptance, or even embrace, of different needs, interests, and pursuits between partners.

At the same time that the Balints were writing about their idea of primary love, Ferenczi (1933) was developing compatible ideas that also seemed to foreshadow aspects of Kohut's selfobject concept. Ferenczi posited a stage of "passive object-love or of tenderness" (p. 163) in which children need "real sincere sympathy" and "identification" with their caretakers (p. 161). Resonating with these ideas in Ferenczi's work, Kohut's concept of selfobject also describes an identificatory relationship: one in which qualities and competencies of an other are shared and taken over as one's own. Loewald (1979b), as well, posited identification as the cornerstone of love between parents and children. Loewald was distinguishing the protective and fostering aspects of early identificatory relationships from the sexual passions and destructive potential of Oedipal relations. In Loewald's view, identificatory relationships include those between parents and children and between analysts and analysands and are hierarchical rather than egalitarian in the matter of self-responsibility. The parents and the analysts are expected to be relatively mature adults who are able to take full responsibility for their own impulses and actions; whereas the children and the patients are seen as needing a period of protection from their own impulses and actions. Because in Freud's, Ferenczi's, Loewald's, and Kohut's theories, *identification* is understood to be a relational process through which psychic structure is formed, it is a concept closely related to Kohut's selfobject theory. For Ferenczi (1933), the identificatory stage of development is a period during which either frustration and withdrawal of love, or oppression in the form of adult passion, can constitute a trauma for the child. In his view, the child has to be met with tenderness at his or her own level of development.

Ferenczi's emphasis on tenderness was a direct response to Freud's theory of infantile sexuality. Ferenczi wanted to highlight the noninstinctual needs of children as opposed to Freud's positing of ubiquitous, instinctually based desires and wishes throughout childhood. Kohut's notion of self–selfobject relating served a purpose similar to that of Ferenczi's childhood stage of tenderness. Ferenczi, along with the Balints, emphasized the importance of protection and tenderness in the adult's attitude to the child and the child's need to be in some way a "passive" recipient of the parental caretaking. I think that these ideas are implicit in Kohut's archaic selfobject concept, in which the child enjoys the benefit of the adult's psychological functioning without even having to recognize it, let alone actively doing anything to attain it.

Bowlby (1958) also made a distinction between an early stage of development in which the object is not recognized as a subject in her own right and a later stage in which such recognition is attained. Additionally, there are passages in Fairbairn's and Guntrip's writings in which they address the psychological needs of young children and thereby seem to anticipate aspects of Kohut's selfobject concept as well. For instance, Fairbairn (1941) wrote of the "unconditional character of infantile dependence . . . not only for his existence and physical well-being, but also for the satisfaction of his psychological needs" (p. 47). And Guntrip (1952), writing, "Hate is love grown angry because of rejection," seemed to join Kohut (and the Balints) in positing a universal and primary love that becomes destructive only in the face of frustration of basic psychological needs for responsiveness and acceptance.

We thus see agreement among Kohut, Loewald, and several object relations theorists that the child (or patient) has a general need for growth-promoting psychic functioning on the part of the caretaker or analyst, which is then used in the child's (or the patient's) psychic development. All these earlier psychoanalysts seem to have described phenomena closely related to aspects of what Kohut meant by selfobject and to have attributed central developmental and curative significance to such experience.

Characteristics of Kohut's Writings That May Have Led to Certain Misunderstandings of His Intent

When Kohut's concept of self is presented independently of his concept of selfobject, misunderstandings of both concepts necessarily abound. This phenomenon seems occasionally to occur even in the writings of self psychology's most outstanding spokespersons and explicators. In what follows, I describe a single instance of such an occurrence and propose ways of understanding this and similar occurrences as inevitable, given certain features of Kohut's writing and the tensions in his overall theory. In selecting an illustrative example of this phenomenon, I turn to authors who are in basic agreement with much of Kohut's self psychology. Furthermore, where these authors genuinely differ from Kohut, they have made valid points that are well supported. Their points of genuine difference are taken up in later chapters, where the original ideas of intersubjective, relational, and postmodern theorists are evaluated on their own terms. Thus, it is not any actual disagreements with Kohut that I wish to highlight here, but rather what I feel are certain recurring misrepresentations of Kohut's ideas as they are discussed in the contemporary psychoanalytic literature.

It is to recent writing of Stolorow and Atwood (1992) that I turn to illustrate what I see as a common misconception of Kohut's self psychology. Stolorow et al.'s (1987) earlier work seemed to embody a very fruitful cross-fertilization of their ideas and Kohut's. Attempting to bridge a perceived gap between Kohut's self psychology and more purely relational theories, Stolorow and his colleagues preserve central tenets of self psychology while emphasizing the intersubjective basis of all experience. In particular, they seek to safeguard Kohut's insistence on the empathic mode of observation as the only approach appropriate to the psychoanalytic encounter.

Stolorow et al.'s (1987) embrace of the empathic mode of observation is directly related to their analytic focus on the intersecting subjectivities of patient and analyst. They agree with Kohut (1959, 1982) on three major issues: 1) that the target of psychoanalytic study should be limited to the subjective experience of analyst and analysand; 2) that objective (or traditionally scientific) modes of observation do not lend themselves to apprehending subjective experience; and 3) that the analyst's vicarious introspection, or empathy, is the only appropriate stance from which to approach the analysand in treatment.

In their elaboration of intersubjectivity theory, Stolorow and his colleagues (1987; Stolorow and Atwood, 1992) have made an invaluable contribution to Kohut's self psychology, to relational theory, and to psychoanalysis. In the years from 1987 to 1992, however, Stolorow and Atwood seem to have moved further away from Kohut's actual text and to have become more identified with relational critics of Kohut's concept of self. For instance, Stolorow and Atwood (1992) include Kohut among those who had hung on to a "remnant of the myth of the isolated mind" (p. 17). They justify this categorization of Kohut by referring to what they describe as his notion of the "nuclear program or inherent design {of the self} . . . locate{d} . . . in the prenatal or genetic prehistory of the individual" (p. 17). But *Kohut never located the nuclear program of the self in the prenatal or genetic prehistory of the individual.* To the contrary, he characterized himself as an analyst "who thought of genetic factors almost exclusively in terms of childhood experiences" (Kohut, 1984, p. 132). Strangely, in making their claim that Kohut perpetuated a myth of the isolated mind, Stolorow and Atwood (1992) refer their readers not to Kohut's own writings, but to Mitchell's (1988) comments about Kohut's ideas! If Stolorow and Atwood had instead turned directly to Kohut's own words, they would have found ample and repeated evidence that Kohut (1984, p. 49, p. 52, p. 61) harbored no such "myth." Among the many other statements that argue compellingly against a "myth of the isolated mind" as a component of Kohut's self psychology, Kohut (1984) wrote as follows:

> Self psychology holds that self-selfobject relationships form the essence of psychological life from birth to death, that a move from dependence (symbiosis) to independence (autonomy) in the psychological sphere is no more possible, let alone desirable, than a corresponding move from a life dependent on oxygen to a life independent of it in a biological sphere. The developments that characterize normal psychological life must, in our view, be seen in the changing nature of the relationship beween the self and its selfobjects but not in the self's relinquishment of selfobjects [p. 47].

Why is it that such passages in Kohut's writings seem to be ignored or underemphasized even among those, such as Stolorow, Atwood, and Mitchell, who find much to appreciate in Kohut's work? Could it be that each new theorist seeks to differentiate himself from those who came before him? This explanation does not fit with the general tenor and tone of Stolorow and Atwood's or of Mitchell's work; these theorists are unusually careful and respectful in their representation of others' ideas and go on to make substantive contributions of their own. Might it be something in the way that Kohut presented his ideas—in the way, for example, he often put forth an opposing viewpoint to sharpen and dramatize the exposition of his own ideas? Or could it be that Kohut's emphasis on the need for a coherent and continuous *sense* of self militated against full comprehension of the selfobject concept as rendering a "self," in the sense of an "isolated mind," a total impossibility within his overall theory? Perhaps this last explanation comes closest to identifying a factor that may have contributed to the diverse interpretations and misinterpretations of Kohut's meaning and intent. Earlier in this chapter, we noted certain tensions and dialectics within Kohut's theory itself which could easily contribute to a reader's tendency to associate Kohut's entire system of thought with one side or another of any such dialectic, rather than grasping how the two sides remained in tension. This seems to be the case with the two strands of his theory representing self and selfobject.

Finally, that Kohut's body of work came to be known as "self psychology" may also have contributed to the general misreading of his ideas in terms of a myth of the isolated mind. After all, the modern idea of self, with which Kohut's concept is widely though inaccurately associated, embodies a degree of separateness and autonomy that Kohut repeatedly told us was not only impossible to achieve, but would be undesirable even if it were attainable. It was Kohut (1984), after all, who wrote, "The self's autonomy is only relative, . . . [A] self can never exist outside a matrix of selfobjects" (p. 61). For this and other reasons, Kohut's body of thought might better have been termed a selfobject theory than a psychology of the self.

An Introduction to the Postmodern Critique of the Selfobject Concept

While Kohut's concept of the self–selfobject relationship seems to have laid the groundwork for the postmodern emphasis on subjectivity and intersubjectivity, it has also evoked an outpouring of critical, or "corrective," literature in contemporary psychoanalytic discourse. Early in his first book, Kohut (1971) defined selfobjects as "objects which are not experienced as separate and independent from the self" (p. 3). This definition focused on the subject's experience of an other and therefore did not address the (subjective) experience of the "object" so perceived. In late 20th-century psychoanalytic discourse, we can no longer speak of an "object" without addressing the issue of that object's status as a "subject" in her own right. Thus, focusing as it does on the experience (or the subjectivity) of one party to a two-party interaction, Kohut's selfobject concept has come to attract the criticism of relational theorists along this dimension. Simultaneously, infant observation researchers have been accumulating data that they interpret as suggesting that even newborns can recognize separateness and difference between themselves and their primary caretakers (Stern, 1983, 1985; Beebe and Lachmann, 1988a, b, 1994; Beebe, Lachmann, and Jaffe, 1997). On the basis of this research, mothers and infants are now seen as cocreators of an intricate system of mutual influence in their moment-to-moment interactions. Aspects of Kohut's selfobject concept have become targets of criticism in relation to these findings as well. (Its various problems will be taken up in later chapters).

In general, postmodern analysts seem to see Kohut's selfobject concept as being unidirectional, one-sided, hierarchical, and reified. In several closely related critiques, the selfobject concept is seen as having neglected the subjectivity of the analyst in the treatment situation and the subjectivity of the mother in the mother–child dyad (Benjamin, 1988; Aron, 1992); as having failed to recognize the importance and centrality of experiences of mutuality in development (Lachmann and Beebe, 1992; Beebe and Lachmann, 1994; Lachmann and Beebe, 1996b); and as having underemphasized the ongoing intersubjective context of all experience (Stolorow et al., 1987; Stolorow and Atwood, 1992; Sucharov, 1994). Finally, it has been faulted for focusing on one aspect of human relationships (the self-supporting or self-enhancing), to the near exclusion of all others (Mitchell, 1996a).

Although, like all of Kohut's concepts, the selfobject eluded precise definition, Kohut made many attempts to spell out his intention in coining the term. Its general meaning, Kohut (1984) said, was "that dimension of our experience of another person that relates to this person's functions in shoring up our self" (p. 49). He also identified a specific kind of selfobject experience designated as archaic; it had to do with "the beginnings" of the development of a sense of self (p. 49). As with his concept of "self," so with his concept of "selfobject": Kohut repeatedly reminded his readers that he was not referring to objects in external or physical reality, but only to personal subjective experiences, to "inner experiences" and to "psychological reality" (p. 50). He urged his readers to allow him the convenience of using these "shorthand" terms without their becoming reified in anyone's mind. These pleas on Kohut's part, however, have not succeeded in warding off the eventuality that other theoreticians would (mis)understand his concepts of self and selfobject as reifications of what are better thought of as fluid and changing psychic experiences and phenomena (see Stolorow et al., 1987; Stolorow and Atwood, 1992). Thus, even theoreticians who grasp Kohut's meaning in his use of the terms self and selfobject have ultimately felt obliged to develop new concepts and new terminology in order to avoid the pitfalls that Kohut's writings did not manage to escape.

For instance, Stolorow et al. (1987) at first reminded the analytic community of Kohut's meaning and intent:

It is often forgotten that the term selfobject does not refer to environmental entities or caregiving agents—that is, to people. Rather, it designates a class of psychological functions pertaining to the maintenance, restoration, and transformation of self experience. The term selfobject refers to an object experienced subjectively as serving certain functions—that is, it refers to a dimension of experiencing an object (Kohut, 1984, p. 49), in which a specific bond is required for maintaining, restoring, or consolidating the organization of self-experience [pp. 16–17].

By 1992, however, Stolorow and Atwood seemed to have abandoned their attempt to keep the general psychoanalytic community mindful of the experiential core of Kohut's theory, and in particular to have resigned themselves to what had in their eyes become an inevitable reification of Kohut's selfobject idea. Addressing this phenomenon, they write: "[T]he pervasive reifications of the concepts of the self, the selfobject, and the self-selfobject relationship threaten to transform self psychology into just the sort of crude interpersonalism or social interactionism that Kohut wished to eschew" (p. 18).

It was partly because of this tendency toward reification that Stolorow and his colleagues (1987, Stolorow and Atwood, 1992) began to devolop a new theory of intersubjectivity. In this new theory, the term subjectivity gradually came to replace Kohut's term self as a way of emphasizing the open-ended and ongoing nature of experience, rather than the "thingness" of the self. The term intersubjectivity helped readers remember that, in speaking of the self–selfobject matrix, Kohut was always conceptualizing a self in need of, and related to, an other. But intersubjectivity theory (Stolorow and Atwood, 1992) goes beyond self psychology by offering as its central tenet the belief that all development accrues in the context of intersecting subjectivities. This tenet accepts Kohut's selfobject relationship as constitutive of the developing "self" but explicitly emphasizes the subjectivity of *both* partners in the developmental or treatment dyad and the never-absent impact of each on the other.

In 1987, Stolorow et al. introduced their theory of intersubjectivity "as a development and expansion of self psychology" (p. 15). They proposed emendations of certain aspects of Kohut's metapsychology in order to rid it of experience-distant concepts, such as, for them, the troublesome notion of self-as-agent. Simultaneously, however, they offered a powerful tribute to Kohut's selfobject concept when they wrote, "Once an analyst has grasped the idea that his responsiveness can be experienced subjectively as a vital, functional component of a patient's self-organization, he will never listen to analytic material in quite the same way" (p. 17).

Stolorow et al. (1987) saw their new theory of intersubjectivity as a direct outgrowth of Kohut's selfobject theory and his empathic-introspective mode of inquiry:

> Our own viewpoint fully embraces Kohut's claim that the empathic-introspective mode defines the nature of the psycho-analytic enterprise. . . . {I}t is our belief that the concept of an intersubjective field is a theoretical construct precisely matched to the methodology of empathic-introspective inquiry. What we investigate with the psychoanalytic method are the origins of subjective experience, their transformations, and the intersub-jective systems formed by their reciprocal interaction [p. 16].

In spite of this explicit linking of intersubjectivity theory to Kohut's self-and-selfobject theory, the overlap between Kohut's and Stolorow et al.'s work seems to be less well recognized among relational theorists. Instead, they see a one-sidedness and unidirectionality in Kohut's archaic selfobject concept, and they often take this out of context and assign it a larger role in Kohut's whole theory than Kohut himself intended. Although Kohut did not always use a language congenial to contemporary theorists to spell out the mutual and intersubjective aspects of self–selfobject relating, from the start his theory of mature selfobject relatonships included mutuality and intersubjectivity as foundational assumptions (Kohut, 1971, p. 51). Kohut insisted that simply because we are human, in one aspect of our relating, *I* will experience *you* in a selfobject dimension, and *you* will experience *me* in a selfobject dimension. This means that, in interactions that are optimal for our mutual psychic growth, we will shore up or enhance each other's self-experience, even as we relate in a myriad of other ways. What intersubjective and relational theorists find lacking in Kohut's writings is the elaboration, in phenomenological and dynamic terms, of the *nature* of these expanded realms of relatedness, a lack that is perceived in his case illustrations as well (Stepansky, 1997, personal communication).

Nevertheless, Kohut (1984) strongly implied the intersubjective dimension and mutuality of his selfobject concept when he wrote:

Throughout his life a person will experience himself as a cohesive, harmonious, firm unit in time and space, connected with his past, and pointing meaningfully into a creative-productive future . . . only as long as, at each stage in his life, he experiences certain representatives of his human surroundings as joyfully responding to him, as available as sources of idealized strength and calmness, as silently present but in essence like him, and at any rate, able to grasp his inner life more or less accurately so that their responses are attuned to his needs and allow *him to grasp their inner life* when theirs is in need of such sustenance [p. 52, italics added].

By including the individual's need to grasp the inner life of his selfobjects, and reciprocally to meet his selfobjects' needs for (self-)sustenance, Kohut conveyed an emergent recognition of the intersubjective and reciprocal nature of mature selfobject relating. But to the extent that this point was often implicit rather than explicit in his writings, and to the extent that the use of an *archaic* selfobject is essentially in the service of psychic development for only one party to a two-person relationship, Kohut's selfobject concept has been criticized as a one-person, unidirectional concept.

Besides the postmodern complaint that Kohut's selfobject concept underemphasized intersubjectivity and mutuality, contemporary analysts sometimes find Kohut's entire theory skewed in what they see as its monolithic emphasis on selfobject relating (Stolorow et al., 1987; Mitchell, 1996a). Kohut (1984) himself was aware of this one-sidedness in his theory and explained it in terms of the need to redress an imbalance in the earlier classical focus on "the self as it desires the 'object.'" Kohut saw this imbalance in classical theory as having precluded investigation of "the vicissitudes of the self as it needs the 'selfobject'" (p. 53). Therefore, self psychology originally "concentrated its efforts on the formerly neglected area" of selfobject relationships. In his final communications, however, Kohut wrote of looking forward "to beginning to investigate the relationship between" selfobject relating and other aspects of relationship (p. 53).

Although early in the development of self psychology Kohut (1971) actively shut out theoretical distractions in his efforts to elucidate his own ideas (p. xix), his comments about expanding the arena of self-psychological investigation, made shortly before his death (Kohut, 1984), suggest that he would have been interested in and open to dialogue with the broader community of relationally minded psychoanalysts as he saw self psychology more securely established in its own right. Although Kohut did not live to see his plan for the future of self psychology come to fruition, the 20th century may end with psychoanalysis having moved from Freud's initial focus on the instinctual basis of relationships, through Kohut's focus on the psychic growth-promoting and self-enhancing (selfobject) function of relationships, and on to the current exploration of any other dimensions of human relating that are seen as having been ignored or underemphasized in both Freudian and Kohutian theories. If there is a particular emphasis in these expanding views of relationships, it is on the inevitability of their being *socially* constructed (Hoffman, 1991) rather than being the product of the psychic organization of one or the other party to the dyad. Kohut's selfobject concept is relevant to this project, for it contains the seeds of a theory of the "social" or relational construction of the self.

With their emphasis on the social construction of relationships, postmodern analysts tend to reject theories that spell out preexisting categories of experience and functioning in favor of focusing on the direct, full, and authentic experience of the relationship itself. Although not altogether joining in this trend, Stolorow et al. (1987) have come to feel constricted by Kohut's finite number of "selfobject" functions; they suggest that we should think of the number and range of selfobject functions as potentially infinite. Stolorow et al. also suggest that, as analysts, we should be attuned to the oscillating figure–ground constellations of selfobject (growth-enhancing) and repetitive/conflictual transferences that our analysands will variously exhibit. Mitchell (1993, 1996a) also seeks to expand the kinds of relational interactions that we see as contributing to the development of the individual self, with an emphasis on the analyst's relational authenticity as a fulcrum for change in the analysand. All these suggestions, however, accept selfobject experience as an aspect of relationships and therefore represent attempts to refine or expand Kohut's theory, rather than throwing it out in its entirety.

A more striking critique of Kohut's selfobject concept comes from a comparison of Kohut's and Renik's recommendations for the clinical approach to the analysand's idealization of the analyst. For Kohut, the ideals constitute one pole of the bipolar self (the other pole constituting ambitions and goals). In normal development, childhood idealization of parental figures is transformed into an internalized set of values and ideals, which guide and enhance the individual's life choices. This is a spontaneous transformation, which takes place in infinitisimal increments, as long as the parents' inevitable weaknesses and limitations are perceived by the child through a gradual and stage-appropriate process, as opposed to being prematurely forced on the child through repeated or cumulative catastrophic hurts or disappointments.

Kohut believed that adult deficits in the idealizing sector of the self could be redressed through a reengagement of the idealization process in the analytic relationship. His view of idealization in treatment, therefore, was that it was among the expectable transference paradigms that might emerge and that it could be used to enhance the patient's development, first through its full and attenuated emergence in treatment, and later through its analysis in terms of its childhood origins and transference manifestations. The analyst was simply urged to behave in ways that *would not interfere* with the patient's idealization. In particular, Kohut recommended that the analyst make no explicit observation or interpretation of the patient's idealizing transference early in the treatment, instead allowing it to blossom fully, to be accepted, and to be understood. Explaining the idealization through interpretations and reconstructions was usually a later step in its treatment.

In marked contrast to Kohut on this issue, Renik (1993) insists that idealization is to be avoided in the analytic situation. Kernberg (1976), following Klein (1952), sees idealization as alternating with and defending against persecutory anxiety, devaluation, and rage. Renik's view differs from both Kernberg's and Kohut's. For Renik, the patient's idealization is incompatible with the postmodern insistence on a certain egalitarianism in the analytic relationship. Furthermore, in the light of the postmodern tendency to circumscribe the clinical use of intrapsychic theory and to emphasize the here-and-now, there seems to be no conceptual framework for understanding the patient's transient, idealizing use of the analyst in the service of psychic development. For Renik, idealization is simply to be taken at face value. He sees it as an end in itself and therefore as an eventuality that diminishes the patient in relation to the analyst. The analyst is encouraged to behave in ways that will *discourage* the patient's idealization. To this end, Renik recommends that the analyst occasionally reveal aspects of his personal experience, explain his thought processes, or point out to the patient her idealizing tendencies as soon as they appear in the transference. Although in his exposition on idealization Renik (1993) does not cite Kohut's writing on this subject, his recommendations read almost as if they were developed out of a need to *counter* the self-psychological approach to idealization. They stand in marked contrast to self psychology's understanding of idealization as a necessary and psychic growth-promoting aspect of relationship.

Although Mitchell (1993), Hoffman (1996), and Aron (1996) seem, like Renik, to be less accepting than Kohut of the patient's idealization of the analyst, these other analysts struggle with its depth-psychological complexities and explore its intricate relationship with aspects of the analyst's authority, in a way that Renik (1993) does not.

Each of our postmodern theorists has at least one important area of disagreement with Kohut's self psychology. As we have seen, Kohut's selfobject concept is particularly problematic for contemporary theorists around the issues of the analyst's subjectivity, the centrality of intersubjectivity and mutuality, issues of gender and female development, and a sense of constriction in the view of relationships exclusively in terms of their selfobject dimensions. In the chapters that follow, I take up these issues sequentially, although each of them is obviously linked to all the others.

PART III

POSTMODERN TRENDS IN
PSYCHOANALYSIS

A DUAL SHIFT IN PSYCHOANALYTIC FOCUS

Self to Subjectivity, Analysand to Analyst

The subjective has tremendous value but is so alarming and magical that it cannot be enjoyed except as a parallel to the objective.

—D. W. Winnicott

[Kohut] has devoted [himself] to the study of the . . . structuralization of human subjectivity.

—Robert Stolorow

[D]elineating the features and development of a full, authentic subjectivity has been the common project of the major visionaries within contemporary psychoanalytic thought.

—Stephen A. Mitchell

The Shift from Self to Subjectivity

In recent years, Kohut's original concept of self has undergone expansions and amendments along several different dimensions. The self has begun to be seen as multiple, as decentered and ever-changing through its dialectic of conscious and unconscious experience, as constituted in an explicitly intersubjective context, and in many ways as less contained and containable than Kohut's theory seems to allow, at least in the postmodern interpretation of self psychology. Furthermore, whereas Kohut concentrated his focus on the subjectivity of the developing child or analysand, the postmodern emphasis has shifted centrally to include the subjectivity of the analyst. In the light of these multiple expansions and amendments, the term self is no longer felt to be adequate to the concept, and the term subjectivity has begun to be widely used in its place.

Implicit in this shift away from the original terminology of self psychology toward the language of *subjects* and *subjectivity* is the suggestion that the language and concepts of self psychology are inadequate particularly to the task of expressing the "requisite multiplicity, ambiguity, and specificity of meaning . . . [or] to convey the psychoanalytic conception of the experiencing 'I' in both a phenomenological and a metapsychological sense" (Ogden, 1992a, p. 522). In re-visioning the "psychoanalytic theory of experiencing 'I-ness,'" Ogden argues for a language that can convey "the ineffable, constantly moving and evolving nature of subjectivity" (p. 521). Ogden acknowledges that "the term *self* is indispensable in the description of aspects of the phenomenology of subjectivity," but he feels that "as a theoretical construct [it] has become weighted down with static, reifying meanings" (p. 522; see also Gedo, 1989). Ogden prefers the term *subjectivity* because it conveys "a sense of 'I-ness' emerging from a continually decentering dialectical process" (p. 522).

Thus, we see that the terms self and subjectivity overlap substantially in their meanings but are not synonymous. Still, since both terms generally refer to the individual's unique sense of "I-ness," perhaps they differ more in their respective potentials for reification than in their actual referents. Ogden's (1992a, b) further views on the distinction between concepts of self and subjectivity are both idiosyncratic and complex, yet they offer ways of understanding some of the difficulties that the postmodern analysts have had with the language of self psychology.

Without actually acknowledging that he has done so, Ogden seems to have placed important aspects of Kohut's self psychology within the Depressive Position of Klein's conceptualization of development, thereby suggesting that a cohesive and continuous sense of self is only one of several different modes of generating experience. Using Kleinian concepts to visualize human experience as a dialectic between "paranoid-schizoid" and "depressive" approaches to self and other, Ogden (1992b) includes in his understanding of the Depressive Position "the presence of an historically rooted sense of self that is continuous over time and over shifts in affective states" (p. 614). He goes on to say that this sense of self enables the individual to enjoy a "relatedness to other people who are experienced as whole and separate subjects with an internal life similar to one's own" (p. 614). In other words, the self of Ogden's Depressive Position closely coincides with a healthy Kohutian self, which has achieved relatively "mature" as opposed to "archaic" self-object relatedness. Ogden continues, however:

> It is important that one not pathologize the negating, de-integrative, decentering pressures associated with the paranoid-schizoid component of the Ps<->D dialectic [the back-and-forth movement between the Paranoid-Schizoid and the Depressive Positions] . . . In the absence of the de-integrative pressure of the paranoid-schizoid pole . . . the integration associated with the depressive position would reach closure, stagnation and 'arrogance' (Bion, 1967). The negation of closure . . . represented by the paranoid-schizoid pole of the dialectic has the effect of destablizing that which would otherwise become static. In this way, the negating de-integrative effects of the paranoid-schizoid position continually generate the potential for new psychological possibilities (i.e., the possibility for psychic change) [p. 616].

Thus, what for Kohut was a healthy self that moved in one direction from archaic to more mature forms of selfobject relatedness, Ogden sees as one pole of a continual dialectical movement between a sense of cohesive and continuous selfhood, compatible with Klein's depressive position, and a decentering, fragmentation-prone, and deintegrating experience compatible with Klein's paranoid-schizoid position.

The concept of subjectivity for Ogden includes states corresponding to these two poles of experience, as well as a third and more primitive one that he has termed the autistic-contiguous position. This third position is "characterized by protosymbolic impressions of sensory experience . . . [in which] rhythmicity and experiences of sensory contiguity (especially at the skin surface) contribute to an elemental sense of continuity of being" (p. 616). Ogden sees autistic-contiguous experience as being "generated [originally] within the invisible matrix of the environmental mother" (p. 616), but later this kind of experience continues in dialectical relationship to the forms of experience represented by the other two (Kleinian) positions. Initially, the three positions are established sequentially in the course of development. The autistic-contiguous possibly corresponds roughly to Kohut's pre-selfobject self of omnipotent merger; the paranoid-schizoid, roughly to Kohut's self of archaic selfobject relating; and the depressive, roughly to the self of mature selfobject relating. But, in Ogden's schema, once all three modes of experiencing have been established developmentally, they form a trialectic in which no mode of experience is privileged over the other two. For Ogden, subjectivity refers to all three of these dialectically alternating ways of generating experience, each creating and destroying the others in turn.

Closely related to subjectivity is the concept of intersubjectivity; in fact, the two cannot really be addressed separately. Thus, although over the next four chapters I attempt to take them up sequentially as they have often been addressed in the psychoanalytic literature, this attempt must to some degree fail to the extent that subjectivity requires intersubjectivity in order to come into being. Stolorow and Atwood (1992) have defined intersubjectivity as the intersection of two subjectivities, and Ogden's (1992b) words make an even stronger case for not trying to separate the discussion of these two closely related concepts:

> The infant requires the experience of a particular form of intersubjectivity in which the mother's *being* is experienced simultaneously as an extension of himself and as other to himself. Only later is this intersubjectivity appropriated by the infant as he develops the capacity to be alone (Winnicott, 1958a), i.e., the capacity to be a subject independent of the actual protection of the mother's subjectivity [p. 622].

Ogden further observes that "the analytic conception of the subject has increasingly become a theory of the interdependence of subjectivity and intersubjectivity. The subject cannot create itself; *the development of subjectivity requires experiences of specific forms of intersubjectivity*" (p. 624, italics added). These words of Ogden's resonate strongly with Kohut's writings on the self and its development within the selfobject milieu. Nevertheless, we have already seen that there are important differences between what Kohut meant by the term self and what Ogden means when he uses the term subjectivity.

The Shift from the Patient's to the Analyst's Subjectivity

In spite of their different language and different notions of what constitutes individual subjectivity, Ogden and Kohut were both very interested in elucidating its original development and how it is played out throughout the human life span. In contrast to this focus, the moderate postmoderns have trained their lenses on the preestablished subjectivity of the analyst and its impact on the analytic situation. Although the postmodern approach to this challenge is completely original, the problem of the analyst's own subjectivity was implicit in psychoanalysis from the start. Freud's (1911–1915) triumvirate of anonymity, neutrality, and abstinence, although partly determined by his drive theory of frustration and gratification, also represented his best effort to assure that the analyst's subjectivity and countertransference would not unduly influence the analytic process. In the eyes of the postmoderns, Freud's efforts in this regard failed (Renik, 1996). Thus, the current preoccupation with the analyst's subjectivity represents the best efforts of contemporary analysts to arrive at an alternative to Freud's recommendation that the analyst remain anonymous, neutral, and abstinent.

The postmoderns do not mean that the analyst's subjectivity *ought* to influence the analytic interaction; rather, they are grappling with growing recognition of the extent to which it inevitably does. With this recognition, the analyst's subjectivity has become the pivotal issue in psychoanalytic discourse of the 1990s. Rather than continuing the analytic tradition of suppressing and denying the analyst's influence, postmodern analysts are confronting it head-on (Mitchell, 1997) through a thoroughgoing reexamination of the analytic situation and its interactive dimensions. Every tenet of classical psychoanalytic theory and every principle of traditional technique has been affected by our more open acknowledgment of the analyst's subjectivity. In the light of this impact, a search for new guiding principles for psychoanalysis is underway.

This search not only represents dissatisfaction with classical psychoanalytic thinking but also is one aspect of the contemporary response to hierarchical implications of the earlier, "one-way" focus of attention on the subjectivity of the analysand in the writings of Winnicott, Loewald, and Kohut. But, surprisingly, Winnicott, Loewald, and Kohut themselves all played a part in laying the groundwork for the current interest in the analyst's subjectivity. Even while these earlier analysts continued actively to advocate an attitude of parental and analytic "provision" in response to chidren's and patients' developmental needs, they each gave explicit recognition to the analyst's subjectivity and took clear initiatives toward the subsequent development of psychoanalytic mutuality. To start with, Winnicott (1951) drew our attention to questions of objectivity and subjectivity as universal developmental issues:

> From birth . . . the human being is concerned with the problem
> of the relationship between what is objectively perceived and

what is subjectively conceived of, and in the solution of this problem there is no health for the human being who has not been started off well enough by the mother [p. 266].

But, even in his recognition of analytic subjectivity, Winnicott still insisted on the mother's overriding responsibility to "start off" the infant.

Even more than Winnicott, Kohut, repeatedly writing of tensions between objectivity and subjectivity within the analyst, seemed to presage current preoccupation with the analyst's subjectivity. Kohut (1984) wrote that "in a matter of speaking, objective reality is always subjective [and that] in principle, the observing agency [the analyst] is always a part of what is being observed" (p. 36). He added that *there is no objective but only subjective reality* (p. 36). Implicitly setting a path for the postmoderns, Kohut went on: "We need an orientation that acknowledges and then examines the analyst's influence *in principle* as an intrinsically significant human presence" (p. 37). Extending his exploration of the analyst's subjectivity and its influence on the analytic process, Kohut wrote, "Prejudicial tendencies deeply ingrained in us often decisively influence what part of the potentially available data we perceive, which among the perceived items we consider important, and, ultimately, how we choose to explain the data that we selectively perceive" (p. 38).

Not long after Kohut wrote these words, Loewald (1986) also took up the question of the analyst's subjectivity, emphasizing its unconscious aspects and their influence on the patient and the treatment. Loewald wrote: "The psychoanalytic study of the analyst's psychic activity in the analytic encounter is still in an early stage. . . . The time is ripe now for proceeding further with that task" (p. 286). These words of Kohut's and Loewald's seem to have marked the beginning of a period in which the analyst's subjectivity and countertransference have been at the center of psychoanalytic discourse. Whether or not the postmoderns have actually been influenced by these specific words from these particular authors, Loewald was correct: the time was indeed ripe.

The Initial Establishment and Analytic Expansion of Subjectivity

Before turning to the extensive literature on the *analyst's* subjectivity that followed Kohut's and Loewald's initial forays into this territory, let us first look at recent theories of subjectivity in psychoanalysis that do not focus on the analyst's subjectivity, but instead look at subjectivity as it becomes established in early development or as it evolves for the patient in the course of psychoanalytic treatment. Mitchell (1993) tells us that "an expanded sense of subjectivity is the goal of psychoanalysis." For Mitchell, subjectivity includes: "1) a full sense of the self as agent, and 2) an experience of the self as the *subject of desire*, as well as sexual object" (p. 39). Mitchell's notion of what constitutes subjectivity overlaps importantly with certain aspects of Kohut's concept of self, namely, the individual's experience of herself as the center of initiative (sense of self as agent) and as the center of experience (this includes but is not limited to Mitchell's sense of self as the subject of desire).

Since Mitchell believes that, as a central goal, psychoanalysis expands the patient's subjectivity, he must view most patients as beginning their analyses with a subjectivity in need of expansion—constricted, impoverished, or otherwise not optimally evolved in the course of earlier development. Thus, although Mitchell does not directly address the original establishment of a full and rich subjectivity in childhood, his thinking seems to be consistent with Ogden's (1986) view of individual subjectivity as, above all, an essential developmental achievement, which may be present in adults to greater or lesser degree.

Ogden tells us that subjectivity is the sense of oneself "as creator of meanings" (p. 217) or "the quality that one is thinking one's thoughts and feeling one's feelings as opposed to living in a state of reflexive reactivity" (p. 209). At first glance, his elucidation of subjectivity does not seem to have much in common with Mitchell's definition. But perhaps Ogden's sense of self as *creator of meanings* overlaps with Mitchell's *self as agent*, since the creation of meaning might be *included* in the sense of oneself as authoring one's own acts. Furthermore, Mitchell's experience of oneself as the *subject of desire* might be subsumed under Ogden's sense of self as *feeler of one's feelings*. Although bringing together Mitchell's and Ogden's views of subjectivity may involve some stretching of language and concepts, one can argue with greater certainty that Ogden's view of subjectivity is compatible with Kohut's (1971) sense of self as the *center of experience*, since Kohut's notion unquestionably corresponds with Ogden's (1986) "quality that one is thinking one's thoughts and feeling one's feelings."

Ogden (1986), elaborating further on these capsule definitions, explains the relationships among the establishment of subjectivity, the sense of creating meaning, and the sense that one thinks one's own thoughts or feels one's feelings. In his view, all these achievements hinge on the ability to distinguish the symbol from that which is symbolized:

> The establishment of the distinction between the symbol and the symbolized is inseparable from the establishment of subjectivity: the two achievements are two factors of the same developmental event. To distinguish symbol from symbolized is to distinguish one's thought from that which one is thinking about, one's feeling from that which one is responding to. For symbol to stand independently of symbolized, there must be a *subject* engaged in the process of interpreting perceptions [p. 224, italics added].

For Ogden, the human being becomes a *subject* only after she can create meaning through the personal interpretation of perceptions, and this capacity presupposes the ability to separate the symbol from that which it symbolizes. Following Winnicott, Ogden tells us that between symbol and symbolized is a *potential space* that allows for the subjective interpretation of meaning. It is in this space that *subjectivity* is born.

The Analyst's Subjectivity: Implications for the Analytic Situation

Although the postmoderns themselves have not made the connection explicit, I see in Ogden's (1986) linkage between the establishment of unique subjectivity and the creation of personal meaning a significant step toward the contemporary preoccupation with the analyst's subjectivity and toward the multiple changes in how we are now conceptualizing the analytic situation. What Ogden has highlighted for us is that the individual *potential* for making different interpretations of experience and for creating idiosyncratic meaning makes every subjectivity singular, unique, and ultimately unknowable. The postmodern analyst is thus newly aware that not only will the patient's unique subjectivity remain to some extent inscrutable to the analyst, but also the analyst's subjectivity will remain partly unknowable even to the analyst's self. It is our uniqueness that makes us partially unknowable to others, and it is the fact that our subjectivities have both "qualities of consciousness and the absence of consciousness" (Ogden, 1992a, p. 523) that contributes to our inability to know everything about our own experience and self-presentation. Gradually, analytic authors have confronted the realization that what is true for the patient's unconscious experience must be true, as well, for the analyst's. It has not taken long for this acknowledgment to dissolve our earlier ideal of absolute knowledge and to nudge us toward letting go an attitude of authority derived from analytic certainties no longer within our reach. Because we no longer are confident that the therapist can know or authoritatively interpret the patient's experience, or that she can even know her own, we are in the process of reexamining the nature and extent of the analyst's remaining claims to authority (Hoffman, 1983, 1987, 1992, 1994, 1996; Mitchell, 1993, 1997; Aron, 1996; Renik, 1996).

With each individual looking out through the limited prism of her own subjectivity, we are less sure about universals of human experience "out there." This recognition of our subjectivity undermines our former confidence in the validity of our theories as guides to an objectively perceived reality. Instead of the search for the *truth* of the patient's experience that characterized classical psychoanalysis, contemporary psychoanalysis seems more to constitute an interactive struggle toward multiple subjective perspectives on the patient's and analyst's shared or coconstructed experience (Hoffman, 1983, 1991, 1992, 1994; Aron, 1991, 1992, 1996; Mitchell, 1993, 1997).

Many analysts now accept that the analyst's subjectivity, like the patient's, consists of a "dialectic interplay of consciousness and unconsciousness" (Ogden, 1992a, p. 524), and that the analyst is therefore no better judge of her own motives than she is of her patient's. Freud (1912) instituted the training analysis and recommended lifelong self-analysis to rectify this problem. But again, the postmoderns feel that Freud's attempted solution has proven inadequate. Many contemporary psychoanalysts write as if the well-analyzed analyst is a myth. They suggest that ongoing self-analysis, even in a previously "well-analyzed" person, is limited in its range and effectiveness at least in "knowing" and controlling the full nature of one's participation in interpersonal relationships. Recognition of these limitations reflects not a disillusionment in relation to the efficacy of psychoanalysis, but rather a reaffirmation of Freud's own recogntion of the power of the unconscious.

This reaffirmation includes acknowledgment of the ongoing flux of unconscious experience in shaping the attitudes, perceptions, and behavior of all individuals, including those who have been previously analyzed. Since postmodern analysts no longer see the central goal of psychoanalysis as involving a process of making the unconscious conscious, or turning id experience into ego, they also have no basis for claiming that their own unconscious experience and their subjectivity can be "known" and controlled so that it has no unintended impact on the analyses that they conduct with their analysands. I would add that with many patients, especially at the more disturbed or traumatized end of the diagnostic continuum, analysts may be confronted with issues that are more primitive and are felt with a greater degree of intensity than anything that spontaneously emerged in the course of their own analyses. Thus, as the widening scope continues to consolidate, many analysts will be dealing with themes and intensities in their work which they have not previously experienced or analytically explored.

This realization led Hoffman (1983) to suggest that the patient, once introduced to psychoanalytic methodology, will inevitably make silent or latent interpretations of the analyst's experience. Why, asks Hoffman, should the patient be any more likely than the analyst to take the other's behavior at face value? Aron (1992, 1996) has extended Hoffman's observation concerning patients' interpretive activity to the point of making it a guiding technical principle: he advocates that the analyst *invite* the patient to speculate *aloud* about the analyst's unconscious motivations and conscious subjective experience. Aron advocates this invitation because he believes that the analyst's countertransference will inevitably be recognized sooner by the patient than by the analyst herself.

The analyst's and the patient's respective subjectivities limit each in her view of self, other, and the world. The best that each can hope for is a collaborative and intersubjective effort to establish a relationship and understand it in terms of what each may bring to it, while recognizing the provisional nature of these understandings. With two analytic partners whose perceptions and interpretations are limited by their respective subjectivities, the analytic relationship is now seen as a more symmetrical arrangement than it was in the past. Although analytic study, training, and control analyses greatly enhance the analyst's capacity to understand her patient's experience and to be aware of her own typical biases and blindspots, the particularities of the relationship with each new analysand may bring out aspects of personality and experience in the analyst that have not been evoked in previous interactions. With this in mind, we can less comfortably claim knowledge, authority, and access to reality as privileged possessions of the analyst. This also means that the remaining asymmetry in the analytic relationship derives primarily from the differential tasks and levels of responsibility carried by patient and analyst. Along with symmetry and asymmetry, the degrees of mutuality and reciprocity in psychoanalysis are also being reassessed. Both Hoffman (1992) and Aron (1992) advocate "a general mutuality" along with a "moderate degree of asymmetry" (p. 494).

Even beyond our loss of analytic knowledge and authority, the recognition of the analyst's subjectivity has changed our view of transference and countertransference, with the realization that the unconscious feelings, ideas, and motivations of each party to the treatment will affect the experience of the other. Important early contributions to these still evolving views of transference–countertransference interaction came from Bird (1972), Racker (1972), and Sandler (1976), among others. No longer can we see the patient's transferences purely as dispositions predating the analytic relationship. The analyst too will develop "transferences" that contribute to the transferences that the patient develops, and vice versa. As early as 1981, McLaughlin suggested that we give up the term countertransference because it implies that only one person in the analytic dyad—the patient—brings *transference* to the situation. Classical analysts proceeded as if the analyst brought no transferences of her own, and they tended to define countertransference as the analyst's *problematic responses* to the *patient's* transferences. Whereas the patient's transferences were understood to be based exclusively on his early experience and psychic organization, the analyst's responses were thought to be purely a current reaction to the patient. This particular asymmetry was rejected by McLaughlin, who argued that transferences (based on early relationships) are elicited in *both* patient and therapist in response to the interactions between them.

Closely following McLaughlin, Loewald (1986) wrote that "it is ill-advised, indeed impossible, to treat transference and countertransference as separate issues. They are two faces of the same dynamic, rooted in the inextricable intertwinings with others in which individual life originates and remains" (p. 277). These early observations by McLaughlin and Loewald concerning the analyst's inevitable participation with the patient through mutual transferences and countertransferences anticipated the now burgeoning literature on intersubjectivity (to be addressed in a later chapter).

To the extent that discussion of countertransference focuses on the *unconscious* feelings and motivations of the analyst, it is a subset of the literature on the analyst's subjectivity. But conceptual distinctions between subjectivity and countertransference are not easily made, since countertransference is often considered to be the totality of the analyst's response to the patient, and the analyst's subjectivity is sometimes considered to consist of her unique ways of perceiving and processing experience or her characteristic ways of creating meaning. In the case of either countertransference or subjectivity, much goes on unwittingly, outside of the analyst's awareness. Aron (1996) prefers to speak of the "organization of the analyst's subjectivity," rather than countertransference, because of the pathological connotation of the term countertransference (p. 70). In stating this preference, he seems to imply that the terms subjectivity and countertransference are otherwise interchangeable for his purposes.

Aron's preferred language may have been influenced indirectly by Atwood and Stolorow (1984), who outlined a phenomenological theory of psychoanalysis, emphasizing *organizations of experience* as "structures of subjectivity." In their view, patterns of organizing experience begin to evolve from birth onward and exert a lifelong influence on perception and relationship quite outside of awareness. Atwood and Stolorow suggest that the need for organizing experience is universal, and they posit it as a primary motivation that *transcends* the organization of either self or object relations alone. With this assertion they have paved the way for an integration of important aspects of object relations theories and self psychology.

By 1987, Stolorow et al. had shifted the focus of their explorations to psychoanalytic *intersubjectivity*. In this context, they are among the first authors after Kohut and Loewald to draw attention to the *analyst's subjectivity*. For them, the analyst's subjectivity includes her earlier organizations of experience, both conscious and unconscious, which inevitably exert an influence on the analytic process. Included in these organizations are the analyst's theories, the choice of which have been influenced by individual subjectivity:

> [W]e do not believe that the analyst possesses any "objective" knowledge of the patient's life or of human development and human psychological functioning. *What the analyst possesses is a subjective frame of reference of his own*, deriving from a multiplic-

ity of sources and formative experiences. . . . *[I]t is essential that analysts continually strive to expand their reflective awareness of their own unconscious organizing principles . . . so that the impact of these principles on the analytic process can be recognized and itself become a focus of analytic investigation* [p. 6].

Nearly 10 years after that statement was written, Aron (1996) suggests that psychoanalysts have not sufficiently followed its directive (p. 82). In particular, Aron doubts that the analyst can recognize either her own general organizing principles or her countertransferences without explicitly seeking the help of her patient. Aron thus writes of his own analytic focus on "the patient's experience of the analyst's subjectivity . . . the patient's implicit interpretations to me about aspects of the countertransference that I may not be conscious of . . . [and on] patients' helping their analysts to recognize aspects of their own participation that they were not aware of" (p. 243).

Aron's clinical focus on the patient's experience of the analyst's subjectivity seems to challenge the outer reaches of the analyst's anonymity. Resonating with this challenge, Renik (1993, 1995, 1996) has explored the optimal expression of the analyst's subjectivity as an answer to what he sees as our earlier, misguided ideal of neutrality. Renik (1996) asks that we move beyond both neutrality and empathy; he suggests that it is the analyst's subjective experience, conveyed by presenting or confronting the patient with "new perspectives" and "supplemental information," that will be most helpful to the analysand (p. 506). Although Renik is contrasting such "new perspectives" with the analyst's empathy, I suggest that an empathic orientation toward the patient's affective life is often a very new perspective for many people seeking analytic treatment. Furthermore, empathy necessarily involves the analyst *affectively* in the patient's life, something that Renik also deems important for analytic success. But, additionally, Renik recommends that the analyst articulate her judgments about the patient's conflicts, and negotiate with the patient "between 'thesis and antithesis'" (p. 506). He believes that patients thrive in response to our "impassioned, idiosynchratic contribution" (p. 507) and concludes that "[w]hat the patient wants—and, [in the] best case, gets—is a perspective different from the patient's own" (p. 508). I think that, regardless of theoretical orientation, few analysts will fail to recognize a great deal of what they do and feel in their offices portrayed in these descriptions and recommendations of Renik.

And yet, these and other clinical implications of the contemporary exploration of the analyst's subjectivity pose quandaries for their authors as well as for thoughtful analysts everywhere. First of all, it often takes considerable time to experience enough of the patient's life, her psychic organization, and her interpersonal patterns so that we can trust our own reactions to what goes on in a treatment. It may take even longer before we become credible messengers to the patient about her self and her life, before, in Mitchell's (1996a, 1997) sense, we have an individually constructed, therapeutic platform on which to stand. Even then, as we acknowledge our subjectivity and its inevitable impact on the development of the analytic situation, how are we to judge whether or not our fuller self-expression has unnecessarily co-opted the patient's emotional, interpersonal, and therapeutic agenda? How are we to let go of the "false" or spurious aspects of our former analytic authority yet not abandon the patient to an ordinary peer relationship? After all, he is paying for our professional expertise and for our therapeutic concern and responsibility. How can we live up to that responsibility without infantilizing our patients or resorting to unhelpful paternalism or maternalism? How, that is, can we recognize the multiple subjectivities of both ourselves and our patients without having the analytic situation dissolve into unprincipled chaos? Renik (1996) acknowledges that, if we are to adopt his new therapeutic principles in place of our fading ideal of neutrality, now more than ever we must count on the individual analyst's integrity (p. 507), and, I would add, his continual self-reflection (Mitchell, 1997), self-analysis, and self-discipline as well.

Recognition of the analyst's subjectivity raises additional questions as well. How can we acknowledge the totally relational and intersubjective context of all therapeutic interaction while still respecting the patient's separateness and difference from ourselves? How can we respect this separateness and difference but avoid traumatizing those who need at least temporarily to feel that we are a part of their selves, that our functioning, for the moment, can be a part of their functioning? How can we acknowledge that the patient has a past that excludes us and a self-organization that prior to treatment was independent of the analyst; and, at the same time, keep in mind that, once the analysis has started, that past as remembered and shared, and that self-organization, will be continually *influenced* by the analyst?

Postmodern Views of Empathy in the
Light of the Analyst's Irreducible Subjectivity

We have noted many ways in which the current focus on the analyst's subjectivity constitutes a critique not just of classical anonymity and neutrality but of self-psychological empathy and the selfobject concept as well. In Renik's (1993) view, for instance, the analyst's empathy is likely to coopt the patient's autonomy (p. 568). This concern of Renik's highlights some central differences between his and Kohut's thinking, inasmuch as Kohut's (1984) selfobject concept rendered individual autonomy neither desirable nor possible. Kohut would have agreed with Renik that empathy indeed tends to co-opt or undermine autonomy, but he saw such co-optation as a positive development rather than as something to be avoided. For Kohut, autonomy was a sterile, isolating mirage. In his view, mutual modification of autonomy in intimate relationships was inherent to selfobject relating and served to foster growth-enhancing bonds throughout the life cycle.

In fact, the different attitudes toward the patient's autonomy in the writings of Kohut and of the postmoderns may account for much of the devaluing of empathy that the postmoderns seem to express. Nevertheless, no single recommended stance in psychoanalysis is without its problems, and many of the postmoderns' concerns about "the use and abuse of empathy" were anticipated by Gedo as early as 1981. Other analysts, as well, anticipated current attitudes toward empathy by commenting on its pitfalls, especially in the treatment of borderline psychopathology (Adler, 1989; Buie, 1981). Elsewhere (Teicholz, 1989), I have suggested that, when patients are in the throes of primitively organized experience, they tend to be made even more frightened and fragmented by overt expressions of the analyst's empathy and often misunderstand these as signs of the analyst's weakness at a time when they are most desperately seeking signs of her strength and indestructability. Patients who are feeling helpless, who are in confused or disorganized states, or who feel affectively overwhelmed (such as with rage, grief, attachment longings, or sexual sensations and desires) may also become humiliated by virtue of having any kind of attention drawn to their experience, even when it is expressed in terms of "sympathy" and understanding. Not usually cited in these critiques of empathy, however, are Kohut's (1984) own comments on the limitations of empathy, particularly what he felt to be his own empathic limitations in working with borderline states or personality organization (pp. 8–9).

But Renik and other postmodern analysts do not specifically address problems of empathy in working with "primitive disorders." Instead, their contributions point to the ways that empathy can undermine the treatment of higher functioning analysands with respect to healthy and normative bids for automomy. I understand Renik to mean that, if a patient is concerned with his autonomy, and if in that context he is trying to establish his separateness and difference from the analyst, then the analyst's empathic stance, to the extent that it tends to highlight aspects of human experience that patient and analyst share, might be felt by the patient to undermine his efforts toward an emergent sense of separateness and difference. But if we accept Kohut's (1982) distinction between a mother's empathy, on one hand, and the actions that are carried out on the basis of that empathy, on the other, then empathy need not be a threat to anyone's sense of autonomy. Let me spell out this claim: a parent or analyst interacting with a child or patient who is trying to establish his autonomy can use her empathic apprehension to *guide* her toward communication or action that will be less likely to "co-opt" the child or patient's emergent autonomy. *Empathy as a stance vis-à-vis the patient's experience leaves the entire field of communication and action open to the analyst*, once the analyst has gleaned some ideas and constellations of feelings that she thinks approximate the patient's experience of the moment. This entire field of communication and action can selectively include, but does not limit the analyst to, a direct expression of what she has gleaned from her empathic "reading." Contemporary discussions often conflate the experience and the expression of empathy, whereas, in fact, the experience of empathy may just as easily point to the decision not to express it.

Whereas Renik's concern with the analyst's empathy centers on impingement on the patient's autonomy, Hoffman, Mitchell, and Slavin and Kriegman have all responded to a sense that empathy is being overapplied and overused and that analysts often resort to a facile and inauthentic mimicry of the real thing. Hoffman (1994) therefore argues against "the conspicuously formal, role-related aspects of the analyst's participation [as] magnets for the patient's mistrust" (p. 192), and seems to include empathy among such "role-related" stances. As an antidote to the dangers of the analyst's rote role performances, empathy included, he recommends "spontaneous personal engagement" (p. 193) and expresses agreement with Slavin and Kriegman (1992), who write:

The attempt to remain exclusively attuned to what appear to the therapist to be the dominant themes and meanings in the patient's subjective world is, in fact, sensed by many patients as self-protective strategy on the part of the therapist. . . . [A]n immersion in the patient's subjective world . . . must be complemented, at times, by what is, in effect, the open expression of the analyst's reality [pp. 252–253].

Mitchell (1997), for his part, emphasizes the *struggle* entailed in arriving at genuine empathy with many patients through trials, mistrials, and corrected misunderstandings. But, since any analytic approach can be poorly executed, should we thereupon move beyond empathy because many of those professing to use it in their work do not do so in an authentic manner or do not arrive at it through a necessarily interactive process in which inevitable trials and errors send us on unexpected detours and delays? Kohut built into his own formulation of empathy what he saw as the inevitable failures in its achievement, and he spelled out the expectable interchanges in an ongoing sequence of disruptions and repairs. To be sure, his discussions of empathy in the 1970s lacked the sense of struggle for the analyst that brings contemporary discussions to life (for instance, Mitchell, 1997). Nevertheless, Kohut never implied an easy and unobstructed road to the analyst's empathy, and, above all, he always granted to the patient the final word on whether the analyst had succeeded or failed in his empathic undertaking. Kohut (1984) wrote that "the analyst focuses his attention on the inner life of his patient, and the successes and *failures* of his understanding activity are the essential motor of the analytic process" (p. 38, italics added). I interpret this to mean that it is the analyst's *struggles* to achieve empathic understanding of the patient that keep the treatment moving and are therefore at the heart of psychoanalysis.

At midcentury, we recall, Kohut (1959) identified empathy as a method of observation that he saw as having become sorely underemphasized in the literature on Freudian interpretation. Empathy gradually shifted in Kohut's (1982, 1984) writings from its origins as a method of observation to become a stance intended to establish or reestablish an affective bond between patient and analyst. Now the empathic stance seems broadly to be seen as having become hackneyed or jaded in its implementation. Thus, Hoffman (1994) encourages us to allow "the analyst's distinctive self expression [to move] into the foreground" (p. 194), and Benjamin (1988) speaks approvingly of the analyst's allowing herself to surface as a desiring subject. These moves or stances are sometimes portrayed as being in dialectical relationship to empathy (Mitchell, 1991; Hoffman, 1994; Aron, 1996), but at other times they are simply presented as *preferable* to empathy: as more therapeutic or as analytically more effective (Renik, 1993, 1995, 1996). Thus, although in his later writings Kohut (1982; 1984) was explicit about the subjective basis of the analyst's empathy, empathy is now often classified with Freudian neutrality and anonymity as a mode of analytic participation that *contrasts* with the articulation and expression of the analyst's subjectivity.

The Dialectic as a Postmodern Solution to Dichotomous Tensions in Psychoanalytic Thinking

Although all the moderate postmoderns grapple with the implications for treatment of the analyst's subjectivity, none of them advocates an exclusive clinical focus on the analyst's self-expression or an irresponsible retreat from the patient's needs. In their search for solutions to new tensions in psychoanalytic awareness, several of the postmoderns have turned to the concept of dialectical thinking. Ogden (1992a), initially referring to "the dialectical interplay of consciousness and unconsciousness" in Freud's work (p. 517), seems to have introduced the concept of the dialectic into contemporary psychoanalytic writings. Ogden writes:

> Dialectic is a process in which opposing elements each create, preserve and negate the other; each stands in a dynamic, ever-changing relationship to the other. Dialectical movement tends toward integrations that are never achieved. Each potential integration creates a new form of opposition characterized by its own distinct form of dialectical tension. That which is generated dialectically is continuously in motion, perpetually in the process of being decentered from static self-evidence. In addition, dialectical thinking involves a conception of the interdependence of subject and object. . . . One cannot begin to comprehend either the subject or the object in isolation from one another [p. 517].

Both Mitchell (1993, 1997) and Hoffman (1994) have expanded on Ogden's (1992a) ideas by acknowledging an interpersonal dialectic in the psychoanalytic situation and seeking a balance between attention to the *patient's* subjectivity and the analyst's elaboration of her own. In Hoffman's (1994) words:

[A] sense of psychoanalytic discipline, which includes restrictions on the extent and nature of the analyst's involvement, provides the backdrop for whatever spontaneous, personal interactions the participants engage in. On the other hand, given our current understanding of how important it is that analysts allow themselves to be affected and known to some significant degree by their patients, the restrictions themselves are more qualified than they were [p. 194].

Hoffman goes on to say that, "although the analyst speaks partly in the context of the role of disciplined expert, his or her *voice* can and should remain personally expressive" (p. 196). Mitchell (1991) also shows an exquisite sensitivity to his patients' needs while trying to contend with the irreducibility of the analyst's intrapsychic and interpersonal realities. He writes: "What may be most crucial is the process of negotiation itself in which the analyst finds his own way to confirm and participate in the patient's subjective experience, yet over time establishes his own presence and perspective in a way that the patient can find enriching rather than demolishing" (p. 164).

Even allowing for sensitivity, caution, and dialectic, however, these new voices cumulatively lead to an impressive insistence on the analyst's expression of a unique self and to the recommendation that she be prepared to spell out her subjective realities and affective experiences, whether or not they overlap with, validate, or affirm the patient's perceptions and feelings. This expression of the analyst's subjectivity is advocated in the interests of the patient's development of a richness of self and in the interests of the elucidation of the patient's relational patterns, which necessarily require an encounter between two individuals perceived as separate and different (Benjamin, 1988; Mitchell, 1993, 1996). Thus, even when these recommendations are not made in the context of a critique of self psychology, they remind us of the serious limitations of Kohut's emphasis on empathy, affective attunement, and availability as an archaic selfobject in the clinical situation. One might even conclude that expression of the analyst's unique and disjunctive subjectivity has become a new guiding prinicple in discussions of postmodern psychoanalytic technique.

THE EXPRESSION OF THE ANALYST'S SUBJECTIVITY

A New Guiding Principle of Psychoanalytic Technique?

*On the one hand there is nothing but the knowing subject; on the other hand
. . . that subject derives from an alien significance that transcends and
overwhelms it.*

—Julia Kristeva

Empathy and the Analyst's Unique Subjectivity

The moderate postmoderns seem collectively to advocate that the analyst be ready to give more spontaneous and authentic expression to her
unique subjectivity than in the past, even though the concept of technique per se arouses concerns about rote performance of learned
responses (Hoffman, 1994). In spite of their convergence on the point
of the analyst's self-expression, there are, among them, complexly argued
differences concerning a continued role for interpretive processes in contemporary psychoanalysis. For instance, Renik (1993) seems almost to
relegate interpretation to a thing of the past, whereas Mitchell (1996)
sees it as uneffective in many instances. Tensions also persist both within
the individual analyst (Aron, 1996; Hoffman, 1996, 1998; Mitchell,
1997) and across paradigms, concerning how freely the analyst can
engage in explicit self-expression without unduly impinging on the
patient's own, often quite fragile, sense of subjectivity (Winnicott, 1960;
Kohut, 1977a, 1984; Trop and Stolorow, 1992).

Long before analyst self-expression was openly debated in psycho-analytic discourse, I sometimes found it invaluable to give myself freedom to engage authentically with my patients or express aspects of my unique experience that I hoped would foster emotional intimacy and trust or provide a useful experience of alterity in the analytic relationship. Similar, I think, to analytic experiences described by Hoffman, Mitchell, and Aron, this sense of freedom has seldom been removed from a complex and profound appreciation of the particular patient with whom I am working, and it is necessarily infused with an attitude of judiciousness and relative self-containment. What I am calling my analytic freedom of expression has also been informed by a recognition of the limits of my capacity for self-observation and the expectation that the ways in which my patients will experience my participation may often take me by surprise. But, regardless of the freedoms of self-expression and relational engagement that I allow myself, I feel that I have only ordinary human empathy, enhanced by psychoanalytic training and ideals, to guide me in what I do. Although the moderate post-moderns do not articulate it in quite this way, sometimes even devaluing the analyst's empathy, they would presumably have us proceed in just this manner.

Not their theoretical discussions, but the case material offered by both Mitchell (1997) and Hoffman (1998) provide support for this belief. For instance, although neither Hoffman nor Mitchell formulates what he is doing in terms of empathy, both seem implicitly to rely on psychoanalytically informed empathy to guide them toward greater or lesser degrees of self-expressiveness and self-revelation with particular patients at specific moments. Hoffman demonstrates an extraordinarily detailed and nuanced appreciation of his patients' past experience and present states, which he brings to bear on his analytic decision making. This is particularly noticeable in the thought processes through which he moved in trying to arrive at a response to a particular patient's unanticipated request that Hoffman accompany him to the elevator at the end of a session. The patient was phobic of heights, and significant to Hoffman's (necessarily split-second) decision to act without visible hesitation in accordance with the patient's request, was the fact that this session had been held in the analyst's downtown high-rise office building, rather than the other office (closer to the ground) where the patient was used to having his sessions. This one-time change of meeting place had been made at the analyst's request to accommodate his own unusual scheduling needs that day. Informing Hoffman's decision-making process, therefore, was his empathically gleaned recognition that the patient's agreement to the change of office had probably entailed a not inconsiderable emotional stretch.

What Hoffman shares of his thought processes in coming to this decision under pressure strikes me not only with the uniqueness of his own subjectivity and how he was able to use it, but, even more importantly, how deeply immersed he was in his patient's subjectivity as well. This immersion enabled Hoffman very quickly to arrive at a course of action that integrated the concerns of two different subjectivities in that particular analytic dyad at a particular moment, and to do so clearly under the dominance of his awareness of the patient's feelings and therapeutic needs. Hoffman did not articulate or openly express to the patient any of his own thought processes or his own needs and interests. He simply acted affirmatively in response to the patient's request, the multiple meanings of which (for the patient) Hoffman seemed to have understood more than adequately.

Although Hoffman (1998) offers this vignette as an illustration of the dialectical tensions in the analyst between ritual and spontaneity, in my reading of it he has also demonstrated an instance of action guided by a profound and richly informed empathy: in fact, we could not ask for a more beautiful, more complete, or more moving illustration of therapeutic empathy than he has given us. His thinking and action most certainly express an instance of spontaneous self-expression to the extent that there was no textbook prescription for how he was to arrive at what he did. Nevertheless, his spontaneous self-expression was at every step of the way oriented toward the complexities of what he understood about the singular subjectivity of that patient at that time and how he could best protect the patient's current vulnerabilities and foster the patient's long-term psychological growth without a humiliating and possibly shattering setback. Thus, although he offers this case fragment in the context of a discussion of dialectical tensions between ritual and spontaneity, the tensions wrestled with in Hoffman's analytic thought processes might be even better understood as three-way, or "trialectic": there is the analyst's sense of obligation to analytic ritual because of what he believes it is able to potentiate, and there is also the analyst's spontaneously expressed subjectivity; but the pull in either of these directions is clearly influenced by the analyst's historically informed, multilayered empathic grasp of the totality of the patient's subjective experience in the moment. Although Hoffman's empathy is thoroughly filtered through and shaped by his own subjectivity, it is nevertheless a personal response to the unique history and experience of this individual, his patient, under the empathy-enhancing influence of the analyst's commitment to carry out his therapeutic intentions and responsibilities.

The current emphasis on the analyst's authentic self-expression and self-disclosure is in part a natural progression from two earlier analytic stances: first there was Freud's interpretive emphasis, which in the hands of some followers seemed to lose Freud's (1913) own insistence on an initial phase of understanding listening toward the establishment of rapport; then there was Kohut's empathy, which, as practiced by some followers, seemed unduly to constrain the analyst's genuine self-expression and a fuller range of authentic relational engagement. Thus, the postmoderns felt constraints emanating from both classical analysis and self psychology, and their elucidation of the analyst's interactive partcipation in the analytic relationship is in part a response to what they have felt to be a misguided emphasis on anonymity, neutrality, and abstinence in classical analysis and a too narrow focus on empathic responsiveness in self psychology. They also sometimes tend to classify Kohut's theory, together with Freud's classical tradition, as a one-person psychology, because both paradigms are seen to focus on elucidating the subjectivity of only one party to the analytic relationship: the patient. The postmoderns' current emphasis on the analyst's subjectivity is therefore an attempt to correct what they see as an imbalance in this area throughout much of psychoanalytic history. They find in the work of Harry Stack Sullivan of the 1940s and 1950s one of the few exceptions to this imbalance. Mitchell and Aron in particular have tried to integrate an updated version of Sullivan's interpersonal analysis into their relational theories, in partial concert with such contemporary interpersonalists as Bromberg and Ehrenberg.

Trying to take into account the many valid concerns about analytic empathy expressed by the postmoderns, many of which were introduced into analytic discourse as early as 1981 by Gedo, I agree with Mitchell that the analyst's authentic empathy is indeed often arrived at only through an arduous struggle and with many failures along the way. Furthermore, I would say that many patients do not want to be understood (Joseph, 1992), cannot trust even the most authentic expressions of empathy, or are terrified of the hopes and longings that genuine empathy may stir up. Therefore, it should go without saying that, once having empathically apprehended such feelings in a patient, the analyst should have it in her repertoire to back off, lighten up, or allow the patient to change the subject. There are other patients who make it almost too easy for the analyst to understand them, and we can only surmise that in these cases there may be pathogenic contributions to an overwhelming tendency to adapt to what the other offers regardless of its fit with the patient's actual needs.

Mitchell (1997) makes a point about the analyst's interpretations that is equally true of the analyst's empathy: the patient will inevitably experience what the analyst says and does in accordance with his earliest formative relationships with significant others. Therefore what the analyst intends and what the patient perceives are often very far apart. Furthermore, I cannot argue with Hoffman's (1996) or Slavin and Kriegman's (1992) concerns that some analysts adopt an *empathylike* stance, or an *automatic* siding with the patient's viewpoint and that every patient can tell this posturing from the real thing. While fully agreeing with these astute observations, I am still unable to imagine any attitude on the part of the analyst other than genuine, hard-won empathy that serves as a guide for helping us choose how and to what extent we overtly express our respective subjectivities or when we might make disclosures to our patients about our feelings or our lives. Such self-expression and self-disclosures are among the large world of interactions in our repertoire from which we can choose, but, if we do not choose on the basis of our *empathy*, then on what basis do we choose? Our empathy, to be sure, is filtered through our subjectivity; indeed it is nothing more than the registration of the affective component of our subjectivity as we explore our potential commonalities with our patients.

It is because I see empathy as thoroughly subjective that I am unable to join the postmoderns in their tendency to set up the analyst's empathy and the expression of her subjectivity as either mutually exclusive opposites or even as dialectically opposed. However, I agree that empathy tends to underscore the affective commonalities between two persons, whereas the expression of the analyst's subjectivity holds the potential for underscoring *either sameness or difference* between the two parties concerned. It is therefore around the issue of confronting the patient with *the analyst's unique and disjunctive subjectivity*, gently or otherwise, that much of the current debate still awaits resolution.

Subjectivity Understood as Developmental Achievement: Implications for the Analyst's Self-Expression

Ogden's (1986) work on subjectivity is relevant to this question concerning the analyst's disjunctive self-expression and has been cited appreciatively by Mitchell (1993, 1996a), Hoffman (1994), Benjamin (1995a), and Aron (1996) in their respective discussions of this and related issues. At the same time that these authors cite Ogden, however, they seem to ignore a central component of Ogden's elucidation of subjectivity in human development and experience. Clarifying and expanding on Winnicott's concept of potential space, Ogden (1986) describes two normal stages *before* the child develops subjectivity. In the first of these, the "mother–infant unit," is in "an original state of 'oneness' that is not appreciated as oneness because *the homogeneity of the situation precedes an appreciation of difference and, therefore, the delineation of meanings*" (p. 225, italics added). In this situation, "there is no need or opportunity for symbols" (p. 214), and therefore no symbolic representation of self or subjectivity. Although infant research has shown infants to be capable of differentiation among concrete or material objects, including the capacity to make distinctions among actions originated by two separate human bodies, recognition of difference in the psychological realm, or recognition of mind in self and other, remains a developmental achievement not attained until later in the first year of life. In Ogden's view, when good-enough mothering prevails, the experience of oneness in the mother–infant pair moves on to a *transitional stage of twoness* (pp. 213–214), still in the absence of separate subjectivities. When things go well, twoness ultimately devolves into the "threeness" of mother, infant, and mother-and-infant, "wherein there is a relationship between symbol and symbolized that is mediated by an interpreting subject. . . . *The infant as subject makes it possible for the infant to become aware of the mother's subjectivity*" (p. 226).

By directly linking the establishment of subjectivity to the distinction between symbol and symbolized, Ogden places the development of subjectivity within the narrative of language development and simultaneously within the narrative of the movement from oneness to greater separateness between mother and child. In this narrative, the child's *ability to recognize the other* hinges on the establishment of the child's own subjectivity. It seems to follow from Ogden's elucidation of a developmental sequence in the achievement of subjectivity that not every patient will arrive for treatment with this achievement firmly established or that its achievement might be destabilized within the regressive pull of the analytic transference. These possibilities, in turn, have implications for the postmoderns' insistence on the overt expression of the analyst's unique subjectivity in the analytic interaction with some patients.

Ogden delineates specific ways that things may go awry along the developmental path to the establishment of subjectivity, since any developmental achievement is vulnerable to delays, detours, or distortions in the face of constitutional and environmental idiosyncrasies, imbalances, or assaults. Self psychology had its beginnings in the context of Kohut's empathic perception that some of his patients seemed to lack a solid sense of subjectivity, not reliably experiencing themselves as the center of their own experience (in Ogden's, 1986, words, not experiencing themselves as the thinkers of their own thoughts, the feelers of their own feelings, or the creators of their own meanings). To help these patients move toward the achievement of their own subjectivity, Kohut emphasized the importance of the analyst's immersion in the patient's experience as *an essential first step* in the therapeutic process. The unarticulated corollary of this focus was that *the overt articulation and expression of the analyst's own experience, to the extent that it differed significantly from the patient's,* might be held in abeyance during these earlier phases of the analytic work. This aspect of self-psychological work seems to be compatible with Ogden's observation that, until the developing child has achieved her own subjectivity, she is incapable of recognizing the subjectivity of an other. It is also compatible with Stern's (1985) research observations that, until the infant establishes subjectivity and intersubjective relatedness toward the end of the first year, he or she has no interest in and no ability to "know" the psychological experience of the other. In keeping with these views, self psychology has suggested that the analyst's participation in the analytic relationship, *as a differentiated and self-revealing other,* must be titrated on the basis of the analyst's empathic apprehension of the patient's subjective experience, allowing for the possibility that some patients at some times are not capable of a nontraumatic confrontation with the reality of a separately perceived other. Meanwhile, even while citing the literature in which these ideas are set forth, the postmoderns often tend to eschew attunement and empathy in favor of the analyst's expression of her unique subjectivity.

Thus, the postmoderns seem to acknowledge Ogden (1986) as an important contributor to their focus on analytic subjectivity at the same time that they seem to ignore certain clinical implications of his understanding that *subjectivity is a developmental achievement directly linked to the capacity to recognize the subjectivity of an other* (p. 226). The postmoderns seem to suggest that, in general, the analyst's unique self-expressiveness, highlighting the differences rather than the similarities between analyst and patient, will contribute to the development of the patient's distinctive and rich subjectivity (Mitchell, 1993, 1996a; Renik, 1996) and to an improvement in interpersonal functioning. They seem not to extrapolate, as I do, from Ogden's (or Stern's) elucidation of the early codevelopment of subjectivity and intersubjectivity to the possibility that such self-expression on the part of the analyst may for some patients be meaningless or even constitute a traumatic impingement.

For instance, Ogden (1986) identifies "a wide spectrum of causes of premature disruption of the mother-infant unity" that can lead to the individual's failure to become a *subject* (p. 215). These include repeated maternal impingements on the infant, constituting "cumulative trauma." Additionally, the infant's constitutional hypersensitivity, trauma resulting from physical illness, and illness or death of a parent or sibling can be disruptive of the normal progression to the establishment of subjectivity (p. 215). Any of these eventualities distort the normal, essential, and stage-appropriate relationship between fantasy and reality for the developing child and result in subsequent difficulties in the use of symbols and the establishment of subjectivity. In Ogden's view, to the extent that the child does not become a subject who can create layered meaning through the distinction between symbol and symbolized, she also cannot recognize the subjectivity of the other (p. 226). How can we take into account the possibility that some patients' presentation in treatment will reflect this inability and still follow the increasingly explicit recommendations of the postmoderns that we more freely express our differential subjectivities?

Clinical Focus on the Analyst's Subjectivity: Containment Versus Expression

The question of whether the analyst should contain or express her subjectivity keeps coming back as we observe contemporary analysts moving from Ogden's (1986) developmental explorations of subjectivity to the role of the analyst's subjectivity in the psychoanalytic situation. In most contemporary discussions of subjectivity, both the analyst's and the patient's subjectivity are taken as givens, and the patient is expected to arrive for treatment with a ready-made capacity to recognize the analyst's subjectivity. On the basis of these assumptions, there are references not only to the inevitability and "irreducibility" of the analyst's subjectivity (Renik, 1993), but also recommendations for the *analyst's deliberate expression of his subjectivity and active exploration of the patient's experience of the analyst's subjectivity* (Renik, 1993; Hoffman, 1996; Aron, 1996).

Analytic exploration of both intentional and unwitting self-revelation is in the forefront of current psychoanalytic discourse. Believing that "[i]nquiry into the patient's experience of the analyst's subjectivity represents one underemphasized aspect of a complex psychoanalytic approach to the analysis of transference" (p. 82), Aron (1996) especially explores the unwitting aspects of the analyst's self-revelation as perceived by the analysand. He pays particular attention to elucidating his patients' "implicit interpretations to [him] about aspects of the countertransference that [the analyst] may not be conscious of" (p. 243). Mitchell (1993, 1996a) believes that the analyst's fuller expression of his unique subjectivity will contribute to the patient's development of intrapsychic richness. And Benjamin (1988) argues that, unless the mother or analyst expresses her subjectivity in relationship to the child or patient, the child or patient will be at a loss in the development of her own subjectivity.

In Benjamin's work, this problem pertains especially to little girls in relation to their mothers, because same-sex identifications between mother and daughter make the little girl particularly vulnerable to following in her mother's footsteps to a future with less than fully expressed subjectivity. But, in Benjamin's view, the problem has implications for children of both sexes and for therapy as well. She writes:

> Only a mother who feels entitled to be a person in her own right can ever be seen as such by her child, and only such a mother can appreciate and set limits to the inevitable aggression and anxiety that accompany a child's growing independence. Only someone who achieves subjectivity can survive destruction and permit full differentiation [p. 82].

Benjamin makes it clear that a primary concern is for the fullest possible development and expression of a differentiated subjectivity for the developing child (or analysand). In this concern, she is in agreement with the goals of development and treatment in Kohut's self psychology. But Benjamin differs from Kohut in the central role she gives to desire in the expression of subjectivity, and also in her notion of the kinds of experiences that are most likely to facilitate achievement of the developmental goal that she and Kohut share. Kohut (1984) agreed with the view of the postmoderns that the analyst's subjectivity is centrally important to the patient as a "human presence" (p. 37). But, in contrast to Benjamin and the other postmoderns, he thought that the analyst's subjectivity was best limited in its disjunctive expression, being conveyed largely through the analyst's general psychological functioning, his warmly affective engagement, and his empathic responsiveness to the patient. In partial contrast to this approach, Benjamin and the other moderate postmoderns suggest that the analyst's fuller expression of his uniquely differentiated subjectivity can facilitate the patient's elucidation and expansion of her own.

In fact, the general drift of postmodern writing suggests that fast disappearing are the old guidelines that once helped the analyst keep her focus on the patient's inner life, a focus that, in spite of other striking differences, classical analysts and self psychologists have held in common. This shift in emphasis from the patient's to the analyst's subjectivity has evoked Bollas's (1989) warning against "a subtle takeover of the analysand's psychic life with the analyst's" (p. 64). Aron (1996) himself acknowledges "a danger that analysts may insist on asserting their own subjectivity . . . [imposing] on patients their own need to establish themselves as separate subjects, thus forcing patients to assume the role of objects" (p. 85). He further suggests that analysts' "deliberate efforts to establish themselves as separate subjects, may be correctly experienced as an *impingement* stemming from their own narcissistic needs" (p. 86, italics added).

But, since any technical principle can be used insensitively or in excess, these caveats alone are not a sufficient basis for turning back the tide on the analyst's expressed subjectivity. Given that Kohut (1984) himself recognized the need for self psychology to broaden its relational focus beyond selfobject experience, it is not surprising that among self psychologists and their intersubjective sympathizers we find an expanding view of the analyst's participation. Stolorow et al. (1987), for instance, make a plea for the analyst's readiness to oscillate between the patient's selfobject and oedipal transferences on the basis of an empathic assessment of the quality of the patient's experience at any given moment. Lichtenberg (1989), having identified exploratory-assertive and aversive motivations, in addition to an attachment-affiliation system, thus recognizes the health-promoting potential, for some patients, of delineating differences and even conflicts between patient and analyst. Fosshage (1995) suggests that the analyst listen "from within and without" the patient's vantage point, "oscillating in a background-foreground configuration . . . [to] illuminate more fully the patient's experience of self and of self in relation to others" (p. 375).

But at the same time that there are self psychologists whose views more closely correspond with those of the postmoderns, there is at least one object relational/interpersonal analyst (Slochower, 1996) who speaks eloquently for the view that "the analyst's dysjunctive subjectivity" must *at times* be "contained within the analyst," rather than directly and overtly expressed to the patient (p. 323). Slochower has observed, at certain times and with some patients, "intensely toxic reactions to 'knowing' the analyst," and she suggests that these patients have an inability "to stand a mutual analytic experience" (p. 323). She joins the postmoderns in more fully endorsing a "collaborative exchange" and "mutuality within the analytic setting," but insists that these kinds of interactions take place only *after* a period during which sufficient holding on the part of the analyst has enabled the patient to tolerate increasing exposure to the analyst's externality and alterity.

We have already identified Winnicott's notion of *holding* as a (pre)selfobject function required of the caretaker in the first year of life. Both Winnicott and Kohut believed that some patients at some times need to use their analysts' psychological functioning in the service of self-development, without recognition that the source of that functioning was in the analyst. Slochower has applied this aspect of Winnicott's thinking to the notion that the analyst sometimes intentionally "holds" or contains her countertransference feelings rather than giving expression to them in the analytic relationship. This recommended containment seems to be compatible with Ogden's (1982) recommendation that the analyst make *silent interpretations* in response to some experiences of projective identification. But attesting to Slochower's attunement and responsiveness to the variable capacities and needs of different patients, she earlier (Slochower, 1991) recommended that, with borderline patients who are "incessantly making demands on [or] endlessly attacking" the analyst, the analyst could effectively express *annoyance* in an attempt to provide a modulated experience of the analyst's affect in response to the patient's angry demands and attacks. Slochower sees annoyance as a restrained expression of the analyst's subjectivity and countertransference, which affords the patient the experience of having had an impact on his analyst at the same time that it offers reassuring evidence that the patient has not destroyed her (p. 713).

Although the postmoderns might feel that Slochower's (1991) suggestion is too prescriptive of a particular response in a specific circumstance, it seems to me that it is no more prescriptive than their own encouragement of greater freedom of self-expression or self-disclosure with patients in general. Nevertheless, in spite of our consensus that every patient, every analyst, and every analytic pairing is absolutely unique, there remain certain familiar, recognizable, and communicable experiences that we are well advised to describe and open for discussion.

With respect to those patients who seem initially unable to tolerate the articulation of the analyst's unique subjectivity, Slochower (1996) makes the point that the analyst does not abandon her subjectivity, nor does she "give it up." The analyst, for a period of time, simply *does nothing to interfere* with the patient's "illusion" of the analyst's absolute resonance (Slochower, 1996) and nothing to interfere with the patient's use and experience of the analyst's psychological functioning as if it were the patient's own (Kohut, 1977a). I share with Slochower the view that the analyst in these cases temporarily contains her disjunctive experience in relationship to the patient, perhaps holding it for later interpersonal exploration and analysis. I suggest further that it is only through the analyst's empathic "sounding" of the patient's experience that she can judge just how much of her disjunctive subjectivity the patient may be able to bear at any given point. This sounding is often undertaken through trial and error, in which the analyst is self-expressive in what seems to be her ordinary way and then is taken by surprise, informed, and redirected by the patient's unexpected feelings of devastation. Not all patients by any means, but certainly some, have such reactions to the seemingly ordinary expression of the analyst's unique subjectivity. Often, the patient's intense negative reaction turns out to hinge on a hidden, idiosyncratic meaning that the analyst's particular self-revelation has for him.

Even while arguing for a freer expression of the analyst's unique subjectivity, Mitchell (1997) describes an interaction with one of his patients in which he (Mitchell) had to "backpedal" when the patient's anxious response to his interpretive use of a countertransference experience dictated such a retreat (p. 41). The countertransference experience that had nudged Mitchell toward the interpersonal interpretation was a "sinking feeling" about the patient's relational repetitions in the transference. In my reading of Mitchell's report, the basis on which he quickly backpedaled was his empathic perception that the patient had become distraught and disorganized by the interpretation, which had included a seemingly minor and sensitively articulated transference–countertransference elucidation. Immediately before this relational observation, Mitchell had felt that the patient "was with [him] point by point" (p. 40). Although it may not have been Mitchell's intention to use this clinical vignette as an example of how the analyst uses his empathy as a guide to choosing between the expression or the containment of his subjective experience, or choosing between the articulation or silent holding of his astute relational observations, for me it exemplifies this principle in action. I have found in the clinical vignettes of both Mitchell and Hoffman persuasive illustrations of the analyst's use of his empathic perception of the patient's complex subjective state as an important component in moment-to-moment analytic decision making about how much and what aspects of the analyst's unique subjectivity will be deliberately expressed. We know now that our unwitting self-expression cannot be avoided, but we still make decisions concerning the vast (intersubjective) field in which we try to give voice to our intentions.

The Phenomenon and Language of Unexpressed Subjectivity

Mitchell (1997) himself identifies several similarities between contemporary interpersonal theories and the ideas of Winnicott and Kohut. Among these, he counts "the emphasis on the patient's subjective experience, the cultivation of the implicit creativity in the patient's own individuality and unique experience, the role of the analyst as instrument for an expansion of the self-experience of the patient" (p. 96). He then goes on to point out important differences; he states that, for the self psychologist, "the analyst's role . . . involves a suspension of the analyst's own subjective experience, and an effort to listen to and to empathize with what the analyst understands to be the 'patient's point of view' " (p. 96). Mitchell suggests that Winnicottian analysts "bracket" their idiosynchratic responses to prevent impingement and to allow the patient's "true" self to emerge without interference. But Kohut (1977, 1984) stated clearly that the analyst's subjectivity cannot be suspended and is always engaged: I think that there is an important difference between suspension of one's subjectivity, on one hand, and the voluntary nonarticulation of it in the interpersonal field, on the other. It was the latter that Kohut might have recommended, but not the former, which, he would have agreed with the postmoderns, is not within the realm of human possibility.

At the risk of being a stickler for fine-tuning the language of our discourse (and inviting a similarly exacting analysis of my own very imperfect formulations), I believe that the same sort of distinction can be made in regard to Winnicott's concept of impingement: I suggest that the mother who allows for the child's spontaneous gesture is "bracketing" her subjectivity only in its overt expression or articulation, but not necessarily in her intrapsychic experience of it. She may hold or contain her affective experience; she may be careful not to draw (undue) attention to it in the interpersonal field by exhibiting or articulating it to her baby; but it is possible for the mother to do these things, up to a point, without diminishing her own sense of subjective experience. Even more than Kohut, Winnicott was sensitive to the mother's potential range of expressiveness. He argued, for instance, that the mother's most important tasks in relation to her baby include allowing the baby the illusion of omnipotence without impingement, but also participating in his gradual but necessary disillusionment at a later stage. And even more germane to our discussion of the analyst's subjectivity and self-expression, Winnicott's (1947) recommendations concerning countertransference hatred, and what he perceived as the universal emergence of a mother's hatred of her baby, argue against interpreting him as having suggested any blanket bracketing of the analyst's experience, at least if what Mitchell means by "bracketing" has anything to do with the analyst's private experience and processing of his affect. Kohut and Winnicott both felt that the analyst's internal experience of her subjectivity is of central importance in the analytic relationship, but that the analyst often chooses not to articulate this experience to the patient, *opting for self-containment rather than self-expression* at certain junctures in a treatment.

Mitchell (1997) also warns of other problems or "dangers" in "the developmental perspective" of these two earlier analysts. In particular, he cautions against "assuming new growth where subtle forms of repetition may be occurring" (p. 52). Here, Mitchell actually speaks to my worst fears each time I continue to the outer reaches of my own endurance in response to a patient's ongoing and seemingly interminable cues concerning the necessary containment of my subjective experience. At these junctures, I recognize that the patient's "repetitions" are occurring with my "help," and I worry that I am supporting their continuation rather than contributing to therapeutic change. However, thus far, with each patient in whose treatment I have felt it necessary to withhold certain aspects of my clinical observation and self-expression, at some point very soon after I think I have reached the limits of my self-containment, the patient himself has taken a step or given me a signal that he is finally more ready to observe himself or to see me in a different light.

On the other hand, on the few occasions when I seem to have "broken down," when intense countertransference pressures and failure of self-containment have led me to impose my subjectivity on a patient who was not ready to handle it, I have felt that our relationship and the treatment process suffered a major setback that sometimes took months or even years to make up. For instance, certain people I have worked with have presented for treatment but then have signaled that they are not able to engage in a process of self-exploration. They may speak of their strengths and accomplishments, all the while suggesting through body language or through cues from their autonomic nervous system that they are extraordinarily fragile in some way. In particular they seem unable to tolerate anything that suggests that I have made an observation of them that goes beyond the way they see or have presented themselves to me. Since interpretive efforts and even simple interpersonal observations lead to extreme autonomic reactivity or actual flight from the treatment on the part of these patients, I have sometimes discovered myself to be narrowly restricted to verbalizations of recognition and affirmation of whatever the patient has presented of himself.

With one such patient—after my professional guilt had been building for 15 months for offering him none of what I then thought of as my psychoanalytic repertoire—I "broke down" and tried to "test the waters" of his tolerance by making a simple observation that went slightly beyond what he was presenting of himself. He reddened, stopped speaking for five minutes, and then fled the session. Until then a patient with "perfect attendance," he missed the following session without even calling to cancel or explain. When he returned he was able to speak only haltingly of the mortification I had caused him by my observation in the previous session. He said, "Until last session, coming to my meetings with you had been like taking a long warm shower, playfully lathering myself with soap, singing off-key at the top of my lungs—reveling in the good feeling and feeling safe and accepted by you. But when I realized you were observing me from the outside, I suddenly felt that I hadn't been alone and private all that time at all. I suddenly felt as if the whole time I thought I'd been enjoying a private shower, everyone I knew, and strangers too, had been standing outside of the shower, watching me through a huge picture window that I'd believed had been an opaque wall or mirror."

Feeling that we were not getting any analytic work done, concerned that I was "allowing" the patient to have too good a time at the expense of his treatment and potential for change, worrying that he did not recognize me as a separate individual, I had made an interpersonal observation of my patient that turned out nearly to destroy the analytic relationship. After these feelings and judgments had persisted in me for several months, I had impinged on my patient with an observation that brought my separateness too much into his awareness. I believe that I disrupted something very important that was going on beneath the surface of our interactions which had to do with the patient's using our sessions to feel my recognition and affirmation. On the basis of my later experience with other patients who showed similar degrees of vulnerablity but with whom I tolerated my feelings of psychoanalytic uselessness longer than with the patient I have just described, I believe that, had I been able to hold on to my interpersonal observations a little bit longer, my patient would have begun to develop the "observing ego" and self-cohesion to begin making useful and growth-promoting observations of himself; and I could have saved the treatment from the unnecessary setback caused by my having exposed him to feelings of mortification.

With the majority of patients I have worked with, the analyst's self-expressiveness has not been an issue at all; but, with those for whom it was, my containment of my disjunctive subjectivity around issues of central importance to the patient seemed to be an essential requirement of the initial phases of the treatment, sometimes extending into the second year of an analysis. To illustrate the changes that can take place in the nature of the analyst's participation over the course of a treatment as the analysand begins to benefit from an earlier period of the analyst's forebearance in relation to expression of her "disjunctive" subjectivity, I have elsewhere presented extensive material from the first and third years of an analysis of another patient who conveyed a similar fragility (Teicholz, 1995).

Not just Mitchell but also feminist psychoanalysts have been critical of certain developmental approaches to analytic treatment. For example, some feminists see in Winnicott's concept of the "good enough mother" a destructively constraining prescription for maternal behavior (Doane and Hodges, 1982, 1992). In apparent synchrony with the postmoderns, these analysts read Winnicott as insisting that the mother *sacrifice* her subjectivity for the sake of her baby. *Although mothers very often do make sacrifices for their children, I suggest that what they most often sacrifice pertains to the pursuit of their own nonmaternal interests and goals, not their subjectivity.* Still, since interests and goals grow out of, and give expression to, subjectivity (Stepansky, 1997, personnal communication), the mother who puts these aside over a period of many years, during which she makes herself available to her children, can suffer considerable damage to her sense of self and her engagement in the world-at-large, with consequent significant loss of confidence, esteem, and even cohesion and continuity.

The empathically responsive analyst, or the analyst allowing aspects of her psychic functioning to be silently used as selfobject experience by her patient, is also postponing the pursuit of her nontherapeutic interests and goals for the sake of her analysand, but the analyst's self-containment is not identical with giving up an internal sense of her own subjectivity. Furthermore, in contrast to the mother who postpones the pursuit of her own goals over a period of many years, the analyst who temporarily contains her subjectivity as needed in work with particular patients, has plenty of other opportunities to pursue interests and goals through which she can give wider expression to her unique subjectivity. Within her professional world alone, she may teach, supervise, do research, administer analytic programs, write, and engage in collegial interactions, all activities that do not usually demand the containment of unique aspects of one's subjectivity to the degree sometimes required of the analyst in the conduct of particular treatments.

To the extent that subjectivity is equivalent to our patterns of organizing experience (Atwood and Stolorow, 1984), to the extent that it is synonymous with the creation of personal meaning (Ogden, 1986), to the extent that it entails our experience of ourselves as the thinkers of our thoughts and the feelers of our feelings (Ogden, 1986), and to the extent that it involves experiencing ourselves as the center of our experience (Kohut, 1977a), we cannot entirely "bracket" it except in transient merger experiences or psychosis. Since there is probably more widespread agreement on this point than the postmoderns seem to realize, the current debates are only spuriously about the *fact* of the analyst's subjectivity itself. More accurately, we are struggling toward a sense of the relative efficacy of expression versus containment of the unique and disjunctive aspects of our subjectivity with different patients at different times.

The Analyst's Irreducible Subjectivity And Mutual Influence: Potential Contradictions

Interestingly, the very analysts who have criticized Kohut and Winnicott for advocating the containment of the analyst's subjectivity, and who themselves advocate strongly for its fuller expression, also seem to suggest that a certain blurring of subjective boundaries inevitably takes place in the analytic interaction through mutual influence. Mutual influence entails changes in the subjective organization of experience of both patient and analyst. Thus, Renik, Aron, and Mitchell have all argued that the analyst cannot put aside her subjectivity; but they have also intimated that the analyst's subjectivity cannot truly remain discrete inasmuch as, both epistemically and pragmatically, it is impossible to "know" who did what to whom in the past, or who is doing what to whom in the present (Mitchell, 1997). These questions must therefore be negotiated (Russell, 1989, personal communication; Pizer, 1992; Slavin and Kriegman, 1992), rather than determined unilaterally by a knowing and authoritarian analyst. The difficulty, I believe, derives not only from the ubiquity, complexity, and ultimate unknowability of unconscious motivation in both parties, but also from the extent to which both patient and analyst, to some degree, gradually and inevitably relinquish their preanalytic subjectivity in the analytic intersubjective mix. Thus, the current literature as a whole carries tensions

inherent in the coexistence of arguments for the expression of the analyst's separate and unique subjectivity, and simultaneous acknowledgment that the respective subjectivities of patient and analyst will never
be the same once they have come together in the intersubjective mix of
the analytic relationship.

Given the duality of these emphases, there are unresolved tensions
in the writings of Kohut as well as in those of the postmoderns. For
Kohut, even the mature selfobject concept entailed a breaking down of
boundaries between selves, or a mutual "borrowing" of psychic functions to sustain or enhance the self. At the same time as he wrote about
this everyday mixing of subjectivities, however, his emphasis on attunement implied that the mother (or analyst) should contain certain
aspects of her disjunctive subjective experience rather than giving it
direct verbal or affective expression in relation to the child (or analysand).
This duality of one-way and two-way selfobject functioning need not
constitute a contradiction if we realize that, in early development or in
the treatment situation, we are usually dealing with the archaic selfobject experiences of a developing individual and therefore focusing on
the one-way provision of needed psychic experiences for that individual. We are speaking not of what might be seen as going on in the eyes
of an outside observer, but only of what the child or the patient herself
might experience, given the limiting effects of her developmental or
traumatic experience up to this point. In this context, the caretaker or
analyst may to some extent remain aware of and "in touch" with her
own subjectivity but choose to express it to the child or patient only
very selectively. Rather than contradictions in Kohut's theory, then,
there may simply be a recognition of different relational needs at different stages of development and in response to different states of mind
for the patient, with differing therapeutic intentions and efforts on the
part of the analyst in the face of these differences.

Even the healthiest of children need some degree of protection
from the harsh realities of the world, and, since these realities are
reflected in the subjectivities of adults, adults do not casually share all
their subjective views of the world to very young children. But, perhaps even more than normal children, our patients who have suffered
earlier trauma need transiently to be protected from certain aspects
of the subjective perceptions and reactions of their analysts. Early
traumatic experience massively calls up primitive defenses that, in
turn, interfere with normal ego development (Coates and Moore,

1997); thus, the "defensive" and "developmental" sequelae of trauma become intertwined, and these issues simply cannot be dealt with separately in treatment.

The idea that previously traumatized patients may initially in treatment need the analyst not to draw attention to her unique or disjunctive subjectivity finds support in recent findings from infant observation research. As reported by Beebe et al. (1997), several studies have found that very high tracking of affect or very intensive attunement between infant and caretaker is associated with a hypervigilant and insecure attachment. The authors found that, in contrast to the unusually high tracking in these insecurely attached infants, "low to midrange values of coordination of vocal timing are optimal . . . [in which] mother and infant significantly influence each other's patterns, but interpersonal constraint is not as tightly coupled as in the very high tracker" (p. 170).

These research observations give us new ways of thinking about the clinical situation, in which some patients arrive with a tendency toward very high affective tracking and seem to command in return a narrowly focused affective attunement on the analyst's part. Although this heightened attunement imposes considerable interpersonal constraints on the analyst and is associated with a clearly psychopathological relational system, it may be necessary as a starting point for work with patients whose patterns of experience and relating were originally laid down in an insecurely attached caretaking dyad. Beebe et al. "speculate that the full range of values [of interpersonal affective tracking], including the extremes, is probably necessary for empathy, so long as mobility across the range is retained" (p. 170). Thus, while "normal" empathy allows for mobility across a range, the clinical situation sometimes seems to call for "abnormal" values of empathy in response to an initially "insecure" and "high-tracking" analysand. The postmodern emphasis on expression of the analyst's unique subjectivity may in part be a reaction to Kohut's emphasis on the "high tracking" empathy that seems to be required initially for work with some patients in whom the original establishment of subjectivity was compromised by early trauma, either singular-event or cumulative. The debates between self psychologists and the postmoderns concerning these issues should make all analysts more aware that patients differ along these dimensions and may need to be engaged differentially on this basis.

Just as certain contradictions emerge within self-psychological writings, so certain tensions in postmodern writings emerge from the dual emphasis on the analyst's unique and separate subjectivity, on one hand, and the mutual influence between patient and analyst, on the other hand. It is understood that this mutual influence inevitably changes the subjectivities of both (Slavin and Kriegman, 1998). Thus, the post-moderns portray an analyst who is acutely aware of the ways in which her subjective experience differs from that of her patient and who seeks ways to communicate those differences in the analytic exchange. At the same time, however, the postmodern analyst recognizes that, through her engagement in the analytic relationship, she opens herself up to the patient's influence on that very subjectivity, which can at least tran-siently be confused with the patient's and which will never be exactly the same as it was before. But how much does the concept of mutual influence require us to forego our concept of a separate and unique sub-jectivity for the analyst? One way that we have dealt with this question is by falling back on the philosophically useful concepts of paradox and dialectic. These notions at least help us to contain the tensions among competing ways of experiencing and conceptualizing our participation in the analytic work and its impact on our patients and ourselves.

But where dialectic and paradox are not invoked, we see a potential split in the analytic community even within the ranks of those who have warmly embraced the concept of intersubjectivity. In one camp, we have the "intersubjectivists," who tend to play down the recognition of the separateness and difference between subjectivities and to focus more on the blurring of boundaries, on shared experience, and on com-monalities (Kohut, 1971, 1977a, 1982, 1984; Stolorow et al., 1987). In the other camp, we have "intersubjectivists," whose primary focus is on the differences and potential for conflict between individuals possessed of unique and often disjunctive subjectivities (Bollas, 1989; Slavin and Kriegman, 1992; Renik, 1993, 1995, 1996; Mitchell, 1993, 1997).

Loewald's writings are unique in that, over the course of his career, they seemed to cover every possibility along this continuum, making it more difficult to suggest that he belongs in one or the other of the two intersubjective "camps." For instance, he preceded Kohut in arguing for the importance of the analyst's affectively focused attention on the patient's subjective experience, but he also anticipated the postmoderns in suggesting that the analyst must become a distinct "new object" for the analysand (Loewald, 1960). In contrast to the postmoderns, how-ever, Loewald believed that the analyst could best become a new object through an interpretive stripping away of the patient's distortions.

Thus, although he emphasized personal qualities that the analyst must embody to facilitate the analytic process, he also adhered to aspects of a classical analytic process.

Loewald (1979b) was also eloquent on the subject of the inevitability of intergenerational conflict. He saw the developing individual as necessarily wresting authority from the parents in order to establish his own autonomy. Loewald thus saw in every "normal" developmental process the inevitability of an experience that would be felt as patricidal enactment. Even though Loewald (1960) had earlier written powerfully about the analyst's developmental love and devotion of attention to the analysand, can we really imagine that he envisioned growth through psychoanalysis as any less fraught than original development with intense feelings of conflict? Or do the different emphases in his 1960 and 1979 papers reflect a striking shift in his world view and experience?

Loewald (1979b) believed that in the negotiation of developmental passages between parents and children (and, I presume, between patients and analysts), one or the other party to the engagement would inevitably be diminished. His view on these matters was far less optimistic than that of either Kohut or the postmoderns. For instance, we have seen that Kohut believed that parents (or analysts) could be enriched by vicarious and identificatory pleasure in the growth of their children (or analysands). Among the moderate postmoderns, Aron (1996) has explicitly noted the optimism implicit in contemporary relational arguments for the patient's growth through mutual engagement with the analyst. Mitchell (1993) has written about dread, but also about hope in the patient. And while both Mitchell (1997) and Hoffman (1998) make much of the limitations of the analyst's powers in the face of human frailty, I suggest that their descriptions of their own clinical work tend to arouse analytic optimism, at least in their readers.

But, while some of these authors seem to lean in their writings a little more toward autonomy and conflict and others more toward interconnectedness and harmony, in all their writings experiences of similarity and difference, harmony and conflict, and separateness and connection are highly valued and are never very far apart. For instance, in Aron's (1996) notion of the "meeting of minds" and in Hoffman's (1991) notion of social construction, we see two paradigms that sit firmly on the cusp of these multiple sets of emphases: separate and unique subjectivities are highly valued at the same time that mutual influence or coconstruction of individual and shared experience is recognized. And even though Kohut did not himself make use of the concepts of paradox or dialectic, I can think of no postmodern writing in which the tension between seeming opposites is more balanced than it is between the self and the selfobject dimensions of experience in Kohut's self psychology.

Empathy and a Two-Person Psychology

Coming back to the clinical implications of these theoretical dialectics, I imagine that all good enough analysts are quite selective about which aspects of their subjectivity they choose to articulate to a given patient and which aspects they choose to remain silent about. I imagine also that these judgments are generally made on the basis of empathic attunement and an in-depth assessment concerning the issues around which the patient's most intense affect is crystalizing. It seems to me that empathy conveys a slightly more interpersonal quality of engagement than either subjectivity or authenticity inasmuch as the latter two, relatively speaking, can express the interests and feelings of a singular individual whereas empathy is by definition an affective connection between two persons. For this reason, in a two-person psychology, empathy remains an optimal guide as to which aspects of our subjectivity and authenticity we choose to articulate and reveal to a particular patient and under what circumstances. I have already argued that empathy, to the extent that it is grounded in a potential affective commonality between patient and analyst (Kohut, 1982), is necessarily an aspect of the analyst's subjective experience. Although each of the three terms has distinct connotations, what the analyst's empathy, subjectivity, and authenticity all have in common is an ultimate reference to and grounding in the analyst's affect.

As noted earlier, Kohut (1982) argued that the mother use her empathy or affective attunement to guide her in choosing from a broad repertoire of possible actions. Similarly, the good enough analyst uses empathy in a necessarily trial-and-error fashion, and with the inevitability of repetitive disruptions and repairs, to guide her in choosing among a broad repertoire of actions and communications that she hopes will be therapeutic or growth-promoting; included in this repertoire are diverse modes of self-expression and extensive interactions that both patient and therapist will experience as authentic relational engagement.

What are we left with here? Inside of self psychology and out, we recognize the inevitability and irreducibility of the analyst's subjectivity and therefore of her idiosyncratic influence on the process, both unwitting and intentional. When analysts try to contain their subjectivity with a given patient, it is done not in denial of two subjectivities, nor to avoid influence. It is not even done in the interests of either gratification or frustration. It comes closer to being intended as a "holding pattern" in response to the often urgent and blatant cues that the patient simply cannot bear to hear from the analyst anything beyond what the patient himself has already thought of or known. (What the patient cannot bear, unfortunately, also includes such practical matters as the analyst's vacation plans.) Since this phenomenon often occurs in work with patients who do not otherwise manifest demanding or entitled behavior, and since the response when we violate these feelings seems to be of catastrophic proportions—even leading to suicidality in the patient—analysts who have worked with such patients feel that, at that moment, they have absolutely no choice in how to respond. Nevertheless, I think that we do not exactly suspend, give up, bracket, or sacrifice our subjectivity; rather we postpone the overt or explicit expression of that subjectivity in a particular context, and only for the time being.

The new guiding principles recommended by the postmoderns are interesting, enlivening, and appropriate to many patients throughout their analyses and to all patients at certain times in their analyses. I am only emphasizing that we have a range of interactive styles and moves in our repertoire and that we use our empathy to guide us in deciding which we employ, when, and with whom. Empathy, understood as constituting a bond between two persons, necessarily entails a two-person psychology and, to my mind, is mistakenly associated with a one-person psychological framework.

We have seen that the concept of the dialectic has been invoked increasingly in this final decade of the 1900s (Ogden, 1992a, b; Mitchell, 1991, 1993, 1997; Hoffman, 1994; Aron, 1996). The analyst's alternating affective attunement and disjunctive self-expression have not been exempt from this way of thinking. Bromberg (1996) has suggested that the analytic relationship is "a negotiated dialectic between confrontation and attunement" (p. 510) or between (the analyst's) empathy and (the patient's) anxiety (Bromberg, 1980). This idea seems to fit with my own experience, and, to the extent that postmoderns such as Hoffman, Mitchell, and Aron invoke the notion of the dialectic, I imagine that it also fits with theirs. Although sensitized to the overuse of empathy as an analytic mode of expressiveness, I doubt that any of the five analysts I have designated as postmodern would ultimately have us do away with empathic attunement as a guide to our broader analytic communication and action. In their critiques of the concept, they seem to be reacting more to what they feel has been an empathic perseveration in the absence of other ways of engaging interpersonally and to its "automization" in the hands of some therapists.

Sometimes it seems as if the postmoderns and the self psychologists are arguing anachronistically about whether the patient's experiences of *sameness or difference* in relationship to the analyst will be the most therapeutic aspect of treatment. Feelings of sameness are elicited most readily in selfobject experiences and empathic attunement, whereas feelings of difference are more likely to be elicited when the analyst is directly expressing or otherwise revealing her disjunctive subjectivity. No one can argue against the idea that patients and analysts alike need both kinds of experiences, not just developmentally but in varying proportion throughout life. Starting with Freud, and continuing through Erikson, Lichtenstein, and Mahler, psychoanalysis has always recognized the child's identification with and differentiation from the parents. Meanwhile, parents (and analysts), for better or worse, try to put aspects of their unique subjectivities in the service of their children (and patients) as needed. Whether this "service" is best provided through the containment or outward expression of the parents' or analysts' subjectivity at any given time can be ascertained only through relational engagement with and attunement to those who seek to grow or change with our assistance.

The Radical and Moderate Postmodern Views of Subjectivity: Unexpected Alliances

As an indication of just how multivarious postmodern thought has become, I close this chapter with an observation concerning the thinking of a "French intellectual" who identifies herself as a feminist theorist, postmodern philosopher, literary critic, novelist, and psychoanalyst. This is Julia Kristeva. Unlike the moderate postmodern analysts whose work I have selected for comparison with Kohut and Loewald's ideas,

Kristeva seems to have an explicitly negative attitude toward both subjectivity and desire. Although she would agree with Benjamin (1988) and others that desire is closely linked with subjectivity—that we achieve subjectivity only when we recognize ourselves as the subject of our desires—nevertheless Kristeva is not in agreement with contemporary American analysts that either subjectivity or desire is a positive development in human affairs. She goes so far as to link individual subjectivity and desire with a "nihilist program" and sees them as major obstacles to making needed human connections (Kristeva, 1987, p. 62). Concerning the mother's subjectivity, Kristeva (1996) has this to say: "[The mother] is willing to set aside all the tokens of her narcissism. . . . [B]ecause she will be rewarded by [the child's] growth, accomplishments, and future, she can subordinate herself to the ideal whom she is trying to raise and who will exceed her bounds" (p. 62).

More than any of the moderate postmoderns, Kristeva belongs to an academic "postmodern tradition" beyond psychonanalysis; and yet, in her comment on the mother's subjectivity, she is more comfortable than either Winnicott or Kohut was with the use of language suggesting that subjectivity can be "set aside." So, on one hand, we have the view of some contemporary analysts that Kohut's emphasis on empathy and his concomitant focus on the patient's subjectivity should be relegated to history (Slavin, 1997); and, on the other hand, we have Kristeva's (1996) description of the mother's involvement with and pleasure in her child, which seems to be entirely compatible with Kohut's (1971, 1977a, 1982, 1984) descriptions of parental/analytic fostering of the other's psychological growth. Both Kohut and Kristeva suggest the possibility of harmony rather than inevitable conflict between the generations. They both invoke the parent's positive capacity for taking narcissistic pleasure in the child's potential for surpassing the parent's achievements. What they mean by narcissism is something both benign and constructive: that the parent's or the analyst's subjective world may be enhanced simply by virtue of participating in the expansion of the subjective world of the child or patient. This participation is understood to diminish the parents' or (analysts') needs to express, articulate, or otherwise draw attention to their unique subjectivities in their interactions with their children (or analysands), at least at times when the children and analysands are thought to need protection from such expression.

Could it be that, at least in part, we are arguing about the different ways that analysts can legitimately fulfill their own narcissistic needs while meeting their responsibilities to their patients? From very different intellectual traditions, Kohut and Kristeva implicitly suggest that patients will be helped most when analysts meet their own narcissisitic needs by curtailing certain aspects of self-expression in order to foster and bear witness to the psychological expansion and enrichment of their analysands. In clear contrast to this suggestion, the moderate postmoderns propose that we can best help our patients by a more overt and fuller expression of our differential selves and by being seen and appreciated by our patients more as we "really" are. What I have tried to highlight throughout this discussion is my perception that our patients inevitably differ in the degree to which they can benefit from one of these approaches as opposed to the other and that we need to come to our analytic work prepard to participate in a number of different ways along this continuum.

All these authors (Kohut, Kristeva, and the moderate postmoderns) recognize that, as an aspect of the analyst's irreducible subjectivity, her narcissistic needs will somehow emerge in the treatment relationship. But they have different notions concerning which aspects of the analyst's needs can be met at the same time that she is fulfilling her professional obligations. These obligations include a responsibility to avoid overwhelming the patient's subjectivity with undue impingement and to avoid co-opting the patient's tentative and emergent subjectivity with the analyst's (supposedly) more fully delineated and more robustly consolidated organizations of experience. The moderate postmoderns are deliberately expanding the possibilities for the analyst's self-expression and interpersonal fulfilment in the course of analytic work. They argue that it is impossible, or at least dangerous (Renik, 1993), for the analyst to try to contain the expression of her subjectivity, as Kohut and Kristeva seem to recommend, and also that it is usually preferable for the patient not to be limited in the degree to which he is exposed to the analyst's unique and disjunctive subjectivity.

The postmoderns have criticized classical analysts for their claims of authority and have challenged self psychology and British object relationists because of what they see as the seductive potential of their developmental approaches. But at least one contemporary relational analyst (Jacobson, 1997) asks whether the postmoderns' own emphasis on the analyst's personal and subjective characteristics might not put us "on the road to a special person/guru version of the desirable analyst."

Seeing in the analyst's self-expression the potential for a new kind of obstacle to the patient's growth, Jacobson asks, "Are we caught between a classical authority and a post classical seduction?" (p. 105). Although we must keep in mind the very real dangers of overstimulating our patients, of coopting their therapeutic and relational agendas, or of getting in "over our heads" emotionally ourselves, we may still answer Jacobson's question concerning a potential for seduction in the analyst's articulated subjectivity with a tentative, cautious, and modified "no." The no is modified in these ways: the analyst's overtly expressed, unique subjectivity should be part of every analytic repertoire, provided that the repertoire is richly variegated and flexibly implemented and provided that the analyst participates in the analytic relationship on the basis of the ongoing empathic readings of her patients' affects and subjective states. The analyst is also aware that, while her unique subjectivity is the primary source of her empathy with others, it is also the "blinder" that renders her empathy only one very limited tool among others in her search for intersubjective understanding. The same can be said for her subjectivity in general and for her unique and differentiated forms of self-expression.

We are helped in moving toward our newly emerging analytic ideals by the fact that in current discourse there are too many vital and interesting voices for any individual voice alone to hold sway. The plurality of voices makes it more difficult than ever before for any analyst to sustain the illusion that he has a monopoly on the "best" theory or the most effective technique. Our communal system of checks and balances is working at full tilt, and the analyst has never had so much support for being honest and bringing her self-questioning somehow into her work with her patients in a way that allows for ongoing self-correction.

Although any technical principle can be seductive in the sense of being used automatically by the analyst or acceded to compliantly by the patient, analysts today have more voices than ever before telling them what to be on guard for in themselves, in their patients, and in the interaction between them. Unfortunately, however, there is still little protection for the patient who runs into a lack of integrity or severe psychopathology in the minority of analysts who bring such serious problems to their work. But the current intensive dialogue among analysts writing more openly from many perspectives offers some kind of safety net when used in conjunction with regular and personal collegial communication. Although we have no choice but to do our analytic risk taking alone, we can examine the consequences of those risks as members of a self-correcting analytic community. Part of our obligation to this community and to our patients is to make ourselves familiar with the risks that other thoughtful analysts have previously taken, as well as with what they thought the consequences were. The more we speak and write about what we do, the more complete will be the reservoir of "experience" out of which individual analysts can make their analytic choices. We can think of this process as one more dialectic: we move continually back and forth between the "evidence" of our own empathically informed sense of what the individual patient can make therapeutic use of and the accumulated "wisdom" of the larger analytic community, which is simply the aggregate at any given time of the personally gathered data of individual empathic engagement, tempered by analytic thought and self-reflection. By way of adding to this communal analytic "knowledge," Hoffman, Aron, and others suggest that we solicit our patients' interpretive and disjunctive readings of our own mental states and behavior, that we make fuller use of the fact that there are two subjectivities engaged in the analytic endeavor. This final recommendation brings us to the concept of psychoanalytic intersubjectivity, which I explore in the following two chapters.

Intersubjectivity in Psychoanalysis

Major Contributions to a Multifaceted Concept

I view the analytic process as one in which the analysand is created through an intersubjective process. . . . Analysis is not simply a method of uncovering the hidden; it is more importantly a process of creating an analytic subject who had not previously existed.

—Thomas Ogden

Ogden's view of the creation of the analytic subject through an intersubjective process is supported by many contemporary analysts and suggests just how far our conceptualization of psychoanalytic treatment has departed from Freud's original uncovering therapy in which the individual was found, not made. In both self psychology and postmodern psychoanalysis, subjectivity and self-experience are generally understood to be constituted in an intersubjective context, which itself is created at the intersection of two individual subjectivities (Stolorow et al., 1987; Stolorow and Atwood, 1992). Because of this inseparable intertwining of subjectivity and intersubjectivity in childhood development and adult experience, the exploration of intersubjectivity that follows will unavoidably include repetitions of material on subjectivity from the previous two chapters, as well as additional ideas about subjectivity that arise in the context of a discussion of intersubjectivity.

Stern: The Subjective Self and Intersubjective Relatedness as Developmental Achievements

Initially as part of a larger effort to clarify, amend, and expand upon Kohut's self psychology, Stolorow and his colleagues (Atwood and Stolorow, 1984; Stolorow et al., 1987) were prime movers in bringing the concepts of subjectivity and intersubjectivity to the center of psychoanalytic discourse. Closely coinciding with these major contributions, publication of Daniel Stern's (1985) book, *The Interpersonal World of the Infant*, also served to refine and amplify our appreciation of the centrality of subjectivity and intersubjectivity in human development and clinical psychoanalysis. Stern's research places the infant's initial development of a *subjective self,* and the concomitant emergence of *intersubjective relations,* between the seventh and ninth months of life. The essence of the subjective self, according to Stern, is the infant's "momentous realization that inner subjective experiences . . . are potentially sharable with someone else" (p. 124). This realization follows the infant's discovery that "he or she has a mind and that other people have minds as well" (p. 124). This new recognition of mind, in self and other, makes it possible for the baby to engage with his caretakers in verbal or nonverbal communication concerning similar feeling states, intentions, or a shared focus of attention. At the moment of this realization, the infant establishes both *subjectivity* (the recognition of his own mind and inner experience) and *intersubjectivity* (the sense that the other, too, has inner experiences and that communication or sharing between separate minds is possible).

In Stern's work, the infant's "subjective self" is characterized by reference to "*inner* or subjective states of experience," whereas the earlier "core self" pertains primarily to "*overt behaviors and direct sensations*" of self and other (p. 125, italics added). The new achievements of a subjective self and intersubjective relatedness, centered on the recognition of inner experience in self and other, do not replace, but, rather, coexist and interact with, core self-experiences and core relatedness. The latter, according to Stern, addresses the sense of "a *physically* distinct and separate self and other" (p. 125, italics added).

Stern suggests that an important aspect of the child's achievement of intersubjective relatedness is that he or she recognizes "that an empathic process bridging the two minds has been created" (pp. 125–126). Once the infant has achieved a fledgling recognition of his or her own and the other's subjectivity, he or she begins not only to seek an empathic bridge that can diminish the new sense of interpersonal distance between separate psyches, but also to express "the desire to know and be known in this sense of mutually revealing subjective experience" (p. 126). Thus, in Stern's view, the child's new-found recognition of his own mind, and its distinctiveness and separateness from the mind of others, leads immediately to an interest in diminishing the gap between minds through experiences of feeling with and knowing the inner life of the other.

Stern hypothesizes that Mahler, Pine, and Bergman's (1975) ground-breaking work on separation-individuation may have "acted as an obstacle to a fuller appreciation of the role of subjectivity" and intersubjectivity in the early years of development (p. 127). He suggests that the establishment of intersubjectivity toward the end of the first year of life "is equally crucial for [its role in] creating experiences of being with a mentally similar other and for further individuation and autonomy" (p. 127n). He insists that "both separation-individuation and new forms of experiencing union (or being-with) emerge equally out of the same experience of intersubjectivity" (p. 127). With these observations, Stern seems to account for both sides of the debate between self psychologists and postmodern analysts, in which empathic resonance is sometimes pitted against differentiating self-expression on the part of the analyst. Stern's findings suggest that proponents of both stances may have merit and that the challenge, clinically, is to establish criteria on the basis of which we can discern when one mode of analytic participation might be more helpful than another. To begin with, analysts can remain alert to the quality of the patient's subjective experience and intersubjective relatedness and be attuned to signals concerning whether the patient's needs for experiences of similarity and closeness or for individuation and separateness are in greater ascendancy. The analyst's responses are then based on her awareness of the quality of establishment of these achievements in a given patient, as well as on some sense of their normal vicissitudes and the possibilities for developmental problems and their sequelae in later life.

Stern's research findings lend support for the view that intersubjective relatedness is something that must initially be established and that there will necessarily be children (or adults) who have failed to negotiate this achievement in a normative and timely fashion. His work leads us to expect that some people will present in treatment with these achievements not reliably in place, and thus we must be alert to signs of difficulty pertaining to the recognition of the differential subjectivity of others. These difficulties are often expressed by patients as an active desire *not* to know the other. Over the years, I have treated a number of patients who specifically articulated a generalized "dread" of knowing me; later in treatment, their progress involved an increasing tolerance for exposure to the details of my life and personhood. These phenomena make sense in the light of Stern's linkage of the desire to know the other with the dual developmental achievements of a subjective self and intersubjective relatedness. It is possible that difficulties in these areas of intrapsychic and interpersonal functioning were contributed to by earlier experiences of traumatic "knowing" about a parent's limitations or hurtfulness such as might be suffered by the offspring of a severely depressed mother or a parent who for other reasons is unresponsive, erratically responsive, or assaultive.

Stern tries to place his own concept of intersubjectivity within preexisting theories of cognitive development in psychology and within developmental and motivational theories in psychoanalysis. He wonders whether intersubjectivity might be "a newly emergent, specific capacity or skill" or whether it is better understood as "the maturational unfolding of a major human need and motive state" (p. 133). He cites Piaget, Bruner, and Bates as among those who approach intersubjectivity from a cognitive or linguistic view and tend to see it as a social skill, acquired through the discovery of "generative rules and procedures for interactions" (pp. 133–134). He cites Shields, Newson, and Vygotsky among those who see the developmental achievement of intersubjectivity following upon *the mother's attribution of meanings* to the mother–infant exchanges from birth onward. In this view, the mother's process of meaning attribution continues until "[g]radually, as the infant is able, the framework of meaning becomes *mutually* created" (Stern, 1985, p. 134, italics added). I have earlier noted that not only Stern, but also Ogden (1986) includes the infant's development of the capacity to create his own meaning among the achievements that coincide with or even partially constitute the initial establishment of subjectivity and intersubjective relatedness.

In contrast to an approach to intersubjectivity in terms of interpersonal meanings, Trevarthan views "intersubjectivity [as] an innate, emergent human capacity . . . present in a primary form from the early months of life" (quoted in Stern, 1985, p. 134). Trevarthan is joined in this postition by Stolorow et al. (1987), Stolorow and Atwood (1992), and Stolorow et al. (1994), who also see subjectivity and intersubjectivity as present in elementary form from birth onward.

In Stern's further exploration of intersubjectivity, he acknowledges that what he calls intersubjectivity—a developmental achievement, arrived at in the second half of the first year of life—Trevarthan calls "*secondary* intersubjectivity," (p. 134*n*, itlalics added). I suggest that the use of such terminology would indeed help us to distinguish between those forms of "intersubjectivity" believed (by Trevarthan or Stolorow et al.) to be present at birth and the later forms of intersubjectivity understood to be a developmental achievement toward the end of the first year (Stern, 1985; Ogden, 1986; Benjamin, 1988).

Ogden: The Original Establishment of Subjectivity and Intersubjectivity

Ogden's (1986, 1992a, 1992b, 1994) view of intersubjectivity closely follows Stern's on several points; but, in his description of a complex series of interweaving processes constituting subjectivity and intersubjectivity, Ogden (1986) makes an additional, unique contribution. He begins by noting that the original establishment of subjectivity is part of the same process through which the child comes to distinguish symbol from symbolized and thereby begins to create personal, idiosynchratic meaning. With this observation, he seems to be addressing the individual and idiosynchratic aspects of personal subjectivity without immediate reference to an "other" in the intersubjective surround. Thus far, then, his description of the establishment of subjectivity could be understood as a one-person, cognitive/linguistic achievement. In keeping with this individual aspect of subjectivity, he spells out the connection between the recognition of self as creator of one's own meaning and the sense of self as thinker of one's thoughts and feeler of one's feelings—again, developmental achievements that do not seem, inherently or necessarily, to include self-in-relation-to-other. But, with Ogden's further claim that the establishment of subjectivity emerges simultaneously with the ability to recognize the subjectivity of the other, he moves from the cognitive/linguistic to the affective/relational realm and brings subjectivity and intersubjectivity into ineluctable relationship with each other.

In fact, everything that Ogden says (1986) suggests that subjectivity cannot begin to evolve outside of an intersubjective context. He reminds us that during the developmental stages prior to the establishment of subjectivity, no distinction can be made between subjectivity and intersubjectivity (and no distinction between self and other as *subjects*) because subjectivity does not yet exist. At these earlier stages in the experience of the infant, there is also no distinction between symbol and symbolized (primarily a cognitive/linguistic consideration), no distinction between infant and mother (primarily an affective/relational consideration), and no need for symbol or meaning, because mother and infant are one (a convergence of cognitive/linguistic and affective/relational concerns).

In his presentation of these several phenomena as part of an integrative developmental process, Ogden is telling us that the child's cognitive/linguistic and affective/relational developments are very much intertwined and that, as subjects (creators of meaning and feelers of feelings) the sense of one's self and the recognition of the other cannot be separated. I have earlier suggested that Ogden's *sense of self* as thinker of one's thoughts and feeler of one's feelings comes very close to Kohut's sense of self as the center of experience. I would add that Ogden's positing of a simultaneous recognition of the other as a similar "center of experience," marking the initial establishment of intersubjectivity within his (or Stern's) framework, might coincide with the transition from archaic to more mature forms of selfobject relating, in the language of Kohut's self psychology.

As we noted earlier, Ogden (1992a, b) characterizes subjectivity as dialectical, as moving back and forth between conscious and unconscious realms of experience. He suggests a dialectical relationship as well between Klein's paranoid-schizoid and depressive positions, pertaining respectively to "part-object" and "whole-object" experiences. The dialectic offers the analyst a way to hold the multiple polarities of human experience and the analytic situation in mind and heart. It has been embraced by several of the moderate postmoderns, its implications for the clinical situation having been explored especially by Hoffman (1994) and Mitchell (1997). If we accept Ogden's depiction of the initial establishment of subjectivity as a developmental achievement, however, we cannot really see subjectivity and intersubjectivity as dialectically related to one another from birth. Rather, we see them as dialectically related only after subjectivity and the concomitant distinction between symbol and symbolized have initially been achieved. The same argument pertains to the dialectical relationship between the paranoid/schizoid and the depressive positions to the extent that the depressive position is initially a developmental achievement. Only after its achievement can we begin to see the two positions in dialectical relationship to one another.

Ogden (1992b) explicitly preserves the developmental perspective alongside of the dialectic:

> It must be emphasized that the negating and preserving interplay of positions evolves along a diachronic (temporally sequential) axis as well as a synchronic one. The interplay of diachronicity and synchronicity represents an inextricable component of the dialectical nature of the concept of positions. A psychological theory becomes untenable if it does not incorporate a recognition of the directionality of time and of life [p. 614].

Ogden's insistence on the developmental achievement involved in the establishment of the depressive position, with its whole-object relations and less permeable self–other boundaries, and his insistence on the developmental achievement of subjectivity with its simultaneous recognition of the differentiated subjectivity of the other have implications for psychoanalytic treatment. We noted earlier that most functional achievements attained developmentally can be vulnerable to delays, distortions, rigidification, and inhibition owing to defenses or destablization under the strain of painful and toxic environmental experiences. For patients who manifest (or are hiding) vulnerabilities in relation to the initial establishment of subjectivity and intersubjectivity, the analyst's presumption that this achievement is securely in place may sometimes be problematic. Once subjectivity has been well-enough established in a given person, that person may indeed seek an opposing other who also "bears {the} lifelong scars" of humanity (Maurensig, 1997); but until subjectivity and intersubjective relatedness are initially established, the "other" cannot consistently be recognized as such. I refer not to an inability to count two *physical* presences in a room, but rather to a difficulty in tolerating the implications of recognizing two separate minds and two different sets of feelings, desires, and interests.

Intersubjective Recognition and Nonrecognition: Stern and Ogden's Ideas as a Meeting Place for Kohut and the Postmoderns

The postmoderns seem only variably to acknowledge the problem of intersubjective nonrecognition on the part of some patients, a problem that derives from the failure of intersubjective relatedness in the sense that both Stern and Ogden have used the term. Bromberg (1996) and Renik (1996) seem not to register this problem as a potentiality at all. Benjamin (1988) and Mitchell (1997), on the other hand, explicitly acknowledge the developmental achievement entailed in the original establishment of subjectivity and intersubjectivity, but they then go on generally to extol the benefits of the mother's (or the analyst's) differentiated self-expression, regardless of the child's (or patient's) immediate position in this particular developmental process. I think that Ogden's work in this area is important exactly because it recognizes an early stage in human life before individual subjectivity and intersubjectivity have been established. He highlights the dialectical nature of individual experience after that developmental achievement is in place but allows for an earlier stage of "predialectical" experience. Ogden's ideas in this regard seem to support Stern's observation that the individual may seek interpersonal experiences that enhance *either* separation/individuation *or* attachment/identification, once subjectivity and intersubjectivity have been established. But before these establishments are initially in place, the developing child, and possibly the adult, cannot yet have an interest in, or a use for, knowing the differentiated other.

The moderate postmoderns seem to have responded primarily to Ogden's very useful elaboration of experience after the individual's establishment of subjectivity and intersubjectivity can be more or less taken for granted. But they seem not to acknowledge the need for different modes of analyst participaton with patients initially needing help to begin moving toward this achievement. It is not difficult to imagine one kind of early experience that might interfere with the normal emergence of a subjective self and intersubjective relatedness: one that entails a primary caretaker who is unable to put aside his or her own agenda, needs, or desires *enough* for the infant to achieve a basic sense of security and an expectation of provision in response to his primary physiological and attachment needs. Such a child might have to resort to primitive defenses against a premature and traumatic confrontation with the other as a separate center of need and desire. And such defenses would inevitably interfere with the normal course of establishing a subjective self and intersubjective relatedness in the Stern or Ogden sense. In treatment as an adult, such a person might understandably experience even the analyst's normal self-expressiveness or self-disclosure as an impingement bordering on retraumatization.

This construction seems consistent with the tentative understanding that I reached with several of my patients who early in treatment manifested strikingly negative reactions to "knowing" me as a differentiated other. These reactions seemed to be related to a fear and expectation, based on early formative experience, that, in the event that the patient's basic psychological needs and interests turned out to be in conflict with mine, my needs and interests would invariably take precedence. The patient's dread included the fear that he would be abandoned to his own needs, which would quickly overwhelm and destroy him. Sometimes the patient's terror of his own destructive rage in reaction to the analyst's anticipated hurtful responses may be an additional complicating factor in the dread of knowing the analyst as a differentiated other.

Diagnostic considerations have always been fraught with difficulty in psychoanalytic formulations, and our awareness of the role of the analyst's subjectivity renders them more problematic still. And yet any hope for resolution of the controversy about what might be the most growth-promoting mode of participation for the analyst, or about how best to facilitate expansion of the patient's subjectivity, seems to hinge on our understanding of the nature and severity of difficulties for which a particular analysand is seeking help. Kohut (1977a) eventually claimed that his self-psychological approach was relevant not only for working with patients who needed support in the initial establishment or consolidation of subjectivity and intersubjectivity (in his language, a robust sense of self and mature selfobject relatedness), but also for working with neurotic patients, for whom issues of enhancement and enrichment may be more central.

"Neurotic" patients were understood to have arrived for treatment with relatively well-established organizations of subjectivity and a capacity for intersubjective relatedness in the sense of Stern and Ogden. What they could be expected to need from treatment was "understanding and explanation" in relation to oedipal struggles and the integration of ideals. But, even if the patient's primary issues pertained to the healthy integration and expression of sexuality and aggression in love and work, Kohut still believed that the analyst's affective attunement and understanding could be pivotal to the unfolding of the analytic process. To some extent, he felt that the analyst's empathic attunement could effectively achieve what a direct defense analysis was intended to bring about in classical technique: the spontaneous emergence of previously repressed and split-off aspects of experience of which the analysand could then become more aware, more accepting, and able to integrate into mature sectors of the personality. Once integrated, the previously split-off aspects of experience could be creatively expressed through ambitions, goals, ideals, and interpersonal relationships (i.e., in love and work). On the analyst's part, both understanding and explaining were important parts of the treatment, which Kohut (1984) presented as an empathic/interpretive process.

But while Kohut believed that a self-psychological approach was useful in working with either narcissistic vulnerability or neurotic suffering, he explicitly warned against using the empathic stance in the treatment of borderline or psychotic-prone individuals. In Kohut's (1984) framework, these patients, by definition, had not established enough basic "self-structure" to protect them from experiences of terrifying chaos once the analyst's affective attunement had broken down their brittle defenses, a breakdown that tended to occur only too easily. In the face of Kohut's claim that self psychology was inappropriate for psychoanalytic work with borderline suffering, it is confusing that Gedo (1997) has judged Kohut's theory, along with Klein's and Ferenczi's, to be relevant only to the treatment of the "primitive psyche" (p. 434). One might assume that Gedo includes within this category of "primitive" those who are usually referred to as borderlines.

Although one need not agree with Kohut (1984) concerning such classifications, he did make a very clear distinction between "borderline" and "narcissistic" psychopathology on the basis of the degree and quality of structuralization of subjective experience (pp. 8–9). Borderline was for him the more primitive of the two and required the development of self-structure *de novo*. It was on this basis that he recommended against trying to treat borderline suffering with a self-psychological approach; he advocated instead the support of defenses.

In spite of Kohut's warnings in this regard, Stolorow and Lachmann (1980), believing that it is possible to apply self-psychological principles to the treatment of the more primitive psyche, describe at length their work with "developmental arrests." How early such "arrests" occurred, what kinds of defensiveness were called into play, and what areas of psychic functioning were affected all contribute to what the patient will need from the analyst in order first to tolerate the treatment and then to get better. These are not inconsequential considerations, because how the analyst understands the quality of a patient's subjective experience, including the intensity of his suffering, must centrally influence how the analyst participates in the work, guiding her toward different ways (and different degrees) of expressing her own subjectivity in relation to the patient's. Again, we can proceed only by broadening our analytic repertoire and increasing our readiness to interact with our patients in a variety of ways (see also Mitchell, 1997), sometimes leading with empathic expressiveness, at other times leading with clarification and interpretation, and at still other times with disjunctive self-expression and intensified interpersonal engagement. In any event, the analyst's moment-to-moment, empathic reading of the patient's state and capacities can guide the analyst's participation and engagement.

The inseparability of subjectivity and intersubjective relatedness in the patient leads to the understanding that, if a patient arrives for treatment with a healthy subjectivity not yet established and consolidated, or if he is in a state in which this achievement is challenged or lost, then he will be unprepared to engage in an intersubjective relationship—that is, he will be unable to recognize and want to know about the analyst as a differentiated other. Thus, I see Stern's and Ogden's conceptualizations of subjectivity and intersubjectivity as holding the potential for opening a pathway along which we may be able to resolve some of the disagreements between Kohutian self psychologists and the moderate postmoderns concerning the analyst's mode of participation in the patient–analyst relationship.

Ogden and the Analytic Third

In the foregoing discussion we have seen at every point of the way the impossibility of separating issues of subjectivity from intersubjectivity. Both Stern and Ogden have made major contributions to our understanding of the complex relationships between the two concepts. Ogden has even coined a new term to refer to a realm of experience in which subjectivity and intersubjectivity, once separately established, come together to produce a third realm of experience. Continuing to track the dialectical nature of human experience after the initial establishment of subjectivity and intersubjectivity has been achieved, Ogden (1994) tells us, "The intersubjective and the individually subjective each create, negate, and preserve the other," resulting in "the analytic third" (p. 64). But Ogden (1992a) had earlier made it clear that there is no dialectic before subjectivity is initially established in the experience of the individual. The analytic third represents the realm of experience cocreated and shared through the interaction of the respective subjectivities of analyst and analysand, once these have been reliably enough established in both parties. Not every patient is able to participate in a true "analytic third," because the creation of the third realm of experience requires two separate subjectivities. The realm of the "third" must evolve as the patient's unique subjectivity and intersubjective relatedness are helped to evolve during the course of treatment.

These ideas are closely paralleled in the work of Stolorow et al. (1987) and were earlier foreshadowed in the infant observation work of such analytic authors as Stechler and Kaplan (1980) and Demos and Kaplan (1986), who charted the infant's affective development through interactive processes of self-regulation and interactive regulation between mother and child. These ideas have received further support in the work of Beebe and Lachmann, to be presented in the next chapter.

Subjectivity and Intersubjectivity in the Work of Stolorow, Brandchaft, and Atwood

Predating Ogden's elucidation of subjectivity, and continuing into the present, Stolorow, Atwood, and Brandchaft (Stolorow and Atwood, 1979; Atwood and Stolorow, 1984; Stolorow et al., 1987; Stolorow and Atwood, 1991; Stolorow and Atwood, 1992; Stolorow et al., 1994) have argued for the intersubjective nature of all human development and experience. Initially working from a self-psycholological perspective, these authors underscored the intersubjective "foundations" of all psychological life (Stolorow and Atwood, 1992). In their view, the intersubjective world shapes the subjective from birth onward. Thus, for them, intersubjectivity is not a developmental achievement, but an unavoidable fact of all human life and relationships. Stolorow and Atwood explicitly differentiate themselves from those they call the "developmentalists" by clarifying that their own use of the term intersubjective refers "to *any* psychological field formed by interacting worlds of experience, at whatever developmental level these worlds may be organized" (p. 3).

Atwood and Stolorow (1984) conceptualize both psychological development and pathogenesis "in terms of the specific intersubjective contexts that shape the developlmental process" (p. 65). Their view of the totally reciprocal nature of subjective and intersubjective experience, however, is highlighted by their assertion that not only is individual psychological development shaped by intersubjective contexts, but also "the evolving psychological field [is] constituted by the interplay between the differently organized subjectivities of child and caretaker" (p. 65). They thus attribute some degree of subjectivity to the infant from birth onward, albeit at first a very "differently organized" subjectivity. For Stolorow and his colleagues, as for Stern and Ogden, where there is subjectivity, there is necessarily also intersubjectivity. But in contrast to Stern and Ogden, Stolorow and his colleagues see subjectivity as present from birth.

Further distinguishing themselves from the "developmentalists" (such as Stern or Ogden), Stolorow and Atwood (1992) do not link the original establishment of subjectivity with any particular cognitive/linguistic or affective/relational achievements. They define it, instead, in terms of the presence of *any* organization of experience unique to the individual, no matter how elementary, incipient, or nascent (p. 8). Also in contrast to the intersubjectivity of either Stern or Ogden, Stolorow and colleagues' intersubjectivity does not imply any kind of mutual *recognition* between subjects. While not including mutual recognition among the criteria for their intersubjectivity, however, they do understand mutual *regulation* to begin at the time of the earliest interactions between parent and child. It is these mutually regulating exchanges that shape the child's ongoing organization of experience and thereby influence the further elaboration of subjectivity within the primary intersubjective context of the first caretaking relationships.

Stolorow et al. have been criticized by those who feel that their enduring focus on the intersubjective entails an abandonment of the prior achievements of classical psychoanalysis in charting the inner life of the individual. By their own report (Stolorow et al., 1994), it has been suggested that they have destroyed "the basis for concepts of character, psychic continuity, the achievement of regulatory capacities, and the development of complex psychological organizations" (p. 204). Responding to these charges, the authors explain that, although they do argue for "the embeddedness of experience in constitutive intersubjective fields . . . [nevertheless] the intersubjectively oriented analyst . . . [remains] committed to illuminating the unconscious organizing principles the patient brings to the analytic encounter" (p. 204). But, significantly, in their view the analyst "understands that the psychopathological phenomena that are seen to unfold [in the treatment] do so within an intersubjective field that includes the analyst as a codetermining influence" (p. 204). They thus try to subsume within their view of intersubjectivity the singular subjectivity of the patient; but, while leaving room for what the patient brings, they also insist that what is evoked from the patient's earlier experience depends on specific qualities of the intersubjective field cocreated by patient and analyst from the moment their psychoanalytic work begins.

Stolorow and Atwood (1992) claim that their concept of intersubjectivity closes "the gap between the intrapsychic and interpersonal realms" and renders obsolete "the old dichotomy between them" (p. 18). Nevertheless, a careful reading of the psychoanalytic literature produced by the moderate postmoderns suggests that some tensions still remain concerning the relative importance of intrapsychic and interpersonal experience and their relationship to one another. Even though the discourse concerning intrapsychic and interpersonal aspects of experience is currently carried out in the language of subjectivity and intersubjectivity, there are gaps as well as contradictions that seem to remain.

The Patient's Subjectivity and the Analyst's Codetermining Influence on the Psychoanalytic Process and Outcome

In fact, the relative weights that differing analytic authors give to the separate but interacting factors of the patient's subjectivity or "organizing principles," on one hand, and the analyst's "codetermining influence," on the other, account for much of the debate and controversy in current psychoanalytic discourse. In the eyes of the moderate post-moderns, the analyst's codetermining influence includes her own organizing principles or subjectivity, her preestablished relational and interpersonal patterns, her affectivity, and her transference and countertransference experiences in relation to the patient. All these have overlapping and interacting elements within the analyst's own experience as well as being subject to influence through the ongoing interactions with the patient.

In contrast to the moderate postmoderns, who are currently undertaking to elucidate aspects of the analyst's influence on the analytic process, classical analysts have historically given exclusive weight to the patient's contribution to the analytic relationship, through his drive-determined transference. Self psychology, on the other hand, has given primary emphasis to the patient's adaptive motivational systems (Lichtenberg, 1989) or to his developmental thrust (Kohut, 1977a; Emde, 1990). At the same time, however, Kohut also recognized the important contribution made by the patient's *selfobject transferences* as they express the earlier derailment of developmental processes during childhood. In addition to acknowledging both the healthy and the pathological contributions of the patient to what evolves in treatment, self psychology also significantly predated the postmoderns in recognizing the analyst's essential contribution to the analytic situation. But the postmoderns expand the modes of analyst participation beyond selfobject function to emphasize authentic interpersonal engagement and the spontaneous expression of the analyst's subjective self.

One aspect of the analyst's contribution, as seen by self psychologists, is that a reactivation of the patient's developmental strivings is made possible by the analyst's successes in being empathically attuned to the patient's experience. The analyst's attunement is understood constructively to stir up hope in the patient for a psychic recovery (A. Ornstein, 1992) and to increase the patient's openness to using aspects of the analyst's psychological functioning to consolidate or enrich the self. But equally influential in the treatment process, as it was understood by Kohut, are the ruptures in the analytic bond that come about through the analyst's inevitable and repeated empathic *failures*. In Kohut's view of the analytic process, it is the *movement* between these two poles of experience for patient and analyst, between affective attunement and rupture and back to attunement again, that enables the patient increasingly to build up and rely on his own self-regulatory capacities. These capacities are seen as having been undermined in an earlier intersubjective context in which a parent or dyadic partner failed to support and enhance the child's inborn regulatory potentials. Kohut's view of the inevitable analytic movement between empathic attunement and failure has been implicitly affirmed in Bromberg's (1980) evocation of the dialectic between empathy and anxiety. I understand Bromberg to mean that the analyst's empathic successes often dispel the patient's anxiety, whereas the analyst's empathic failures allow the patient's anxiety to prevail and therefore to be brought into the analytic experience. This entire dialectic contributes to the forward movement of the treatment.

To the extent that we think of the patient's anxiety as a response to the analyst's empathic failures, it is closely related to Kohut's notion of frustration, a concept that for him was far removed from Freudian instinct theory. In Kohut's view of cure, what was inevitably frustrated were not the drives but the patient's wish for perfect understanding. Partly because of the longstanding association of frustration with drive theory, there is a significant self-psychological literature today that rejects Kohut's inclusion of frustration in the formulation of how psychoanalysis cures. The concept of optimal responsiveness has replaced the terminology of frustration in more recent discussions of therapeutic action (Stolorow et al., 1987; Bacal, 1988; A. Ornstein, 1988; Terman, 1988). My own resolution of the tensions expressed in this debate is to underscore Kohut's focus on need and not drive and to suggest that his word optimal, as a ubiquitous qualifier for frustration, revealed his own recognition that although frustration was an inevitable aspect of human experience, it could be present in every individual's life in either too little or too great quantities. His emphasis was on the parent's and the analyst's responsibility to do whatever was possible to keep the unavoidable frustrations of life within optimal or manageable bounds, neither depriving nor overstimulating, and to offer understanding and acceptance in response to the child's (or the patient's) distress when success in these efforts turned out not to be within the parent's (or the analyst's) capacities (Kohut, 1977a; Teicholz, 1996). This, in Kohut's (1984) view, was an important aspect of the analyst's influence on the analytic process, and he believed that it could be expressed as an integral part of the interpretive process of understanding and explaining.

While articulating the analyst's contribution to the analytic process through affective attunement and its failure, however, Kohut did not spell out other aspects of the analyst's participation that also have an impact on the analytic process, aspects that go hand-in-hand with, or even extend beyond, the analyst's empathy and its failures. For the most part, Kohut seemed to be saying that in reinstating developmental processes of self-development that have earlier been derailed, only the dimension of analyst participation that pertains to affective attunement and its rupture will have a significant impact on the therapeutic outcome for the patient. On this point, it seems, the moderate postmoderns heartily disagree, arguing instead for the analyst's differentiated self-expression and for a broad-based and variegated engagement with their patients, beyond or even in lieu of the analyst's persistent efforts toward affective attunement.

Interaction, Interpersonal Engagement, and Intersubjectivity in Psychoanalysis

Before turning to the postmoderns and their individual varieties of intersubjectivity, I would like to comment on three closely related terms, which are sometimes used interchangeably in analytic discourse, but which I believe should be distinguished from one another: these are *interactive, interpersonal,* and *intersubjective.* Psychoanalysts today from every paradigm, including classical, interpersonal, object relations, self psychology, and postmodern, acknowledge the interactive nature of the analytic process. However, the term interactive refers only to the intersecting *actions* of the patient and analyst, and not necessarily to how either participant *experiences* himself or the other. Thus, although the interactive nature of psychoanalysis applies across the board to all patients, regardless of the level of their psychic organizations and regardless of the nature of their problems, it was of little interest to Kohut because he saw it as encompassing an extrospective, as opposed to an introspective, viewpoint.

Interaction is an unavoidable consequence of the fact that analysis involves two persons in some kind of communication with each other, whether that communication is primarily the patient's free associations and the analyst's interpretive activity, the patient's selfobject needs and the analyst's affective attunement and explanation, or authentic relational engagement between two individuals who will influence each other mutually. The term interpersonal simply refers to all aspects of the personal relationship between two individuals, including feelings, actions, and communication. In the common usage of both terms, interactive and interpersonal, it is not essential that the partners to the exchange be perceived and experienced by each other in any particular way, nor that the "psyches" of the two parties to the engagement possess any particular level of psychic organization or capacities. Two people, then, can interact and can also develop an interpersonal relationship, even if one or both parties to the dyad have not reliably established "subjectivity" or intersubjective relatedness in the sense of recognizing self and other as subjects in their own rights. As opposed to the terms interactive and interpersonal, only the term intersubjectivity (as defined by Stern or Ogden) includes this last achievement. The terms interactive and interpersonal seem to refer primarily to data gathered extrospectively, whereas the terms subjective and intersubjective refer to the individual experiential world that is best approached through (vicariously) introspective processes.

Closely related to the concept of intersubjectivity is that of mutual influence. In current psychoanalytic discourse, mutual influence usually refers to that aspect of human relationship in which the behaviors and feelings of each party to a dyadic system affect and therefore serve to regulate (possibily even to predict) the behaviors and feelings of the other (Lachmann and Beebe, 1992, 1996b). If we were to define intersubjectivity only as the exchange of mutual regulation or influence, then the views of Stern, Ogden, and Stolorow et al. would line up in more complete synchrony than they usually do in analytic discourse. However, one way of formulating the distinctions between Stern's and Ogden's intersubjectivity, on one hand, and Stolorow et al.'s intersubjectivity, on the other, is on the basis that, while all three authors (or groups of authors) include mutual regulation and mutual influence in their understanding of intersubjectivity, only Stern and Ogden additionally include mutual recognition as an inherent and necessary aspect of intersubjectivity. What "recognition" refers to in both their frameworks is the individual's understanding that experience pertaining to a unique psychic life is a property of both oneself and others and that these separate psychic experiences can be the basis for either sharing and identification or differentiation and individuation. Benjamin (1988) joins Ogden and Stern in emphasizing recognition, but her understanding of how recognition is achieved is diametrically opposed to their understanding.

In summary, the capacity for recognition must be established through relational experience over time, but from birth onward the child's experience is at least partially regulated through interactions with caretakers. We now have empirical evidence that the influence between mother and infant is mutual (see chapter 9). Thus, if we all agreed to define intersubjectivity only in terms of mutual regulation and influence, there would be consensus that intersubjectivity pertains from birth or even before. In contrast to this notion, if we insist on including the later achievement of recognition in our definition of intersubjectivity, then intersubjectivity cannot be understood as a given capacity at birth. Since these are two very different ways of understanding intersubjectivity, it is important that in any discussion of these issues, we declare our specific meaning in using the term.

Combining the multiple and partially overlapping contributions of Ogden, Stern, and Stolorow et al., we can understand the emergence of subjectivity and intersubjectivity as a complex set of interpenetrating processes involving the following intrapsychic and interpersonal phenomena: processes of mutual regulation and influence from birth onward (Atwood and Stolorow, 1984; Stolorow et al., 1987; Stolorow and Atwood, 1992; Stolorow et al., 1994); the later achievement of recognition of both oneself and the other as separate centers of experience (Stern, 1985; Ogden, 1986; Benjamin, 1988) and also as unique creators of meaning (Ogden, 1986); and interchanges in which the "postintersubjective" infant has opportunities to experience the caretaker as capable of both similar or resonating experiences, on one hand, and differentiating experiences, on the other (Stern, 1985, p. 127).

Let us bring together these varying psychoanalytic views of intersubjectivity. At its most generic, the intersubjective field is the realm of experience created by the interaction and intersection of two differentiated subjectivities. Within this framework, subjectivity refers to any unique organization of experience, regardless of how primitve or undeveloped. This most generic definition satisfies the requirements of Stolorow and his colleagues in their less complex notion of intersubjectivity seen to pertain at birth. If we add to this definition that each party in the intersubjective field must be capable of recognizing the other as a separate subjectivity, the source of either similar or different intentions and feeling, then we have met the requirements of Stern's and Benjamin's intersubjectivity. And when we add further that each party to the dyad also experiences herself and the other not only as separate centers of experience but also as idiosynchratic creators of meanings, we have met the criteria for Ogden's intersubjectivity.

Ogden's (1994) "analytic third," pertaining to the whole constellation of experiences constructed in the intersubjective field by two interacting subjectivities, evokes the potential for new experience and creativity in the intersubjective space between patient and analyst. The analyst and the patient both contribute to the creation of the analytic third and, in turn, are influenced by what they have created. These ideas represent a creative extension of the elucidation of the intersubjective dimensions of the analytic relationship begun as early as 1984 by Atwood and Stolorow, which, with Brandchaft, they have continued to expand to the present time. But, while the combined efforts of all these authors have effectively established the ubiquity of mutual influence, we also understand that the two parties to any intersubjective engagement are never infinitely malleable: each individual initially brings to the engagement the complex totality of limitations and potentials, realized and unrealized, from previous intersubjective contexts. Each individual also brings the strengths and problems developed in response to the omissions and commissions—beneficial and destructive—from participation in previous intersubjective contexts.

INTERSUBJECTIVITY

Implications for the Psychoanalytic Situation

What you have to be willing to do is to stand in the crossroads of ambiguity.

—Anna Deavere Smith

Intersubjectivity: Regulation and Recognition

I earlier noted that postmodern authors differ among themselves in the extent to which their notions of intersubjectivity center on the regulation of affect or on recognition of separateness, sameness, and difference in others. For Benjamin (1988), as with Ogden (1994), intersubjectivity importantly concerns the mutual recognition between two subjects. Stern (1985) seems to underscore the importance of both regulation and recognition: in his view, the mother's earlier successes in establishing a mutual regulation system between herself and her baby contribute to the baby's later success in achieving intersubjectivity, that is, a sense of mutual recognition between a subjective self and an intersubjectively recognized other. Once the subjective self and intersubjective relatedness are established, they are maintained and enhanced by "bridges" of empathy, by further mutual recognition, and by fulfilment of the desire to know and be known. For Stolorow and Atwood (1992), and Beebe and Lachmann (1994, 1996a, b), the importance of intersubjectivity lies primarily in its potential for mutual regulation of affect between the members of a dyadic system, something we have already noted begins at birth, or even earlier in the more purely physiological processes and exchanges in the intrauterine world.

Winnicott's concept of holding, Bion's concept of containing, and Kohut's concept of omnipotent merger are ways of understanding the mother's role in regulating the infant's affective experience early in life. Additionally, Kohut's concepts of mirroring, twinship, and idealization emphasize the caretaker's recognition of the developing individual in both her uniqueness and her relatedness to others. Infant researchers who rely on empirical findings as well as contemporary analysts who work with adults are currently more struck with the mutuality of both the regulation and recognition within relationships; they feel that earlier authors, such as Winnicott and Kohut, placed too much emphasis on these processes as unidirectional from parent to child or from analyst to analysand. This has been the context within which the moderate postmoderns have begun to insist on the expressed subjectivity of the mother (Benjamin, 1988) and to explore the subjectivity of the analyst (Hoffman, 1983; Mitchell, 1988, 1993, 1996a, 1997; Aron, 1992, 1996; Renik, 1993, 1996). The question of mutual regulation has expanded to broad considerations of mutual influence in psychoanalysis (Aron, 1996; Mitchell, 1997), far beyond its original elaboration in regard to affective development in the infant–caretaker surround (Stern, 1985; Demos, 1988, 1989).

Each of these emphases seems to open up to a world of its own, yet be inextricably bound up with all the others. I suggest, however, that if we make a clearer distinction between the mutually *regulating* aspects of intersubjectivity and the mutually *recognizing* aspects, some of the controversy may spontaneously drain out of our discourse. More explicitly, we might agree that mutual regulation and influence pertain at least from birth onward and therefore need to be taken into account in every analytic situation. On the other hand, mutual recognition is necessarily an achievement either of the "subjective self" and intersubjective relatedness, as in Stern's (1985) schema; or of the child who has arrived at the point in development where she is able to distinguish symbol from symbolized and thereby has a sense of both self and others as creators of meaning, as in Ogden's view of intersubjectivity. With both the regulatory and the recognition aspects of intersubjectivity in mind, and especially including the complex, cognitive/affective/relational achievements that Stern's and Ogden's notions of intersubjectivity entail, analysts are in a position to use their observational powers and their empathy to assess their patients' sometimes fluid experiences along this continuum and to act and communicate accordingly.

Winnicott (1955) explicitly acknowledged a time before which the child normally establishes what he variously labeled as an intact ego or a self. He exhorted us to participate in the analytic relationship differentially, on the basis of whether the patient could or could not take this achievement for granted. In order to refer to the person of the child or patient, but still recognize the normative or pathological absence of what Stern (1985) called the *subjective self* and *intersubjective relations*, Winnicott coined such terms as "going-on-being," the "spontaneous gesture," the "feeling of aliveness," and "the experience of the impulse." All these terms enable us to talk about aspects of the child's or adult's experiencing, without attributing to him a functional degree of cohesion, organization, or self-and-other recognition.

Kohut's selfobject concept actually tries to explain the initial development of subjectivity in an intersubjective context. To a large extent, we have simply changed the language in which we talk about these phenomena, in order to underscore the fluidity, ambiguity, diversity, and bidirectionality of individual and relational experiences, aspects usually underemphasized in Kohut's writings. Nevertheless, Kohut's four selfobject functions of omnipotent merger, mirroring, twinship, and idealization all refer to interpersonal experiences of affective regulation and recognition that contribute to the establishment of subjectivity or to the child's sense of self as center of her own experience. To this extent, Kohut's self psychology lay some of the groundwork for the contemporary psychoanalytic focus on subjectivity and intersubjectivity, focusing on its initial establishment in childhood and its consolidation and enrichment in treatment. Furthermore, we can interpret Kohut's view of the coexistence of and constant movement between self and selfobject experience, throughout the life cycle, as nudging self psychology toward a dialectical understanding of the human psyche. But Kohut's language of self and selfobject and his emphasis on intrapsychic structure have been found to be too reifying and rigidifying for many of today's analytic authors. Furthermore, his emphasis on the child's (or patient's) subjective experience, and on what the child (or patient) requires of the caretaker/other, has been found by many to be too one sided and unidirectional (see, e.g., Benjamin, 1988). Even though Kohut acknowledged the influence of the parents' (or the analyst's) subjectivity and even though he articulated a methodology through which the analyst could bring her participation into the psychoanalytic dialogue during discrete disruption–repair sequences, the moderate postmodern analysts argue for a much broader expression, acknowledgment, and use of the analyst's subjectivity than Kohut articulated in his clinical writings.

Intersubjectivity in the Works of Kohut and the Postmoderns: Similarites and Differences

It seems that the moderate postmoderns all begin with certain agreed upon tenets of self psychology, which include the central importance of individual subjectivity in human development and psychic growth, as well as a consensus concerning the relational and intersubjective context out of which subjectivity emerges. With the exception of Benjamin (1988), who takes up questions of mutual recognition, the postmoderns do not explicitly address issues of regulation and recognition as such; yet they might all agree that interpersonally achieved affect regulation and recognition of both one's uniqueness and similarity to others are essential for the normal or "mature" establishment of subjectivity. Where there are differences among the postmoderns, they appear to center on the relative importance of mutual regulation versus recognition in the establishment, maintenance, and enhancement of individual subjectivity. Differences between Kohut and the postmoderns, on the other hand, appear to center on 1) the degree of fluidity, multiplicity, fragmentation, and ambiguity in "normative" subjective experience; 2) the role of the unique subjectivity of the other in the original, childhood establishment of subjectivity, as well as questions concerning how early and how fully, in childhood development, the other's uniquely differentiated subjectivity can be recognized and accepted; and 3) questions concerning the optimal degrees of mutuality and symmetry in the exchange between the developing individual (child or patient) and the significant other.

Both Kohut and Loewald insisted on a "one-way" psychoanalytic relationship in the sense that the analyst was there for the sake of the patient and not the other way around. Today these views, which were intended to protect the patient from the untoward effects of the analyst's subjectivity, are often seen as paternalistic. It is a challenge for all of us, now, to conceptualize the analytic relationship in a way that alerts the analyst to the seriousness of his professional and relational obliga-

tions to the patient while at the same time not undermining the
integrity and competencies of the patient. The same kinds of tensions
prevail in relation to our updated conceptualizations of the new, interpersonally competent infant. Loewald (1979b), Aron (1996), Mitchell
(1997), and Hoffman (1998) all address issues of analyst responsibility
while struggling to recognize the patient's need for autonomy.

<hr>

Expanding the Analyst's Participation, Broadening the Repertoire

Stolorow et al. (1994) identify a paradigm shift that Kohut was instrumental in starting but that has now gone places that Kohut probably
could not have foreseen. They point to relational models, dyadic systems, social constructivism, and intersubjectivity (cited by Aron, 1996,
p. 18), all labels for current ways of thinking psychoanalytically, but
each with a different emphasis. What distinguishes all four of these
"paradigms" from self psychology proper is the increasing recognition
of the analyst/other as an expressive or desiring subject in her own
right, having significant influence on the patient and the analytic relationship far beyond her intended therapeutic impact. An unofficial consensus seems to have developed among the moderate postmoderns that
it is better to make this influence the focus of explicit psychoanalytic
inquiry than to allow it to continue its influence hidden and unrecog-
nized. This consensus leads them to recommend an overt exploration
of the patient's experience of the analyst's subjectivity and countertransference (Aron, 1996) and to include in the analyst's repertoire of
interventions a readiness for deliberate self-disclosure (Renik, 1993,
1996; Aron, 1996).

From a self-psychological perspective, the primary role of the analyst
is to facilitate the patient's consolidation, elaboration, and enhancement
of subjectivity and intersubjective relatedness. In self psychology it is
believed that the analyst can best fulfill this function through empathic
resonance and understanding. The benefits and pitfalls of the analyst's
fuller self-expressiveness and self-disclosure, especially as a differentiated
other, were therefore not explored in Kohut's major works. Qualities of
the analyst's (subjective) affective experience, however, are necessarily
revealed through her empathic resonance with her patients. And to the
extent that empathy is understood as vicarious introspection, the analyst

is clearly drawing on her own experience whenever she attempts to res-onate affectively or to communicate empathically with her patient. We earlier noted that Kohut (1984) eventually felt that the analyst's empathic participation was sufficiently emphasized to "correct" Freud's earlier (and misguided) insistence on the analyst's neutrality and objectivity; thus, Kohut suggested, future self psychologists might begin to explore a broader base of interactions in the analytic exchange. This exploration has begun to take place within self psychology (Stolorow and Atwood, 1992; Stolorow, 1994; Fosshage, 1995a, b, 1997; Lichtenberg et al., 1996), even as it is proceeding at an ever more rapid pace in more purely rela-tional or postmodern paradigms.

At this point in history, however, the moderate postmoderns are far more likely than are traditional Kohutians to recommend the analyst's explicit self-expression and self-disclosure in the analytic relationship. Each strives toward an intersubjective analysis and believes that, if psy-choanalysis is to be truly intersubjective, the subjectivities of both par-ties to the analytic relationship must often be brought explicitly into the dialogue. The bringing together of two subjectivities is important both for a richness of self to develop in the patient (Mitchell, 1993, 1996a) and also for the analysis to have a platform (Mitchell, 1996a, 1997) from which to address, and be able to change, the patient's preestablished pat-terns of organizing experience and relating to others. In Mitchell's thinking, this platform is also something on which the analysand can stand, so that he will not have to pull himself up by his own bootstraps! Mitchell believes that the analyst's personal subjectivity, and her will-ingness to share it, can become that platform the patient lacks. Bromberg puts it this way: "I would argue that the human personality, in order to grow, needs to encounter another personality as a separate center of subjective reality, so that its own subjectivity can oppose, con-firm, and be confirmed in an intersubjective context" (p. 176).

Bromberg's interpersonal analysis is thus explicit about the role for both confirmation and opposition in contributing to growth in early development or analytic cure. Kohut's self psychology articulated the affirmation or mirroring needed by the developing self but was not explicit about the developing child's (or patient's) need for oppositional interactions. In Kohut's view, however, the mirroring selfobject mirrored all manifestations presented by the developing other; and, to the extent that things are going well, these manifestations eventually come to include self-assertive and oppositional behavior and attitudes. There is a difference, of course, between affirming the child's (or patient's) own oppositional moves and presenting oppositional moves of one's own as parent (or analyst). It is also a challenge both to affirm the child's opposition and to present the opposing force or content against which she can sharpen her own edge. However, by positing a primary motivational system based on aversive experiencing, Lichtenberg (1989) offers a self psychological framework within which these interpersonal and postmodern ideas concerning opposition can be clinically and theoretically "at home" and within which self psychologists and postmoderns alike can struggle to meet the challenges.

Fully agreeing that we must include within our analytic repertoire a readiness to oppose and be opposed in the analytic relationship, I find no general fault with the varying approaches of Lichtenberg, Bromberg, Mitchell, and others. With many analysands at various times, I have felt called on to keep a firm hold on my own differentiated viewpoint, or to take a stand contrary to that taken by my patient on some point of greater or lesser urgency between us. I also wonder, though, whether such opposition might best be brought forth in the analytic situation at times when there are signs that the patient is secure in his establishment of some requisite modicum of individual subjectivity, without which more psychoanalytic sensitivity to issues of impingement must prevail.

Mutual Influence and Responsibility
In the Intersubjective Dyad

Presenting another conceptual challenge, as I see it, is that, while the moderate postmoderns recognize mutual influence between patient and analyst, they also rely on the analyst to remain "a separate center of subjective reality, so that [her] own subjectivity can oppose" or confirm that of the patient (Bromberg, 1996, p. 176). To the extent that we recognize the mutual influence between patient and analyst and insist on the intersubjective nature of the exchange, are we not giving up the possibility of having a firm enough hold on our own subjectivities to be effective in opposing or confirming the subjectivities of our patients?

Although both parties to the interaction are inevitably influenced, it is the patient who is seeking help to make important changes in his life, and therefore it is incumbent on the analyst to have relatively "more" influence than the patient if there is to be a therapeutic outcome.

If the patient is influenced by our subjectivity and we are influenced by his, how do we account for the greater influence that the analyst's organization of experience must have on the psychoanalytic process in order for the necessary therapeutic change to take place in the patient? Loewald (1960) wrote of the analyst's higher level of (ego) organization, as compared with the patient's, but such language has hierarchical implications not acceptable to the postmodern sensibility. Hoffman (1996) confronts the ironies of the analyst's influence in his discussions of the analyst's authority, and Lachmann and Beebe (1996b) address these problems by suggesting that the quality and quantity of influence between mother and infant or between analyst and patient are not necessarily the same. In asserting that the influence goes both ways, they mean only that the interactive behavior of one partner to a dyad can contribute to accurate predictions concerning the subsequent interactive behavior of the other.

That the behaviors of both mother and child or of both patient and analyst influence and thereby contribute to predictions concerning the subsequent behaviors of the other leaves open the question of who changes whom in which ways and to what degree in the longer term. There is the danger that our collective enthusiasm in response to the recognition of mutual influence could, in the wrong hands, lead to new opportunities for "blaming the child" or "blaming the patient" when things go wrong, a possibility not usually realized in the writings of the postmoderns, but a possibility nevertheless. For instance, in a discussion of a case presented by Trop and Stolorow, Mitchell (1992) assures the reader that he is not suggesting "an accusatory confrontation in which the patient is blamed for running away from something" (p. 452); yet, in the same discussion, he earlier referred to the patient's initial behavior in treatment as an "opening gambit" (p. 447). The word gambit carries the meaning of a "calculated move, to gain an advantage in position" (Webster's New Collegiate Dictionary, 1977); thus, implicit in this use of language is the suggestion, if not of blame, then at least of a holding of the patient responsible for the very behaviors that Mitchell himself empathically views as reenacted "features of [the patient's] relationships with his parents . . . based on terror and deep convictions about threats to his own survival" (p. 449). Loewald (1979b), on the other hand, insisted that responsibility for one's feelings, behavior, and instinctual life is something that analytic treatment must help the patient grow into over time.

Inherent in our present recognition of mutual influence in psycho-analysis is a new tension in the analyst's attitudes of concern, empathy, caring, and responsibility, which can veer toward one extreme—co-opting the patient's sense of responsibility and autonomy (Renik, 1993; Mitchell, 1997)—or, at the other extreme, placing the burden of responsibility for the treatment on the shoulders of an already vulnerable patient (Loewald, 1979b; Teicholz, 1995). We noted earlier that Aron (1992) and Hoffman (1994) have provided some degree of resolution to these tensions by portraying the optimal analytic relationship as one in which there is more general mutuality (of influence) but only a modest degree of symmetry (in roles and responsibility). Again we may have to invoke a dialectic of mutuality and hierarchical responsibility because the asymmetry recognized by Kohut and the postmoderns alike necessarily compromises a full or general mutuality (P. Stepansky, personal communication). The way this works in clinical practice is that the analyst inevitably is influenced by, and unwittingly enacts with the patient, aspects of her own and the patient's unconscious motivation and conflict; but all the while struggles to understand and use these enactments to further the analytic process and the patient's growth. That the analyst as well as the patient "grows" and changes, to the extent that such understanding is achieved, is increasingly acknowledged in the literature (Slavin and Kriegman, 1998).

But Mitchell (1997) rightly underscores the analyst's ultimate responsibility "for safeguarding the process and the well-being of the analysand" (pp. 167–168). I suggest, further, that the clinical arrangement recommended by Mitchell echoes the mother–infant relationship: the mother holds the ultimate responsibility for the baby's well-being because the good enough or "average expectable" mother comes to the interactions with her infant in possession of an individual subjectivity already established, whereas the infant enters the mother–child interactions with only a rudimentary sense of self in place (Teicholz, 1998). The infant possesses a "subjectivity" that is only in the process of becoming. Thus, although each member of the mother–infant dyad clearly affects the immediate mood and response of the other in the exchange between them, it is only the infant whose *primary establishment of subjectivity* will be affected by these exchanges.

Because of this differential in the mother–child relationship, we recognize far-reaching consequences of the mother's influence on the baby's primary development as compared with the baby's influence on the mother. I have given this naturally occurring, mother–child asymmetry the label of *normative inequality* (Teicholz, 1998). Normative inequality suggests neither inferiority nor lesser rights on the part of the child or patient, but rather a greater degree of vulnerability to being exploited (Renik, 1993, 1996), hurt, damaged, or interfered with, based on developmental considerations and the unavoidably regressive aspects of the psychoanalytic treatment situation.

Regardless of the mother's mental health or "illness," regardless of the quality of her historical psychic development and its effects on the quality of her mothering, her functional capacities, as compared with the baby's, and the fact that the baby is dependent on these for survival, will give her much greater *power* than the baby has in their relationship. To the extent that, consciously or unconsciously, the psychoanalytic situation stirs up these old experiences of dependency and vulnerability, the analyst will be felt by the patient to retain some measure of this "maternal" power, regardless of how much the analyst herself may be aware of the limitations of her own knowledge and authority and regardless of how much symmetry she may try to structure into her conduct of psychoanalysis. This is a double-edged sword, as it adds affective leverage to the therapeutic action at the same time that it amplifies the possibility of doing harm. Similarly, the entire concept of psychoanalytic intersubjectivity makes it possible for analysts to assume more responsibility for what does not go well in the analytic relationship than was possible using a classical analytic framework. But, at the same time, some analysts may use the concept to feel less responsible for things that go wrong analytically: they understand the concept of mutuality to mean that patient and analyst are on an equal footing and that the analyst contributes no more to the outcome than the patient does.

Intersubjectivity and the Analyst's Authority

Hoffman (1996) engages the problem of symmetry and mutual influence through his explorations of the analyst's authority. He acknowledges that, although psychoanalytic authority has changed from its Freudian version, in which the *knowing* therapist makes *objective* interpretations of the patient's experience, it nevertheless remains an essential aspect of the therapeutic leverage that the analyst is able to bring to the analytic encounter. Regardless of how the analyst perceives her own participation in the dynamic interplay of two subjectivities, and regardless of how explicit and how mutual is the exploration of the analyst's influence on the patient's transference experience, the patient still needs to be able to hold the analyst in high enough regard at some level of experience so that the analyst's behavior and communications, and her willingness personally to engage with the patient, has the power to make a difference in the patient's characteristic organizations and interpretations of experience.

Likewise, Mitchell (1997), compellingly exploring the relationship between the analyst's knowledge and authority, has struggled to find a new basis for our authority now that we recognize the perspectival nature of our subjectivity. This recognition has confronted us with the relativity of our perceptions of ourselves and of the world, a world we can know only fleetingly and through the lenses of our limiting and distorting subjectivities. Among these distortions are our psychoanalytically informed, empathically grasped views of our patients and their inner lives.

But Mitchell valiantly struggles against a mindless or "irresponsible relativism" as a replacement for our now "anachronistic objectivism" (p. 211). He struggles to remain convinced and concludes that psychoanalysis has generated many ideas over the years that are "worth believing" (p. 212). In his effort to capture in words what these ideas might represent, however, he speaks of some phenomena that seem to be very ephemeral indeed. As examples of the analyst's areas of expertise, he suggests the following: mythologies that "shimmer with complication" (p. 213); an ability to compose and arrange the events in the patient's mind, on the basis of better or worse guesses, but with no possiblity of "best guesses" (pp. 218–219); and an expertise in "coconstructing and helping to transform" patients' narrative histories "in useful and illuminating ways." This expertise is based on special knowledge of "the way . . . systems of meaning become constructed and change" (p. 212).

In spite of the analytic humility suggested by Mitchell's reference to our mythologies and guesses, there is a large world of psychoanalytic mastery conveyed in his belief that our expertise concerns the way systems of meaning become constructed and involves the ability to transform patients' narrative histories in useful and illuminating ways. Nevertheless, in conclusion to his chapter on the analyst's knowledge and authority, Mitchell tells us that the analyst tries to facilitate in the patient "a tolerance of and a sense of excitement about" the unknowns of psychic life (p. 230). For me, all these articulations on the extent and limits of the analyst's knowledge and authority ring true, and we are fortunate to have Mitchell, with an honest and often poetic rendering of our position, as a companion in the uncharted territory of each new psychoanalysis we undertake. Mitchell speaks from the undeniable authority of his own and others' accumulated psychoanalytic experience, without claiming that it is any more than what it is.

Unacknowledged by the postmoderns, however, is that the analyst's empathy itself can facilitate a balance between outdated concepts of analytic knowing and authority, on one hand, and the irresponsibility threatened by the new relativism, on the other. To the extent that we acknowledge the inevitably subjective nature of the analyst's empathy, we are able to make every effort to focus on and plumb the depths of the patient's experience, while recognizing that the only medium through which we can do this is our own personal affective experience (see also Sucharov, 1994, 1997).

Interpersonal and Intrapsychic Aspects of Intersubjectivity

In their acknowledgment of mutual influence in psychoanalysis, all the postmoderns are struggling with the tension between their recognition of preestablished patterns of individual subjectivity in patient and analyst and their acknowledgment of the potential for bidirectional change in the analytic situation. Beyond the writing of the moderate postmoderns, these issues have been interestingly addressed by Sucharov (1996) in a discussion of mutual empathy in the analytic encounter and by Slavin and Kriegman (1998) in an exploration of the ways in which the analyst must change. Continuing to struggle with the balance between subjective and intersubjective influences in early development and treatment, Beebe et al. (1997) have told us: it is true both that "interactions patterns are co-created," and that "early patterns are reproduced in adult dyadic life" (p. 217). It is because both assertions reflect aspects of human experience that change may come about in the patient's previously established patterns of experiencing and relating.

First, the patient's early patterns are reproduced in the analytic situation through the analyst's unwitting cooperation. Later they may be changed to the extent that the analyst's preestablished patterns of experiencing and relating are different from the patient's and are anchored well enough to have an influence that surpasses that of the patient on how things evolve in the analytic dyad. Especially in the face of the sometimes overwhelming pull into the patient's preestablished modes of experiencing and relating, which are often very painful and destructive for both patient and analyst, the analyst's willingness and capacity to struggle repeatedly toward and regain an empathic stance vis-à-vis the patient is essential. The alternative may be an impasse that is weighed down with the analyst's unyielding hatred or withdrawal in the face of the patient's witting or unwitting attacks on her being.

The patient's preestablished patterns of experience and interaction used to be labeled as intrapsychic structures (of self or ego) and internalized object relations. Such terminology is now felt to underemphasize the relational and intersubjective dimensions of development and the fluidity of individual experience, open as it always is to mutual influence. Still, as we try to correct old problems in our theories, new solutions sometimes miss the mark in one direction or the other: sometimes we seem precariously close to having constructed a psychoanalytic picture of patient and analyst as two combatants in conflict, while other writings call up a view of the analytic dyad as a puddle of similarity and togetherness. From the domain of empirical infant research, some alternative solutions are beginning to emerge that help us avoid both of these easily caricatured extremes.

Lachmann and Beebe (1992), in particular, have met the challenges of balancing our understanding of the differential roles of individual subjectivity and mutual influence in human development and treatment. They write, for instance, that "psychic structure is interactively organized," and that "the infant has an extraordinary array of early social, perceptual, and cognitive capacities with which to engage the caretaker in an active construction of both the interpersonal and subjective worlds" (p. 146). They suggest that transference "reflects in microcosm the patient's inner life as well as being generated by both patient and analyst" (p. 143). They go on to further our understanding of therapeutic action as intrapsychically and interpersonally determined: "The contributions of analyst and patient [to transference] are neither similar nor equal but, through their interaction, the patient's rigidly retained structure can be engaged, responded to analytically, and transformed" (p. 145). These words call to mind similar comments by

Stolorow and Atwood (also published in 1992), which explicitly bring together the intrapsychic and interpersonal worlds in the concept of intersubjectivity: "The concept of an intersubjective system brings to focus both the individual world of inner experience and its embeddedness with other such worlds in a continual flow of mutual influence" (p. 18). Among the moderate postmoderns, Hoffman, Benjamin, Mitchell, and Aron all manifest in their writings an appreciation of the depth and complexity of intrapsychic experience at the crossroads of the interpersonal world.

Lachmann and Beebe (1996a, b) continue their synthesis of old and new concepts by seeing both the mother–infant and the analyst–patient dyads as "interactive system[s] within which self- and mutual regulation must be integrated" (p. 2). They go on to say that intrapsychic or interactional "organization is an emergent property of the dyadic system as well as a property of the individual" (p. 2). In this statement, Beebe and Lachmann (1988a, b, 1994) continue to meet their earlier commitment to integrate one-person and two-person psychologies. As noted earlier, the groundwork of our understanding of this integration of self- and mutual regulation was laid over the years by other psychoanalytic infant researchers, including Stechler and Kaplan (1980) and Demos and Kaplan (1986). Although explicitly committed to intersubjectivity and to a two-person psychology, Mitchell, Benjamin, Aron, and Stolorow and his colleagues all struggle to articulate their own ways of recognizing the individual differentiated subjectivities or organizations of experience that make up the intersubjective dyad.

Intersubjectivity: Separate Subjectivities in Conflict vs. the Breakdown of Boundaries Between Selves

Overall, it seems the recognition of the intersubjective nature of human development and of the psychoanalytic situation seems to have led us in two opposing directions. Taking one path from intersubjectivity and emphasizing the significance of two separate selves, we can open up an exploration of their differences and inevitable conflicts: Bollas (1989) follows this path in his *dialectics of difference*; Mitchell (1993) emphasizes relational conflict; Pizer (1998) suggests the twoness of subjectivities in his *negotiation of paradox*; and Slavin and

Kriegman (1992) arrive at a recognition of ubiquitous relational conflict in their reexamination of psychoanalytic concepts from an evolutionary biological viewpoint. Slavin and Kriegman further remind us that, to the extent that no two individuals have identical gene pools, no two persons can ever share identical interests and goals. Thus, conflict is inevitable even between parents and children, who share some, but not all the same genes.

But at the same time that all the moderate postmoderns have pursued a concept of intersubjectivity in which there is an emphasis on two *separate and different* subjects conflictually involved in a given dyad, other authors tend to place greater emphasis on the blurring and overlap of subjective experiences in interpersonal interactions. Approaching intersubjectivity from strikingly different starting points, the radical postmodern philosophers and psychoanalysts Barratt (1993, 1995) and Kristeva (1987, 1996) seem to join Stolorow et al. (1994) and Kohut (1984) in arriving at a view of the inevitable and even *desirable blurring of boundaries between initially separate subjectivities in interaction with one another.*

In earlier chapters, I have documented at length Kohut's arguments for the inevitable and desirable blurring of boundaries between selves and his insistence on the impossibility of individual autonomy in human experience (for example, Kohut, 1984, pp. 29, 52, 61). His entire selfobject concept attests to his understanding of subjective development in an intersubjective context (in the sense of both mutual regulation and influence and interpersonal recognition). Although Kohut did not explicitly break down the relational elements of development into articulated categories of mutual regulation and recognition, he saw affective regulation as the central need of the infant in the first months of life (omnipotent merger). Affect regulation is then followed by increasingly differentiated experiences of recognition (mirroring, twinship, and idealization) contributing to primary self-development through age three. In his archaic selfobject concept, he was clear that benefits outweighed losses for the developing individual when premature or precocious recognition was not forced in relation to the differential intrapsychic experience of a separate other.

Starting with self psychology as their platform, Stolorow and his colleagues went beyond Kohut in their explicit emphasis on the intersubjective nature of all human development and experience. Echoing Kohut's (1984) own words, Atwood and Stolorow (1984) argue that *"[p]atient and analyst together form an indissoluble psychological system,* and it is this system that constitutes the empirical domain of psychoanalytic inquiry" (p. 64, italics added). But, whereas Atwood and Stolorow, as well as Kohut, assert that the indissolubility between patient and analyst is a given—an inevitable quality of human relationships—the more radical postmodern analysts and philosophers Kristeva (1987, 1996) and Barratt (1993, 1995), see a breaking down of boundaries between individual selves not as a given but as a moral goal to be struggled for. Both Kristeva and Barratt speak eloquently against the isolated and bounded self, which, paradoxically, is implicit in the relational theories of the moderate postmodern analysts.

In their commitment to articulate the relational and intersubjective aspects of the analytic situation, and in their reaction perhaps to Kohut's earlier and almost exclusive emphasis on empathy and the self-object aspects of relationships, the moderate postmoderns have focused almost entirely on the ways that the analyst establishes herself as a separate and differentiated entity. In this emphasis, they end by approaching the very image of a bounded and isolated self that they unanimously reject. From this contemporary American relational view, the emphasis is on the analyst's establishment of herself as a differentiated subject through both deliberate and unwitting self-revelation and planned and spontaneous self-disclosure. This emphasis is indeed ironic, because the very analysts who want to rescue their discipline (and their analysands) from the isolating confines of classical theory and technique seem to be articulating a psychoanalysis that, in the interests of both enrichment of self and relational development for the patient, emphasizes the difference between patient and analyst and therefore militates against the possibility of a breakdown of boundaries through empathic connections between them. Of course, their occasional exaggeration of the benefits and values accruing from the analyst's unique expressiveness has been influenced by what they see as Kohut's unvarying emphasis on empathy and selfobject relating, which Kohut (1984) himself, in his final writings, anticipated moving beyond. At their best, the moderate postmoderns all engage in struggles to balance these aspects of human relational experience; and, to the extent that they invoke the notions of paradox and dialectic, I think they succeed.

As the postmoderns strive to distance themselves from Kohut's overriding emphasis on empathy, empathy has become an increasingly devalued aspect of the analytic exchange, a commodity that is seen as anything but postmodern. In self psychology, empathy is a mode of relating that underscores the potential for similar and shared experiences at the affective level; whereas the moderate postmodern emphasis on the analyst's subjectivity and authentic self-expression tends to underscore the potential for disparate and differentiated human experiences. The moderate postmoderns vigorously acknowledge and explore mutual influence, and yet this recognition seems not to have modified their conviction about the possibilities for, and the value of, the analyst's maintenance of a separate subjectivity and differential self-expression.

Meanwhile, Barratt and Kristeva see the establishment of separateness and difference in a way that seems to be in contrast to the views of the moderate post moderns. The positions of the radical postmodern authors are more closely aligned with Kohut's notion of a lifelong attitude of openness to, mutual exchange with, and acceptance of others, as expressed in his notion of selfobject relating. Is it perhaps significant that none of these authors—Barratt, Kristeva, or Kohut—was born in this country and that the collective American analytic subjectivity of the moderate postmoderns was shaped in a strikingly different context, leading to a different emphasis?

For instance, Barratt's (1993) rejection of "self" compels us to acknowledge that too much emphasis on separate identities in our century has contributed to two World Wars and countless other organized and spontaneous acts of destruction, to worldwide tribal wars and racial tensions, and to "ethnic cleansing" in Bosnia and other parts of eastern Europe. Either identity, or the self, in Barratt's view, forecloses on all possibilities other than the paths chosen and tends too much to underscore separateness and difference between individuals and groups of individuals, to no good end. Would the moderate postmoderns' emphasis on the multiplicity of selves, and their appreciation of the ubiquity of mutual influence, be capable of countering Barratt's rejection of our notions of identity and the self, including our current analytic emphasis on the analyst's subjectivity? And how much would the moderate postmoderns' insistence on the analyst's self-expression in relation to her patients offend the sensibility of one like Barratt, whose clinical emphasis is on the unfettered flow of the analysand's unconscious experience?

Kristeva (1996), like Barratt, speaks of having tried to break free of "identificatory thinking" and highlights instead the "multifaceted nature of the psychic apparatus, and thus of human experience itself" (p. 259). Kristeva (1987) suggests that, when analysis is successful, the analysand, through his relations with the analyst, sheds his "old self" (p. 61). In fact, unlike all the moderate postmoderns, and in contrast to Kohut and Stolorow et al. as well, Kristeva goes so far as to reject individual subjectivity altogether. She links it ominously with desire and the "nihilistic program" and sees in it nothing more than the narcissistic pursuit of fulfilment of one's own greed and lust at the expense of the other. Kristeva thus looks "forward to *the ultimate dissolution of desire . . . to be replaced by relationship with another, from which meaning derives*" (p. 63, italics added). The moderate postmoderns agree with Kristeva that desire is at the heart of individual subjectivity (Benjamin, 1988), but, in sharp contrast to Kristeva, they honor desire as that which keeps subjectivity alive. Whereas Kristeva sees subjectivity as that which keeps individuals isolated and apart and tending toward exploitation, the moderate postmoderns see subjectivity—in Stern's and Ogden's sense of the possibility for mutual recognition—as that which makes it possible for individuals to come together, or as Aron (1996) puts it, to achieve a meeting of minds.

On the issues of desire and subjectivity, Kohut and Loewald saw desire as shaped in an intersubjective context. As such, it can become a vitalizing aspect of the individual's subjective self-experience and interpersonal relatedness, provided that the human environment continues to respond in a way that affirms (while not exploiting) the individual's desire. Desire is not just originally but continuously intersubjectively organized (see also Winnicott, 1958, 1960); it therefore requires ongoing interpersonal containment, organization, and responsiveness in order to enhance rather than undermine the individual's subjective experience. Like the moderate postmoderns, Winnicott, Kohut, and Loewald all built their theories around a meeting of minds, but each of them also had an interest in the beneficial effects of not just a meeting but also a melding of minds. This interest is reflected in Winnicott's concept of transitional space, in Kohut's concept of selfobject relating, and in Kohut's and Loewald's concepts of internalization.

A Meeting or Melding of Minds

Do individual minds simply meet, while maintaining some degree of separateness within the intersubjective field? Or do they inevitably meld and lose their former distinctiveness? These questions continue to be a subject of psychoanalytic exploration, as we struggle to elucidate the basis of the analyst's contribution to the patient's behavior, experience, and therapeutic change. Earlier notions of internalization, as formulated in Freud's, Kohut's, and Loewald's work, account for the "taking in" or "taking over" of psychological traits and functions in the course of psychic development and change but are no longer accepted in postmodern discourse. Kohut's and Loewald's notions of internalization were very compatible with one another: both men saw an intimate caretaking bond as necessary to begin the process but saw the internalized psychic functions as becoming the uniquely integrated "property" of the developing individual once the process was underway (Teicholz, 1990).

For Kohut and Loewald, internalization was not explicitly conceived as a two-way process in which parents and analysts were enriched through their interactions with their children or analysands, although Kohut certainly implied narcissistic enrichment for the parent who fostered psychic growth in her child. There is no conceptual reason that this possibility could not have been considered more generally. It was largely ignored because at that particular juncture in psychoanalytic history it was felt that the treatment situation demanded a singular focus on the experience and psychic growth of the analysand alone, and also perhaps because only the analysand was thought of as sustaining a regression sufficient to render him open to ongoing internalizations.

The moderate postmoderns see the notion of internalization as problematic in several ways: the concept emerged from, and is integral to, the structural theory in psychoanalysis, which is no longer in ascendancy in analytic discourse; it relies on spatial rather than temporal metaphors, the latter now seen as preferable (Mitchell, 1993); and as it was presented in the history of psychoanalytic thought, it was unidirectional rather than bidirectional, suggesting a one-person rather than a two-person psychology. The postmoderns do hypothesize, however, that exposure to a broad range of interpersonal functioning in the analytic dyad and to the richly expressed subjectivity of the analyst will somehow contribute to a more richly elaborated subjectivity for the patient. It is not clear from their writings how they see this gain coming about; they certainly do not ascribe it to identificatory processes or to any other form of "internalization."

Starting with Kohut's self psychology, and then taking early giant steps toward a psychoanalysis that is increasingly postmodern, Stolorow et al. (1987) seem to have expressed some of the collective and over-lapping concerns of Kohut, Loewald, and the moderate postmoderns in their ongoing struggles to elucidate the relationship between the sub-jective and intersubjective worlds:

> Exploration of the specific *meanings* that the analyst's activities have for the patient, together with reconstructions of how these meanings were acquired developmentally, then become possible. It is the full and continuing articulation of the patient's affective experience of the analyst that establishes an intersubjective con-text in which the arrested process of self-differentiation can become reinstated" [p. 52].

Kohut and Loewald kept their focus on the inner subjective world of the patient's experience. They believed that the patient's intrapsychic and interpersonal growth was determined by the particulars of the ana-lyst's participation in the analytic relationship. The important particu-lars for them were the analyst's centering of attention on and empathic responsivity to the patient. Meanwhile, it has become almost a marker of the moderate postmodern analytic literature that it is concerned with the "continuing articulation of the patient's affective experience of the analyst" (Stolorow et al., 1987, p. 52; see also Aron, 1991, 1996; Hoffman, 1996, 1998). Kohut also advocated the analyst's exploration of the patient's experience of the analyst's behavior and subjectivity, but he did so primarily in the context of discussing disruption and repair sequences in the analytic relationship. And, although emphasizing the analyst's function as a new object for the patient, Loewald did not make explicit reference to analytic exploration of the patient's experience of the analyst's subjectivity.

Even while the *meeting* of analytic minds is still being debated in the literature, it seems that a *melding* of analytic minds has already taken place without our prior explicit intention. Certainly, I have been influ-enced by every one of the theorists whom I have undertaken to discuss. What is left for us as readers is to continue to tease out the threads of our similarities and differences. Where we differ, we seek agreement on which patients might benefit more from one approach than from an other and when this might happen. This subject is difficult to discuss in the abstract owing to the unique subjectivities and intersubjective con-texts created by every analytic dyad. Surely, however, few would disagree with Mitchell's (1997) argument for the "highly cultivated skill" of "self-reflective responsiveness," in which the analyst follows "different levels of meaning at the same time, [learning] to track and engage in, simultaneously, different lines of thought, affective response, self-organization" (p. 194). In Mitchell's view, all these activities can facilitate in the analyst "the freedom to respond variously at different times and to be able to draw on a wide variety of potential responses in [his] repertoire when it seems useful" (p. 194).

Through the recognition of our individual and idiosyncratic subjectivities, and our acceptance of a different kind of authority, one no longer based on knowledge, we may be led to join the poets in their embrace of not knowing. As W. S. Merwin (1983) wrote of a conversation he had with his fellow poet John Berryman:

> he said the great presence
> that permitted everything and transmuted it
> in poetry was passion
> passion was genius and he praised movement and invention
>
> I had hardly begun to read
> I asked how can you ever be sure
> that what you write is really
> any good at all and he said you can't
>
> you can't you can never be sure
> you die without knowing
> whether anything you wrote was any good
> if you have to be sure don't write

[from *Opening the Hand*]

I think that Mitchell and all the postmoderns are telling us that, if we have to be sure, we cannot be psychoanalysts. If we cannot be sure, perhaps we can at least join Merwin and Berryman in singing the praises of constructive movement and invention, which we hope will emerge from our passionate pursuit of learning with our patients, through our work on their behalf. We accumulate not knowledge but experience—each new patient represents an opportunity to enter into a brand new subjective world and to participate in the creation of a new intersubjective realm that never existed before and never will again in exactly the same way.

THE IMPACT OF FEMINIST AND GENDER THEORIES ON PSYCHOANALYSIS

The Interface with Self Psychology and the Moderate Postmoderns

After long maintaining that the orchestra's superior sound and style came partly from its maleness, the members . . . voted to welcome women to their annual auditions . . . when positions would be available for a violist, a tuba player, and a trumpet player. . . . Beyond the possibility of the women destroying their special sound, the orchestra had [earlier expressed fears about women] and also argued that it would suffer financially if women took maternity leaves and had to be replaced. But the new Austrian Chancellor, Viktor Klima, publicly told the orchestra members . . . that there was "creative potential in the other half of humanity and this should be used."

—Jane Perlez

Men no longer barbecue in our movies; instead they are the ones being skewered. But why did they barbecue in the first place? Because we once lived in a gendered world built out of piled-on oppositions: outdoors versus indoors, work versus family, production versus reproduction, salaried versus unsalaried, competitive versus cooperative, hard versus soft. . . .

But now those distinctions have been blurred. Women are in the workplace, where they are more productive and less reproductive. . . Men are being downsized and losing their jobs. . .

What happens to the minds of men and women in this brave new con-
fusing world? Men fall out of love with themselves and into doubt. They
look into the void and ponder ultimate questions: Are women more
evolved because they can be productive and reproductive at the same time?
If you take away a man's economic function as breadwinner, does anything
of value remain?

—Richard Shweder

To do full justice to the topics of female psychology, gender development, and sexuality in psychoanalysis would require three separate
books beyond this chapter. There has been an explosion of richly creative activity on these closely interrelated topics, and I am painfully
aware that in any overview I must leave out more than I am able to
include. And yet one cannot undertake to explore the emergence of
postmodern influences in psychoanalytic thought without a serious
attempt to represent the major changes in these three areas of conceptualization since the 1960s. In undertaking this effort, we shall see that,
just as feminist and gender theories are today nearly identical on certain points, so too is there extensive overlap between postmodern theories and these other areas of study.

This convergence covers broad territory: it is at its clearest in the
valuing of egalitarianism and mutuality over hierarchical arrangements
and earlier notions of analytic authority; in the acknowledgment of
ambiguity and uncertainty as opposed to claiming knowledge and certainty; in the recognition of subjectivity or intersubjectivity where an
ideal of objectivity used to reign; in the effort to place individual experience and personal narrative where analysts formerly saw hard-wired
and bodily essences and universals; in the substitution of social constructionism for biological positivism; and in the embrace of paradox
and dialectical thinking over dichotomization and linear conceptualizations of development. Indeed, all the issues that we have already
explored in relation to Kohut, Loewald, and the postmoderns could be
taken up again in the presentation of psychoanalytic feminist thought
and gender theory. Although I shall try to avoid undue repetition, I
hope that as this chapter proceeds it will become clearer how these
more abstract conceptualizations pertain to the issues of female psychology, sexuality, and gender. The chapter may also shed light on how
the feminist and gender projects have both contributed to these gen-

eral shifts in psychoanalytic thinking—many of them epistemological in nature—and have been enhanced by them in turn.

Some of the complex interrelationships among the overlapping issues of feminism, gender, and sexuality are suggested by Chodorow (1989):

> Feminist understanding requires a multiplex account . . . of the dynamics of gender, sexuality, sexual inequality, and domination. It is the focus on relations among elements . . . along with an analysis and critique of male dominance, which define an understanding of sex and gender as feminist. . . . I no longer think that one factor, or one dynamic, can explain male dominance. . . . An open web of social, psychological, and cultural relations, dynamics, practices, identities, beliefs, in which I would privilege neither society, psyche, nor culture, comes to constitute gender as a social, cultural, and psychological phenomenon [p. 5].

Thus, Chodorow not only highlights the inseparable interrelationships among issues of female psychology, gender, and sexuality, but simultaneously notes the web of social, psychological, and cultural factors contributing to our understanding of each. Chodorow is not alone in pointing to the inseparability of these ideas. For instance, Young-Bruehl (1996) writes, "It is not surprising that a term and topic like gender, which for a quarter of a century did such ubiquitous service in the feminist/sexual/cultural revolution as well as in the process of psychoanalytic revisionism, should have come to be a whirling traffic circle of meanings and debates" (p. 17).

In the feminist contribution to psychoanalysis, the inevitable focus on problems of gender and gender roles brought the discourse to the crossroads between psyche–soma, on one hand, and culture and society, on the other. It is therefore fitting that one of the founding texts of late 20th-century psychoanalytic feminism, *The Reproduction of Mothering*, was written by Chodorow (1978), who came to her interest in psychoanalysis by way of previous studies in anthropology and sociology. Chodorow's own journey is one that moves from a greater initial emphasis on social and cultural factors (1978) to increasing respect for the power of the intrapsychic, dynamic, and relational experiences within individual families (1989). In addition to Chodorow's contribution, other influential texts on feminist thought and gender have come from the academic fields of anthropology, philosophy, sociology, women's studies, and cultural criticism (e.g., Rubin, 1975; Foucault,

1980, 1984; Butler, 1990). These and other contributions heighten our awareness that, in addition to the difficulties of teasing apart the separate contributions of feminist and gender studies to psychoanalysis, it is no easy task to find a balance between our attention to sociocultural factors and those pertaining to individual psychology as we approach feminist issues and concepts of gender.

Given the complexities in the fields of feminist and gender studies, the nature of the relationship between these contributions and the major tenets of self psychology is not always clear. For instance, although self psychology has sometimes been included in the broad category of relational theories that are felt to be in some ways compatible with feminist theory (Chodorow, 1989), self psychology has been somewhat out of the loop of excitement generated within psychoanalysis by new developments in feminist and gender theories. Self psychology seems neither to contribute significantly to, nor to be greatly enriched by, the ongoing debates.

Unlike Kohut, Loewald did not overtly reject the Freudian view of sexuality. But in his writings, sexuality was frequently subordinate to ego and relational considerations (Loewald, 1960) or to concerns for autonomy of the self (Loweald, 1979b). Presumably, Loewald shared Freud's views on sublimation but ultimately had in common with Kohut a focus on the noninstinctual aspects of development and experience. This focus resulted in his writings' being fairly devoid of commentary on the specifics of sexuality and gender experience. For the most part we must read between the lines to infer what his position might have been in relation to contemporary feminist and gender theories, and even then we have very little on which to rely.

For instance, in Loewald's (1977) book review of the Freud–Jung correspondence (McGuire, 1974), he presented the respective arguments of Freud and Jung concerning the importance of sexuality versus spirituality in human experience. Although Loewald (1977) acknowledged that the views of both men were colored by their personal interests or quests, he went on to say: "But one cannot simply dismiss Jung's impressions and 'intuitions' in regard to Freud's deep concern with sexuality as nothing more than expressions of Jung's own preoccupations and inclinations" (p. 416). From this comment we might infer that Loewald was supporting Jung's suggestion that Freud's interest in sexuality betrayed a personal and emotional overinvolvement not in keeping with his observations on other topics (in McGuire, 1974, p. 150).

But Loewald (1977) soon followed this comment with statements suggesting agreement with Freud

> that superpersonal and transcendental aspects of human exis-
> tence and of unconscious and instinctual life (so much stressed
> by Jung) can be experienced and integrated convincingly . . . only
> in the concreteness of one's own personal life, including the ugli-
> ness, trivialities, and sham that go with it [p. 426].

With this observation, Loewald seemed slightly to tip the balance of his support back in the direction of Freud's grounding of his theory in the body, with relationships perhaps included as part of what constitutes one's "personal life." For the most part, the paucity of Loewald's exploration of specific issues of sexuality and gender has led me to stretch toward an interpretation of his position on the basis of meager material in his writings. This absence alone probably speaks for itself.

While contemporary relational theorists often share with Kohut and Loewald the tendency to downplay sexual issues, we have seen that feminists, gender theorists, and the moderate postmoderns neverthe-less converge in a certain critique directed at the concepts of self, iden-tity, and gender identity. In arguments that bear a striking similarity to one another across the varying contemporary paradigms, notions of self, identity, and gender identity are faulted for their apparent assumption of unity and coherence. Eschewing a privileged position for these qual-ities of self or identity, contemporary feminists, gender theorists, and the moderate postmoderns alike all place a greater emphasis on multi-plicity, fluidity, and even chaos in their conceptualizations of normative self and gender experience.

Many interesting and successful efforts have been made to summa-rize late 20th-century developments in feminist and gender theories from varying psychoanalytic viewpoints (for example: J. Mitchell, 1974; Fast, 1979, 1984, 1990; Person and Ovesey, 1983; Mayer, 1985, 1991, 1995; Cherazi, 1986; Benjamin, 1988, 1991, 1995b, 1996; Chodorow, 1989, 1994, 1995; Person, 1990; Coates, 1990, 1997; Coates, Friedman, and Wolfe, 1991; Harris, 1991b; Coates and Wolfe, 1995; Stack, 1995; Mitchell, 1996b; Young-Bruehl, 1996; de Marneffe, 1997). Relying on this impressive body of literature, I will provide only a brief and selec-tive summary. I hope to bring some of the feminist and gender contri-butions into relationship with aspects of self psychology and with the postmodern concepts of subjectivity and intersubjectivity.

Countering Male Supremacy from
Within and Outside of Biological Positivism

From the start, there have been many diverse issues at stake in the separate but overlapping feminist and gender debates. Most of the early discourse took as its starting point direct statements in Freud's writings that, from the viewpoints of feminism and gender theory, had to be countered. Among the statements that early feminists and emergent gender theorists alike felt impelled to challenge were those in which Freud (1905, 1924, 1933) repeatedly expressed the view that female sexuality and feminine personality development were secondary to all that was male and masculine. Feminist critics and gender theorists also identified certain contradictions within Freud's evolving commentary on sexual development over the decades of his professional life. For instance, they perceived contradictions between his concepts of biological determinism and male supremacy, on one hand, and the broader psychoanalytic theory and methodology that tended toward enlightened theories of male and female psychologies and gender development, on the other. As examples of further contradictions that have been cited in Freud's theory of sexuality are his assertion that bisexuality is universal and that homosexual love is not necessarily pathological (Freud, 1905); yet his theory of the Oedipus complex was so weighted in a heterosexist direction that he labeled as "negative" the eroticized relationship between a child and his same-sex parent while calling love for the opposite sex parent the "positive" oedipal (Freud, 1917).

Freud's extensive writings on sexuality (see, e.g., 1898, 1908, 1910, 1912, 1918, 1920, 1923b, 1925) focused on the anatomical differences between the sexes and what he saw as the "bedrock" psychological consequences of these differences (1925). Although his psychoanalytic method and its assumptions allowed for infinite variety in the personal construction of meaning attributed to any biological or anatomical "given," he was primarily interested in identifying the universals of psychological experience emanating from what he saw as central and inescapable biological "realities," namely, the male phallus, the female "absence" or lack of a penis, and the normality and desirability of heterosexual reproduction.

Especially in the area of reproductive sexuality, Freud's views were influenced by concepts derived from Darwin's theory of evolution, which carried the weight of such notions as survival of the species. From the viewpoint of today's feminist and postmodern critics, Freud's theory of male supremacy, his heterosexist views, and his derivative emphasis on reproductive sexuality all are understood as having been multiply determined by a mix of the intellectual/sociopolitical climate of his times, the limiting effects of his personal subjectivity, certain unanalyzed aspects of his childhood misperceptions, and defensive unconscious fantasy (see Stolorow and Atwood, 1979). It is commonly recognized today that, for all analysts, similar factors influence our individual preferences for one theory among the multiple available paradigms.

For example, in keeping with changing times and social/intellectual climates, some contemporary analysts tend to be less fascinated with Darwin and more interested in Einstein's theory of relativity (Eagle, 1987); Heisenberg's uncertainty theory (Greenberg and Mitchell, 1983); and chaos theory (Schwartz, 1995; Mayer, 1996b). Astrophysicists almost daily provide new metaphors with which we can enhance our ability to characterize our psychoanalytic theories of mind. But these accelerating findings from the empirical sciences also give us new ways of seeing and thinking about human experience. Currently, most new ideas tend to emphasize the randomness and discontinuities in nature or the multiplicity and fragmentation of experience (Elliott and Spezzano, 1996; Goldner, 1991; Dimen, 1991; Barratt, 1993; and others), as opposed to an ordered and predictable biological determinism, or reliable experiences of unity and coherence.

I earlier noted the differences in the prevailing intellectual climates of Freud's versus our own times. I suggested that Kohut's self psychology and Loewald's relational ego psychology can be seen as important waystations between classical and postmodern theories, looking both forward and backward and manifesting elements of both essentialism and constructionism. For instance, Kohut rejected Freud's biological determinism but clung to a belief in the possibility of psychic order and coherence on the basis of certain kinds of relationships available to the individual during childhood. Loewald's (1979b) work more than Kohut's straddled the line between relational and biological determinism; for example, he maintained the centrality of the Oedipus complex as posited in Freud's theory but reinterpreted it as a universal striving toward autonomy, with a greatly diminished role for the sexual and aggressive instincts.

We shall soon see that the earlier noted criticisms leveled by the postmoderns at Kohut are echoed in the feminist and gender theorists' critiques of Freud and some aspects of self psychology as well. But, interestingly, the feminist and postmodern critiques of self psychology are not at all directed toward Loewald's very similar ideas. Chodorow (1989) in particular sees in Loewald's work a significant compatibility with feminist psychoanalytic interests and cites his writings at length in putting forth her own feminist object relations viewpoint. But the ideas Chodorow wishes to appropriate from Loewald's writings for feminist psychoanalysis are not incompatible with Kohut's thinking, even though they may be more explicitly and poetically elaborated by Loewald than by Kohut. For instance, Chodorow credits Loewald with having provided a bridge between the two "sometimes disparate dialogues" pertaining to psychoanalytic treatment on one hand, and the early mother-child relationship on the other (p. 12). I submit that Kohut too provided such bridges; he saw the selfobject relationship as constitutive of both early development and later growth in psychoanalysis. Additionally, Chodorow points to Loewald's success in having captured "the ways that unconscious processes resonate with conscious and thus give conscious life depth and richness of meaning" (p. 12, referring to Loewald, 1960). She also cites Loewald's (1976) appreciation of the interplay between fantasy and reality and between rationality and irrationality (Loewald, 1979b). I already cited passages in which Kohut too argued for a measure of irrationality as well as rationality in human affairs, and I have singled out his notion of omnipotent merger as one instance in which he recognized the normative value of fantasy. In fact, Kohut's self psychology is generally constructed on the basis of his conviction that the grandiose fantasies of childhood have to become a "tamed" but integral part of the adult personality if healthy relationships, creative pursuits, and a general sense of well-being are to prevail in an individual's life. Thus, although Kohut's writings failed to capture the imagination of the feminists, his ideas often significantly overlapped with those of Loewald, from whom Chodorow borrows heavily.

All the pasaages cited by Chodorow to bring together Loewald's ideas with her own object relations feminism involve juxtapositions of opposites. These juxtapositions foreshadow the enthusiastic embrace of the dialectic as a way of containing intellectual and affective tensions in psychoanalytic theory and practice in the 1990s. I have pointed out that Kohut's *self* is constantly immersed in a selfobject milieu that simultaneously undermines and contributes to its autonomy. Although

Kohut did not use the terms paradox or dialectic in his theory, his concepts of self and selfobject seem to meet the criteria for Ogden's (1986) use of the term dialectic, namely, opposing poles of experience that simultaneously create and destroy each other's meaning.

In postmodern thought and current feminist views of gender, an attempt is often made to resolve the dichotomy between masculine and feminine by invoking a dialectical relationship between them. For example, Benjamin and Sweetnam have applied Ogden's concept of dialectically related modes of organizing experience to issues of gender. Bringing together Fast's (1979, 1984) ideas of gender inclusiveness in young children with Ogden's (1986) dialectical "positions," Benjamin (1996) has suggested that children move from a preoedipal, overinclusive stage in their conceptualization of gender, through a dichotomous oedipal stage (the resolution of which represents the developmental endpoint of classical theory), to a more fluid and complex postoedipal period in which the overinclusive and the dichotomous experiences of gender are combined in dialectical relation to one another. Similarly turning to Ogden's modes of organizing experience, Sweetnam (1996) argues for a dialectical relationship between qualities of rigidity and fluidity in the experiencing of gender. Harris (1991a), while not explicitly invoking the concept of the dialectic, nevertheless speaks of gender experience as having qualities of both tenaciousness and evanescence (p. 198).

Although Kohut made no reference to the feminist and gender literature emerging simultaneously with his own theorizing in the 1970s, his selfobject concept helped to move psychoanalysis toward one of feminism's central goals by replacing Freud's universalist biological determinism with a new personal/relational "determinism," laying the groundwork for later contructionism. In Kohut's version of development, the current and future health of the self is tied not to biology but to the quality of the selfobject relationships and milieu. Although not always explicitly recognized as such, Kohut's emphasis on relationship in the construction of individual experience and meaning turned out to be compatible not only with the more purely relational theories of the moderate postmoderns, but also with many strands of feminist and gender theory as well (Chodorow, 1989).

In an earlier discussion, we noted that the primary difference between Kohut and some of these other theorists was in the kinds of relational experiences believed to be pivotal for psychological development.

Whereas Kohut usually limited his discussions of the relational field to four specified selfobject functions, the moderate postmoderns leave the field more open to include other kinds of interactions; they emphasize in particular interactions in which the analyst makes herself known as a differentiated subject. But among the moderate postmoderns, Benjamin (1988) singles out *recognition* as a relational experience pivotal to the development of subjectivity and intersubjective relatedness. Beyond the fact that her emphasis is exclusively on mutual rather than one-way recognition, it is not clear how her notion of recognition differs from Kohut's concept of mirroring in self psychology.

Certainly, in Kohut's theory, the capacity for mutual recognition is one of the primary goals of development. And, while he posits a stage before which this achievement is established, so too does Stern (1983, 1985), of whose work Benjamin (1988) is appreciative. We may conclude that both Benjamin and Kohut place a high value on mutual recognition but differ in their notions of how individuals acquire this capability. Whereas Kohut believed that children (or patients) will develop this ability if they are reliably the recipients of the other's recognition or mirroring, Benjamin focuses on the child's need for interactions with important others, who, through expressions of their own subjectivities, serve as models or identification figures for *self-recognition*. Benjamin sees Kohut's theory as demanding that the mother (or analyst) sacrifice or downplay expressions of her own subjectivity and argues for an approach to both mothering and psychoanalysis that runs counter to this tendency.

In spite of these important differences, certain similarities between Benjamin's *recognition* and Kohut's *mirroring* may have been missed by Benjamin. Moreover, many femininist and postmodern critics have failed to grasp the limitations that Kohut's notion of the selfobject places on the autonomy of the self. Nonetheless, the widespread criticism of Kohut's emphasis on coherence in healthy self-experience does need to be addressed. Resonating closely with postmodern emphases in general, late 20th-century feminist and gender theories suggest that any sense of coherence is either "a necessary fiction" (Goldner, 1991; Harris, 1991a), a defense against the confusions of multiplicity, or both.

Would Kohut have disagreed with this rendering of a coherent sense of self (or coherent gender identity) as a necessary fiction? Although he saw the coherent self as adaptive rather than defensive, he would certainly have agreed with the adjective "necessary." Also, his concept of coherence was not as far from postmodern and feminist views of the self as it is sometimes taken to be; it was clearly meant to include the integration of multiple and varied strands of experience. Be that as it may, Kohut would probably have been uncomfortable with the designation of "fiction" to the individual's sense of coherence. His view emphasized the (psychic) "reality" rather the fictional status of anything *felt* by the individual. Thus, if an individual had a *sense* of coherence, Kohut might well have said that it mattered little whether or not an epistemologist judged the feeling to be a fiction. The critical issue for Kohut was whether or not the sense of coherence functioned in such a way that the individual was able successfully to pursue personal ambitions, goals, and ideals and to engage in mutually satisfying and enhancing relationships with important others. In other words, for Kohut, the significance of the sense of coherence was in its functionality. Its "truth" value—whether it was fact or fiction—was more or less irrelevant.

Still, in keeping with radical postmodern thought, today's feminist and gender theorists tend to focus on what is lost through coherence, self, or identity rather than on what is gained. This psychology of loss is currently being applied even more to gender identity and sexual orientation than to other aspects of selfhood. While "fictions" of self, gender, and sexual identity are seen as necessary for functional purposes within our present culture and society, they are also seen as foreclosing alternative identities (Barratt, 1995), as inhibiting life choices and limiting realms of relating (Goldner, 1991), as entailing lost connections never adequately mourned (Butler, 1990; Layton, 1997), and as being generally destructive to many individuals whose psychic realities or fictions do not fit with society's prescriptive norms (Goldner, 1991).

Thus many contemporary feminist and gender theorists go beyond critiquing our psychoanalytic concepts of self and gender identity to criticize a society that pressures individuals into complying with these necessary fictions under threat of exclusion from many of society's comforts and rewards. This argument pertains more to issues of gender and sexual identity than to the concept of self, for there are not only strong cultural pressures but also *laws* regulating some aspects of sexual identity and orientation. Even though there are no such laws directed toward the more generic concept of self, a self that is fragmented and unstable is considered, if not illegal and immoral, then at least unwell. Yet the writers who understandably criticize rigid and unitary gender and sexual identities seem to ignore the coexisting problem that people

whose self-experience is fragmented or very unstable are suffering profoundly, are often unable to enter sustaining relationships, and cannot
set and work toward goals that provide them with some sense of purpose and worth.

Early History of Feminist Views in Psychoanalysis

The earliest challenges to Freud's psychology of women came from
Jones (1927, 1933), Horney (1924, 1926, 1933), and Klein (1928), all
of whom argued against his notions of female sexuality as secondary
and inferior. But, despite these strong and eloquent voices, Freud's
views managed to prevail as the official psychoanalytic pronouncement
on female psychology until what has become known as the "second
wave" of psychoanalytic feminism in the 1970s and 80s. Elucidating the
"first wave," or "prehistory," of psychoanalytic feminism, Chodorow
(1989) credits Horney with having recognized the "male-dominant
society and culture" while providing us with "a model of women with
positive primary feminine qualities and self-valuation, as against Freud's
model of woman as defective and forever limited" (p. 3). Chodorow
similarly credits Klein with having turned psychoanalysis "from a psychology of the boy's relation to the father to a psychology of the relation to the mother in children (people) of both sexes" (p. 3), thus
shifting the analytic focus from oedipal to preoedipal. She sees Klein's
theory as "attentive, in an unmediated way, to the emotions and conflicts that relations rooted in gender evoke in the child and in the child
within the adult" (p. 3).

By attributing to Klein an important role in the prehistory of psychoanalytic feminism, Chodorow takes little note of a biological determinism in Klein's work that is more extreme even than Freud's. Of
course, unlike Freud, Klein did not use her version to promote a view
of women as inferior to men but, rather, saw it as an explanation for the
ubiquity of aggression in human experience and interactions.
Furthermore, although Klein granted to the mother, more than to the
father, central significance in early childhood development, her emphasis on the drives and their constitutional basis tipped her theory in the
direction of holding the baby responsible for destructive elements seen
to be universal in mother–infant relations. This destructiveness came
about through the biologically determined creation of the bad object—

the inevitable result of inborn aggressiveness deriving from the death instinct—and the negative and painful object relations established in its wake.

Although the Kleinian narrative can be seen, problematically, as letting the mother off the hook at the expense of blaming the baby, some contemporary femnists (Doane and Hodges, 1992) have viewed Klein's work in a positive light: her theory is praised and contrasted with that of Winnicott, whose work is seen as prescribing an impossible ideal of motherhood that entraps women by suggesting that they give up all aspects of their lives and subjectivity not directly involved in mothering. But Winnicott's "good enough" mother does not have to be *perfectly* available—she only has to be available "enough." And although Winnicott's theory does encourage the mother initially to meet her baby's omnipotence and allow him the illusion of having created his own fulfilment, it places equal emphasis on subsequent phases in which the mother naturally disillusions the baby through gradually diminishing attunement and responsiveness. Winnicott's (1960b) concept *of primary maternal preoccupation* covers a very brief period of time at the beginning of the baby's life, and he also spells out the mother's need, during this time, to be supported by the father so that she can transiently but safely put aside outside interests and relationships. Thus, although Winnicott assigns roles on the basis of traditional notions of gender, never questioning that mothers do all the mothering, he does seem to appreciate, if only in passing, the family as a system, and he does not view the mothering role entirely in isolation from other family members.

Because women have traditionally and overwhelmingly been the primary or exclusive caretakers, the problem of parenting has been a central issue for feminists inside and out of psychoanalysis. Initially the feminist movement saw mothering as a problem only for women. But Chodorow (1978), Benjamin (1988), and others then began to elucidate the problems created by our usual parenting arrangements, problems not just for women but also for men and for children of both sexes. Although Klein, focused as she was on the instinctual origins of behavior, seldom suggested that the aggression of children toward their mothers was mobilized in part because of the isolation of mothers and the absence of fathers from the caretaking scene, many contemporary feminists believe that children's all too common destructive rage toward their mothers, or sometimes crippling defenses against it, could be greatly diminished if caretaking were shared by mothers and fathers rather than carried out by mothers alone (Chodorow, 1978).

Taking a position almost diametrically opposed to the biological determinism of either Freud or Klein, Simone de Beauvoir (1949), in *The Second Sex,* made a lasting contribution to feminist literature outside of psychoanalysis. She argued, decades before postmodernism, that women are relationally and socially constructed rather than biologically determined by their sex. But at the same time that de Beauvoir's feminist existentialism turned Freud's phallocentrism and male supremacy upside down, she credited psychoanalysis with the recognition that

> no factor becomes involved in the psychic life without having taken on human significance; it is not the body-object described by biologists that actually exists, but the body as lived in by the subject. Woman is female to the extent that she feels as such. . . . It is not nature that defines woman; it is she who defines herself by dealing with nature on her own account in her emotional life [p. 42; also cited in Young-Bruehl, 1996].

In spite of de Beauvoir's groundbreaking treatise, two decades were to pass before new responses to Freud's psychology of women began to emerge within psychoanalysis. When they did, the earliest efforts to counter Freud's psychology of women took a path very different from that of de Beauvoir. In France, for instance, Chasseguet-Smirgel (1975) argues for a maternal and paternal law, each essential to human development. Under the maternal law, children of both sexes long to return to the womb, and this infantile dependence must be acknowledged rather than denied. Facilitating integration of the maternal law is the subsequent identification with paternal law, which represents separation and the oedipal order. Chasseguet-Smirgel (1986) believes that both men and women fear the "primitive Mother," a fear that prompts them "to control the female powers and to accord inferior status to women" (p. 4). Thus, Chasseguet-Smirgel rejects Freud's particular biological determinism but maintains his gender binary, reinterpreting women's inferior status on the basis of universal psychological experiences and solutions. She does not question the necessity of women's power over their children but seems to accept it as a given.

Chasseguet-Smirgel's contribution, although unique and original, has in common with the work of several other female analysts the attempt to offer complex object relational interpretations of behavior and attitudes in women that Freud explained only in biological terms. Important examples of this approach include works by Torok (1964), Bernstein (1993), Benjamin (1996), and Harris (1997) on penis envy; by Bernstein (1983) on the female superego; by McDougall (1964) on homosexuality in women; by Mayer (1985, 1995) on castration anxiety; and by Tyson (1982) on object choice. These and other contributions propose equally valued, parallel or complementary lines of development for boys and girls and suggest that neither masculinity nor femininity is primary for both sexes. An exception to this recurring egalitarian theme appears in the work of Stoller (1976), who went so far as to reverse Freud's ordering of things by arguing that femininity, not masculinity, was primary in both boys and girls.

Another body of psychoanalytic responses to Freud's psychology of women generally tended to accept his biologically determined terms of the debate, but then tried to find evidence that he was wrong in his devaluation of women and femininity. Most of those who first argued with Freud on the subject of women looked specifically for evidence of primary femininity (Kestenberg, 1956, 1968, 1976; Schafer, 1974; Chasseguet-Smirgel, 1975; Galenson and Roiphe, 1976; Meluk, 1976; Parens et al., 1976; Ritvo, 1976; Stoller, 1976) or for ways to valorize the different qualities and traits that women seemed to exhibit (Miller, 1976; Gilligan, 1982). The division of all humanity into two sexes was not questioned, and the direct relationship between one's given sex and one's emergent gender continued to be seen as fixed and immutable.

Among those who undertook logically or empirically to "prove" the existence of primary femininity, many sought evidence of early genital awareness in preoedipal children of both sexes, or of "maternal" instincts (Benedek, 1959; Kestenberg, 1976; Galenson and Roiphe, 1976; Kleeman, 1976). Kubie (1974) and Fast (1979, 1984) have argued that both girls and boys go through an early stage of believing that they have or could have the genitals, personal characteristics, and gender roles of both sexes. Fast suggests that narcissistic injury is entailed for boys and girls alike in the subsequent recognition that this is not so. This view repositioned girls' penis envy in relationship to boy's womb or reproductive envy. The case for primary femininity continues to be made in an ongoing literature exploring the multiple aspects of female sexuality and feminine identity (Bernstein, 1990; Kulish, 1991; Mayer, 1991, 1995; Richards, 1992, 1996; Lax, 1994; Tyson, 1994).

Preceding most of these efforts were studies by Money and Eberhart, (1972), later elaborated by Stoller (1976), that established the concept of core gender identity. Money, Hampson, and Hampson (1955a, b), cited in Coates and Wolfe, 1995) reported on one such study in which each child in a group of infants born with indeterminate genitals was arbitrarily assigned to either the male or female sex at birth. With the goal of creating a sex for each child that would make later heterosexual activity possible, surgeons constructed the indeterminate genitalia of each child into either a penis or vagina, and the child was then labeled and raised as either boy or girl. Despite their preexisting theoretical commitments to biological determinism apropos gender, the researchers who followed the development of these hermaphroditic children found that most of them attained "normal" gender identity in accordance with the genitalia and gender label assigned to them at birth. This was the case even for children in whom there was a discrepancy between their sex chromosones and the gender and genitalia chosen and constructed for them. These and other gender studies, carried out and reported independently of the early feminist movement, established a new way of looking at problems of masculinity and feminity. This approach was soon taken up by feminist psychoanalysts as well, who moved their focus from female psychology to problems of gender.

The feminists were able to make constructive use of Money's, Stoller's, and others' work on gender to bolster their own attempts to pry apart the conflation of sex and gender, or body and psyche, in Freud's instinct theory. Thus, while within psychoanalysis the search continued through the 1970s to establish evidence of primary femininity in an effort to counter Freud's view of women as the second sex, a parallel movement was soon launched in which feminists began to question the biological/sexual roots of gender (Goldner, 1991; Layton, 1997). In this questioning, the acquisition of language, the culture at large, and parental attitudes and interactions were understood to play a much larger role in the establishment of gender identity and gender roles than had previously been believed (Coates and Wolfe, 1995; Benjamin, 1995a; de Marneffe, 1997). At the radical edge of this postmodern view, "there is no precultural, presocial, or prelinguistic body; the body is a 'social and discursive object, a body bound up in the order of desire, signification, and power'" (Schwartz, 1997, p. 198).

A quick review of the language of sex and gender is useful here (taken from Coates and Wolfe, 1995, pp. 10–11). *Sex* refers to the external genitalia, which normally correspond with the chromosomal status of 46 *xx* chromosomes for females and 46 *xy* chromosomes for males. *Gender*, by contrast, is a social/psychological construct designating how persons are categorized by others and how they categorize themselves. *Gender role* is the outwardly observable activities, proclivities, and attitudes that are consistent with either the male or the female stereotypes currently afloat in a given time and place; *gender identity* is the complementary intrapsychic sense of being either male or female in accordance (or discordance) with one's social roles. *Core gender identity* is the affectively laden sense that one is the "right" sex. Benjamin (1995b) and de Marneffe (1997) suggest another designation, *nominal gender identity*, the child's earliest ability to name his or her gender correctly, regardless of the affective loading this holds for the child.

The study of gender, removed from biological determinsim, ultimately opened the door to late 20th-century gender and queer[1] theories, particularly the idea that, if gender is not biologically determined, then it must be "performative" (Butler, 1990; Goldner, 1991; Layton, 1997). Each act performed in accordance with a male or female stereotype contributes to the individual's sense that he or she is masculine or feminine. Society rewards gender behavior that is concordant with one's sex and punishes gender-discordant behavior. Repetition of unigendered acts in childhood eventually leads to a core sense that one is masculine or feminine. An important aspect of the masculine stereotype is that men are sexually attracted to women. Similarly, an important aspect of the feminine stereotype is that women are attracted to men. Therefore, inherent in the gender stereotypes is the notion of normative heterosexuality.

In contemporary gender and queer theories, these stereotypes or gender prescriptions are seen as greatly compromising the choices available to both men and women as to how they may live their lives and with whom they may form emotionally intimate, romantic, and sexual relationships. Butler (1995) therefore sees gender as a melancholy phenomenon, in which vast segments of the population are unable to grieve their lost identifications (with opposite-sex parents and partners) or their lost relationships (with same-sex parents and partners). At least as far as identifications are concerned, Benjamin (1995a, 1996), taking

---

[1] Scholars of gay and lesbian life have chosen to call their academic discipline "queer studies."

a more optimistic view, suggests that children of both sexes can benefit from identifications with both parents. She places special emphasis
on the identifications that children of both sexes are able to make with
their fathers and that facilitate movement away from the mother of
early childhood and out into the world. Traditionally, the importance
of the girl's identifications with her father has been neglected. But in
the view of more radical postmodern thought in both feminist and
queer theories, Benjamin's emphasis on the beneficial effects of girls'
identification with their fathers entails a problematic acceptance of the
polarized differences between mothers' and fathers' gender roles and
characteristics.

Feminist Theory, Gender Theory, and Self Psychology

Self psychology's emergence in the early 1970s overlapped with some
of the ground-breaking empirical research on gender (Stoller, 1968;
Money and Eberhardt, 1972) and preceded only slightly the "second
wave" of feminist writings within psychoanalysis (Chodorow, 1978;
Benjamin, 1988). In spite of this near-convergence, there seems to have
been little cross-fertilization between self psychology, on one hand, and
feminist and gender writings, on the other. Because Kohut intended his
theory of self to apply equally to men and to women, and because self
psychology can be understood to transcend issues of gender (Lang,
1984), one might have expected the feminists to seize upon his writings for support. Kohut's lack of offensiveness in matters of gender (as
opposed to Freud's ubiquitous offense) might have been used to counter
Freud's theory of sexuality in which he highlighted differences between
the sexes both anatomical and psychological, to women's disadvantage.
Chodorow (1989) does recognize the gender-neutral quality of object
relations theory and in some of her remarks seems indirectly to have
included Kohut in that category.

That feminist analysts did not generally turn to self psychology for
support in countering Freud's phallocentrism and male supremacy can
be understood to be at least partially related to the fact that feminist
analysts at first accepted the central importance that Freud placed on
biology and sexuality in human psychic development. In the early 70s
they did not usually argue with his essentialist stance; they simply
thought that Freud had gotten it wrong where women were concerned.

Therefore, instead of seeing in self psychology a liberating, gender-free theory, they saw in it little of interest or use at all: very little nuanced discussion of sexuality, female or otherwise, and no new insights into gendered relationships. But a question that still remains is why Kohut's work was ignored for these reasons, while, for instance, Winnicott's, Loewald's, and the moderate postmoderns were not. Explicit issues of sexuality and gender generally play no greater role for these latter theorists than they did for Kohut.

The feminist movement of the 1960s and early 70s was concerned primarily with equality between the sexes and the attempt to reverse pervasive social patterns of male privilege and dominance. Within psychoanalysis, the feminist effort was directed toward finding a basis on which to reject Freud's explicit phallocentrism, his understanding of femininity as derivative of masculinity, and his belief in the "bedrock" inferiority of the female sex. Kohut shared with the feminists a wish to re-vision Freud's psychosexual theory of development, but the different pathways taken to this end by feminist psychoanalysts and self psychology could not have been more different. Whereas Freud saw sexuality at the root of all normal and pathological development, Kohut, in a 1981 letter to Stolorow, stated his belief that conflicts around drive experience were only secondary to self-deficit (cited in Cocks, 1994). Consonant with this view, Kohut constructed a theory in which sexuality plays a minor role as one of many aspects of experience contributing to the vitality of the self. In Kohut's view, a firm and robust self, in turn, contributed to the possibility for satisfying relationships in which sexuality could play its part.

Kohut predated the feminists in his efforts to counter Freud's belief that biology was destiny; he argued that sexuality became a problem for men and women alike only in the absence of self-cohesion. For Kohut, it was the parent–child relationship, not biologically determined drives, that contributed centrally to the child's psychological and sexual development. In particular, it was the parents' selective responsiveness to the child from birth onward that led to the development of the child's sense of self and to her greater or lesser ability to live richly and fully in close and satisfying relationships, in accordance with her ambitions, goals, and ideals. The self evolved similarly in both male and female children: for both men and women, ambitions and ideals were seen as its "poles."

Kohut did not elaborate on the different ways that boys and girls might develop because of their different sex or genders, nor did he attribute great significance to the different sexes in parental selfobject functioning. Although he suggested that the mother was usually the first mirroring selfobject and that the father was more likely to function as an idealizable parent imago, these assignations derived from the (unquestioned) roles traditionally played by mothers and fathers in their families. He was explicit that the selfobject functions were interchangeable between mother and father (Kohut, 1971, p. 185; 1977a, pp. 179, 185). Thus, although Kohut was no feminist and although he did not directly question the gender status quo, his theory did provide a framework for "equal opportunity" parenting and equal opportunity childhood development.

Kohut's emphasis on the importance of gender-neutral ambitions and goals in self-development could have been used by feminists to underscore the necessity for children of both sexes to receive encouragement and support in developing talents and skills and in constructing lives in which those assets would gain broad expression. Furthermore, given that in Freud's theory the ego ideal was a substructure of the superego, Kohut's emphasis on the importance of internalized ideals for all persons might have served indirectly to counter Freud's notion that girls develop superego functioning inferior to that of boys. For Kohut, the ideal self was a gender-transcendant concept: it was equally important in male and female development, and he did not suggest a difference between the sexes in its achievement. Kohut's theory also allowed for children of both sexes to turn to the father for idealizing identifications, thus implicitly anticipating Benjamin's (1991, 1995) ideas. But the feminists within psychonanalysis seem not to have turned specifically to self psychology for support on any of these points. Benjamin and Chodorow are virtually alone among major feminist psychoanalysts in even bringing Kohut into the discourse by name.

Although Kohut and other early self psychologists did not directly address the nature of the relationship between self-experience and gender identity, others have struggled with aspects of this issue. Chodorow (1995) has urged us to acknowledge that "the 'solution' of gender problems involves the solutions of general problems of personal subjectivity and . . . intersubjectivity" (p. 297). Corbett (1997) has argued for recognition of the need for primary self-cohesion as the basis on which gender identity can be established. He proposes that we distinguish between gender problems that derive primarily from deficits in the primary establishment of self and those which have their origin in later periods of development when issues of guilt and desire are prevalent. While acknowledging a certain validity in the postmodern and gender theorists' critique of linear thinking and developmental stages, he nevertheless reminds us that there is "an order in which things cannot happen" (p. 262). He offers a metaphor to illustrate his meaning, suggesting that, just as we cannot hang a door before we have built our house, we cannot construct a gender identity before we have built a self.

Approaching the relationship between self and gender from a slightly different angle, Stack (1995) distinguishes between a generic sense of self—"the enduring quality of self-recognition that forms when primary caretakers provide the developing infant with a safe enough and loving holding environment"—and the more politically and emotionally specific "choices," both conscious and unconscious, involved in the establishment of sexual and gender identities. These latter are more subject to change than is the abstract sense of personal existence involved in the concept of self (p. 335). Resonating with a point made earlier in this chapter, Stack notes that in valuing flexibility and fluidity of self and gender identity, many postmodern theorists have failed "to distinguish between a fluid sense of self that is flexible and highly functional and the fragmented self that underlies the tortured lives of many of our patients" (p. 335). She rightly asks whether we can "envision a model that allows optimal flexibility for sexual identity without undermining the necessary psychological work of self cohesion" (p. 335).

Differing Feminist Approaches to Psychoanalytic Theory

We have already noted that early analytic feminists did not initially see the concept of gender as a problem in its own right. They simply saw Freud's theory of male supremacy and primacy as the problem, and they worked to attain recognition for a theory of primary femininity that revolved around equally valuable female traits and qualities. Following this line of thinking, and taking it one step further to privilege and valorize women's traits as opposed to men's, Miller's (1976) work attracted a large feminist following. Under her founding leadership, scholars at the Stone Center for Women's Studies have emphasized women's differences and special capacities, mostly relational and cooperative (Stiver, 1983, 1986; Surrey, 1984; Jordan, 1984, 1986). Also in this tradition is the work of Carol Gilligan (1982), who emphasizes the different "voice" of women and their responsibility and caring in the relational orientation.

In work coming from the Stone Center, the qualities valued in women, especially empathy (Jordan, 1984, 1987), closely resemble qualities Kohut associated with the optimal development of both sexes. Yet Kohut is barely mentioned, only to be faulted once more for his alleged emphasis on autonomy (Jordan, 1987). In one such instance, almost simultaneously with offering this critique of self psychology, Jordan makes a statement of her own supposedly different viewpoint but makes no mention of its striking similarity to Kohut's central ideas: "The expectation that someone will listen and make an effort to understand greatly enhances the clarity and sureness of the message" (p. 2). Furthermore, although the Stone Center's emphasis on relational needs has much in common with Loewald's (1960) viewpoint, its authors cite Loewald not at all. Nevertheless, the Stone Center participants have been outstanding contributors to the feminist effort to respond to society's gender inequality; they have challenged Freud's theory of male supremacy by identifying and valorizing women's unique qualities and contributions while problematizing what have historically been seen as men's more healthy and successful adaptations. Not directly addressed in this literature is the question of whether women mother because they are relational by constitution or whether they are relational because they are socially constructed to mother.

The whole question of mothering was first comprehensively addressed in psychoanalytic terms by Chodorow (1978). Although today there are multiple significant feminist voices and issues being taken up within psychoanalysis, I am singling out Chodorow and Benjamin, whose early and comprehensive explorations of mothering and of the relations between the sexes continue to exert broad influence on feminist and gender theories within psychoanalysis. My overview of their contribution in this context will necessarily fail to convey the richness, depth, and complexity of their respective writings.

Nancy Chodorow

In her first book, *The Reproduction of Mothering*, Chodorow (1978) emphasized societal and cultural contributions to women's mothering role and the negative impact it had on children of both sexes. She thought that the organization of society, in which mothers alone raised their children, produced women who have "relational capacities and needs, and psychological definition of self-in-relationship, which commits them to mothering" (p. 209). In contrast, "men develop . . . a self based more on denial of relation and connection and on a more fixed and firmly split and repressed inner self-object world." She concluded that "the basic masculine sense of self is separate" (p. 160). In Chodorow's view, the only way out of this infinite reproduction of mothering, and the resulting incompatibilities between men and women, was to reorganize society in such a way that men and women would share parenting.

By 1989, Chodorow had become increasingly impressed with the unique ways that individuals internalize societal prescriptions as they are variously communicated in the intimate relationships between parent and child in the nuclear family. As her view became more identified with psychoanalysis, Chodorow was convinced that not only the social and cultural promotion of the notion of male superiority, but also the specifics of mother–child relationships, reproduced and sustained the system in which male supremacy prevails. She wrote:

> If I were to discover that the 'central dynamic' or 'cause' of women's oppression were located outside of the personal, interiorized, subjective, and intersubjective realm of psychic life and primary relationships that psychoanalysis describes, I would still be concerned with this realm and its relation to gender, sexuality, and self [p. 7].

In Chodorow's (1978) view, the fact that both male and female children are raised primarily by mothers leads the little boy forcefully to separate in order to establish his male gender identity. The ramifications of this phenomenon, earlier observed by Greenson (1967), continue to be explored by feminist psychoanalysts today. They see in it an explanation of the value that men, more than women, have historically placed on separation and autonomy. It offers a way of understanding as well what is now seen as men's defensive stance against emotional intimacy and the widespread occurrence of male aggression against women. The personal and societal losses from this state of affairs include the reproduction of mothering exclusively by women, polarized roles for children of both sexes, and the resulting profound incompatibility between the sexes. Chodorow concluded that women gain in relatedness and in empathic connections but remain dependent on men who do not reciprocate these needs and interests. Men gain in the independent pursuit of personal goals, reaping the narcissistic and financial rewards granted by society for such endeavors; but they are cut off from their emotional and relational selves, with widespread negative repercussions for themselves, their wives, their children, and society at large.

In later work, in which she moved toward theories that are more decentered, Chodorow (1989) acknowledged that women's inequality may be "multiply caused and situated" (p. 6) and that she had earlier emphasized the mother and the preoedipal period as a reaction to "the nearly exclusive Freudian focus on the father and the oedipal complex" (p. 6). Despite this broadening of her understanding, however, she avowed that she had "yet to find a convincing explanation for the virulence of masculine anger, fear, and resentment of women, or aggression toward them, that bypasses—even if it does not rest with—the psychoanalytic account, first suggested by Horney, that men resent and fear women because they experience them as powerful mothers" (p. 6). Thus, through the 1980s she seemed alternately to move away from, and then come back to, the reproduction of mothering.

Reflecting multiple current shifts of interest in feminist psychoanalysis, Chodorow's (1994) most recent book examines notions of difference and variation in our understanding of gender categories and questions what is increasingly perceived as the heterosexist bias in both psychoanalysis and society at large. In this exploration, she observes that "sexual feelings are psychological, charged, and subjectively meaningful" to an extent that individual psychodynamic history and cultural/linguistic location offer far better ways of understanding than biological explanations (p. 41).

Chodorow finds a deficiency not only in Freudian, but also in most subsequent, psychoanalytic attempts to elucidate normal heterosexual experience and behavior. She suggests that authors as diverse as Kernberg, Stoller, Person, and McDougall tend to stress defense and compromise formation, while a certain richness and vitality seems to escape most interpersonal explications. She suggests that we need to treat sexuality per se as problematic since psychopathology seems to be more or less equally distributed among those who prefer homosexual and those who prefer heterosexual relationships.

But, while arguing for a balanced look at both hetero- and homosexual relationships, Chodorow comes back to the problematic differences that she finds to be pervasive in adult love attachments between the sexes. She suggests that women more than men seem to seek an unconscious, internal affective dialogue with their prelinguistic and pre-oedipal mothers in which self–other and gendered differentiations play a small role. Although in intimate relationships men often experience similar regressive pulls in relation to their internalized mothers, these unconscious longings tend to push men toward a more exaggerated expression of their masculinity. That very masculinity is understandably threatened by an invitation to internal dialogue with the preoedipal mother in a way that women's corresponding sense of femininity is not. We see how Chodorow has moved away from her initially exclusive focus on mothering while continuing to struggle with the differences and incompatibilities between the sexes. In her continuing quest for understanding, she asks, "[H]ow [can we] consider gendered subjectivity without turning such a consideration into objective claims about gender difference [?]" (p. 91). With this question she brings us back to properly postmodern epistemological tensions among objectivity and subjectivity, essentialism, and constructionism. In other words, feminist and postmodern analysts alike undertake to deconstruct the status quo but struggle not to create inadvertently an ever new suggestion of "givens" to be questioned by themselves and the next generation of critics.

Jessica Benjamin

Expanding beyond problems of mothering to a broad examination of the relationship between the sexes, Benjamin (1988) has provided one of the most thorough, complex, and original accountings to date of the interlocking difficulties of male and female development. I have included Benjamin among my highlighted group of moderate postmoderns because she has in common with the others a focus on subjectivity and intersubjectivity without sacrificing the complexity and richness of psychoanalytic understanding. But Benjamin's feminism means that her exploration of intersubjectivity is consistently carried out in a gendered context which distinguishes her from the other post moderns in my group.

Consonant with Chodorow's earlier project, Benjamin's approach to feminism entails a study of society's entire system of gender, refusing to see the problems of women in isolation. The link that Benjamin makes between societal structures of mothering and the relationship between the sexes hinged most importantly on society's support of mothers' sacrificing their subjectivity in the process of caring for their children. She sees this phenomenon as leading to several destructive aspects of development for men and women and in the relations between them.

Benjamin believes that, in sacrificing their subjectivity, mothers fail to provide a model for their daughters in the later establishment of the daughters' own subjectivity. Although boys similarly lack such a model from their mothers, boys tend to develop by forceful separation from their mothers and a turning toward their fathers during the separation-individuation process, whereas girls are more likely to remain identified with their mothers. Thus, boys alone have an alternative model for identification, with their father's subjectivity. This bifurcated developmental path preserves societal norms for girls, who then grow up without a strong sense of their own subjectivity, while boys have a monopoly of this sense. Societally this situation tends to result in heterosexual couples consisting of a man as subject and a woman as object. It is because of this perceived mismatch in the developmental achievements of men and women pertaining to subjectivity that Benjamin focuses on intersubjectivity as the necessary goal in gendered relations.

Where there has historically tended to be one male subject and one female object in every heterosexual dyad, Benjamin wants to see two subjects in recognition of one another. She feels that such mutual recognition of subjectivity in the gendered relationships of adulthood has to originate in the mother's earlier insistence on recognition of her own subjectivity in parent–child interactions. Benjamin argues generally for the expression of the mother's unique subjectivity, even though she recognizes and accepts Stern's (1985) positing of a developmental progression through which modes of experiencing are built upon and added to in the first years of life and lead to late first-year achievements for the child in the area of subjectivity and intersubjective relatedness. Thus she is aware that the early caretaking interactions hold a potential for either a relatively smooth or a less successful movement along this pathway for individual children in relation to their mothers.

Stern's theory suggests that, during the first several months of life, the mother's empathy has to be more or less taken for granted, because the child has not yet attained a capacity to recognize either his own or an other's mind. Only following the achievement of such recognition, in Stern's view, can the mother's expression of her own subjectivity become meaningful for her baby. And, even then, empathy remains important as a way to reassure the newly cognizant child that, even though mother's and child's minds are separate, affective connections can still be established and sustained.

In Benjamin's (1988) focus on women's problems and on gendered relationships, however, she refers only to the problems that come about in the wake of mothers' common tendencies to sacrifice too much of themselves for their children. She does not address the different but equally destructive outcomes for children whose parents are unable to decenter enough from their own subjectivities to empathize with their children. The very problems for girls which Benjamin claims are the consequence of mothers' *absent* subjectivity are sometimes also seen in the wake of cumulative parent–child interactions in which the mother's subjectivity is *too much* in the foreground. In other words, parents who can imaginatively enter into no one's subjectivity but their own are likely to do as much damage to the development of robust subjectivities in their children of either sex as are parents who too consistently sacrifice their subjectivities in the name of good mothering or fathering.

These comments raise further questions but do not diminish Benjamin's very original contribution to elucidating male and female development on the basis of parenting practices rather than biological determinism. For instance, whereas Freud saw a biologically determined passivity at the root of women's apparently less active desire, Benjamin offers a social/psychological explanation of this phenomenon. She suggests that it is because girls are raised by mothers who deny their own subjectivity and desires that they tend to grow up to do the same. They then easily and even willingly become slaves to men who embrace their own subjectivities and desires. This master-slave relationship, in Benjamin's (1988) view, is the basis of strong sadomasochistic trends in the relations between men and women:

> [T]he splitting that is so typical in sadomasochism is in large part a problem of gender. The defensive masculine stance promotes a dualism, a polarization of subject and object. The assumption of subject status to male and object status to female flows from the simply unavoidable fact that the boy must struggle free with all the violence of a second birth from the woman

who bore him. In this second birth, the fantasy of omnipotence and erotic domination begins [p. 81].

Although in this particular passage, Benjamin emphasizes the male fantasy of omnipotence and domination, her book generally distributes the weight evenly between men's and women's contribution to the establishment and maintenance of master–slave relationships: just as current parenting arrangements tend to create dominant men, they simultaneously create women who lack their own subjectivity and sense of agency and therefore long to surrender to one who enjoys these enlivening and direction-enhancing qualities.

To summarize Chodorow's and Benjamin's early contributions: Chodorow's (1978, 1989) view emphasizes how the mother's undiluted power over her children by virtue of her functioning alone in the role of day-to-day parent has had negative consequences for persons of both sexes: it has led women to deal with their early experience of mother's domination by becoming dominant mothers themselves; and, for men, it has led to a compensatory and vengeful assertion of power over women in adult life. Adopting a different emphasis, Benjamin (1988) argues that it is the mother's abdication of her subjectivity and desire that has led insidiously to both male domination and female submission. Therefore, while Chodorow makes a plea for the sharing of parenting between mothers and fathers, Benjamin (1988) supports a two-pronged attack on the problem: that mothers retain and express their subjectivity throughout their mothering years and that girls as well as boys be encouraged to turn to their fathers for identification with a more fully expressed subjectivity and desire (Benjamin, 1991). Both Benjamin and Chodorow have moved on to address broader issues in the ongoing discourse on women's development and gendered relationships.

Gender Discourse in Psychoanalysis

Chodorow's and Benjamin's earlier approaches to feminist problems by way of investigation of the developmental situation for both men and women and the relationships between the sexes are increasingly yielding to a psychoanalytic study of the problems inherent in the concept of gender per se. One of the most widely influential contributions to psychoanalytic notions of gender in recent years has come from Goldner (1991), who set out to establish a new psychoanalytic goal consisting of "the ability to tolerate the ambiguity and instability of gender categories" rather than the previous "goal of 'achieving' a single, pure, sex-appropriate view of oneself" (p. 249). Furthering this viewpoint, Harris (1991a) presents both theoretical support and case material to underscore the "constructed and complex dynamics" of gender and sexual identity (p. 200). Because of largely unconscious dynamics, the external sex of the participants in a relationship does not necessarily correspond to their sexual identities and orientations at a psychological level. This means that, in Harris's view, a relatonship between same–sex partners is not necessarily homosexual and that some outwardly heterosexual relationships carry a primarily homosexual meaning to one or both participants.

Whatever the simultaneous influences coming from social/political/intellectual ferment interacting with feminist psychoanalytic contributions, once Chodorow had suggested mothering was socially constructed rather than biologically determined, and once Benjamin had suggested that male dominance was coconstructed with female submission through mothers' "voluntary" sacrifice of their subjectivity and desire, then we could begin to wonder what other gender attributes might be constructed rather than biologically determined. Such wondering occasionally seems to be moving in the direction of complete social construction. But some analysts, even though attuned to the new gender literature, still struggle to maintain a continuing awareness of the *body* in psychoanalytic thinking even while embracing social constructionism. This struggle has yielded such terminology as "embodied subjectivity" and "psychic corporeality" (cited in Schwartz, 1997, p. 198).

If we accept social constructionism as an explanation for our organization of gender, however tentatively, then we must begin to question vigorously the seemingly arbitrary bifurcation of gender such that every individual feels a coercion to "perform" in accordance with either masculine or feminine stereotypes (Butler, 1990; Layton, 1997). And, to the extent that sexual orientation is understood to be an aspect of gender relations, then we must question the privileged position that heterosexuality has until now enjoyed in our culture as well (Domenici and Lesser, 1995). In the thinking of theorists participating in this questioning, there is a strong recognition that where gender and sexuality are concerned, classical analysis has actively maintained the status quo rather than leading the exploration in accordance with its revolutionary potential (Goldner, 1991; Dimen, 1991; Corbett, 1997; Mitchell,

1997). And, although Kohut's gender-neutral concepts held the promise of a positive alternative to Freud's devaluing of women and heterosexism, self psychology seems generally to have avoided many of the problems raised by feminists and gender theorists, neither contributing to the debate nor undertaking to solve the thorniest issues. Therefore, whereas we have seen that self psychology simply bypasses the problems of sex and gender by providing a relatively gender-free theory in which gender and sexuality of any kind play but a relatively small role, the feminist and gender theorists tackle the many problems of Freud's psychosexual theory head on, offering great detail, nuance, complexity, and richness in their alternative ways of thinking about human sexuality and gender.

Thematic Convergence Among Feminist Critics, Gender Theorists, and the Moderate Postmoderns

We have seen that issues of subjectivity and intersubjectivity have arisen in the feminist and gender literature simultaneously with the emergence of a parallel but distinctive discourse in relational postmodern discourse. Whereas Benjamin (1988), for instance, introduces subjectivity and intersubjectivity as a problem in women's mothering and in gender relations, we have earlier seen that Stolorow and his colleagues (Atwood and Stolorow, 1984; Stolorow et al., 1987; Stolorow and Atwood, 1992; Stolorow (1994), Stern (1985), and Ogden (1986) have focused on the significance of subjectivity and intersubjectivity in the development of all individuals, without explicit recognition that in our culture such development has generally been more problematic for women than for men.

And yet the very focus on subjectivity has made it easier to question all theories and approaches to understanding. It engenders a rightful humility in all theorists, male and female alike. Whereas it is now a truism that psychoanalysis was founded with a decidedly male and heterosexist bias, feminists and moderate postmoderns are currently trying to move beyond their earlier efforts to right that balance by a compensatory focus on female development and to include multiple viewpoints on understanding healthy development in males and females alike. Furthermore, whereas the current emphasis on the analyst's own subjectivity poses a significant risk of intrusion and burden for the patient, it also helpfully confronts the analyst with the limits of her knowledge and authority, leading her clinically to take the patient's perceptions very seriously and theoretically to remain open to others' viewpoints.

As exemplars of this openness, Mitchell (1996b) and Aron (1995) have kept fully abreast of innovations in the feminist and gender literature and have been stimulated to original thinking in attempting to integrate the concerns of these theorists into their own relational theories. Mitchell (1993), for instance, has reminded us that we are not gendered in isolation but in relation to significant objects and the cultural-linguistic matrix into which we are born. He adds, "There is no way to ascertain what it is like to have a male as opposed to a female body, apart from a particular culture and its gender definitions within which the meanings of those bodies are shaped" (p. 127). Of course, the cultural gender definitions can be supported or countered in individual families, significantly adding unique content and texture to every individual's sexual and gender development. Mitchell (1996b) has tried to maintain a balance between a qualified biologism and a qualified constructionism. This makes sense to me, given that we do have bodies and that our experience is shaped by what we feel in those bodies even as our personal relationships, language, and sociocultural milieu structure the meanings and valuations of those experiences.

Interested in reworking previous psychoanalytic concepts in the light of new theoretical developments, Aron (1995) has revisited the child's experience of the primal scene in an attempt to integrate into his thinking the deconstructed notions of sexuality and gender available in the contributions of contemporary feminist and queer theories. Sounding quite Kohutian as well as postmodern, he suggests that we take "a more affirmative approach" to "the omnipotent wish 'to have it all,' to fulfill symbolically the phantasy of being both sexes" (p. 197). He argues that "we need both a notion of gender identity and a notion of gender multiplicity; more broadly, we need an emphasis on people both as unified, stable, cohesive subjects and as multiple, fragmented, and different from moment to moment" (p. 195).

From this passage, we get an impression of why Aron has labeled himself and his fellow relational theorists "moderate" rather than "radical" postmoderns. What we see in their approach to gender and sexuality, as in other areas of their theorizing, is an attempt to bring ideas together, to preserve what they identify as useful in old ways of thinking but also to integrate and apply what they perceive as valid in the postmodern. Kohut deliberately tried to close himself off to other ways of thinking while he developed his theory of self and selfobject. The moderate postmoderns have done the very opposite, creating a sense of great uncertainty and flux as they rapidly shift in response to each other's ideas and ideas from multiple contemporary psychoanalytic quarters. This uncertainty and flux may keep all of us just a little off balance as we try to keep up with the latest integrations, but it also makes this a very enlivening time to be a psychoanalyst.

PART IV

KOHUT, LOEWALD, AND THE POSTMODERNS AT CENTURY'S END

THEORIES OLD AND NEW

A moment of crisis is a moment when something has crumbled, some-thing is rejected, but it is also the moment when new sources appear, and in postmodernity I myself see this aspect of renewal, which interests me.
—Julia Kristeva

My thesis is that Kohut and Loewald helped lay the groundwork for the postmodern revolution in psychoanalysis. Both authors repeatedly drew attention to the subjectivity of the analyst, thereby beginning to chip away at the position of knowledge and authority previously enjoyed by the analyst as objective observer. They suggested that the actual personal qualities and behavior of the analyst had a significant impact on the patient's analytic "material," his psychopathology, and the treatment outcome. Thus they began shifting psychoanalysis away from an exclusive focus on the intrapsychic, drive-based fantasy of the patient toward the direction of the intrapsychic and interactional "realities" of both patient and analyst. Finally, they highlighted the relational, as opposed to the instinctual, determinants of self, along with the relational elements of cure. In their writings, therefore, although insight remained important, it was subsumed within the all-important and structure-building therapeutic relationship.

Both Kohut and Loewald focused on aspects of the analytic experience evocative of the early caretaking functions and affective intensity involved in the mother–infant relationship. This emphasis diminished the importance of the oedipal period in their writings and rendered its triadic relationships and paternal order less central to early development than it was in classical theory. And while Loewald did retain a place for universal oedipal struggles in his theory, his view of this rite of passage highlighted the autonomy of the self as both its motivation and crowning achievement. He thus placed far less emphasis on either sexual or aggressive instincts than did classical theory.

Kohut and Loewald also recognized the adaptive element in defensive activity and were more reluctant than most classical analysts to analyze "resistance" early in treatment or to address it in a confrontational manner. Loewald (1986) wrote, "Defenses are necessary to remain sane or to return from immersion in the irrational unconscious to rationality. They are needed as protectors of ego organization and at times must be supported, even though or because genuine analysis unhinges and goes beyond them" (p. 284).

For further examples of postmodern leanings in the writings of Kohut and Loewald, consider how Kohut (1984) seemed to anticipate later developments in gender theory and to foreshadow the late 20th-cenutry embrace of diverse sexualities. For instance, he wrote:

> Although the attainment of genitality and the capacity for unambivalent object love have been features of many, perhaps most, satisfying and significant lives, *there are many other good lives, including some of the greatest and most fulfilling lives recorded in history, that were not lived by individuals whose psychosexual organization was heterosexual-genital or whose major commitment was to unambivalent object love* [p. 7, italics added].

Kohut was also able to imagine a time when the importance he placed on coherence or unity of self might be questioned, a time when analysts might "discover certain specific discontinuities in the self that do not stand in the way of a fulfilling life—a finding that would necessitate a revision of our theory" (p. 211). That time clearly has come, and, as forward looking as both Kohut and Loewald were in their frequent flashes of insight, not only are the shifts they made in psychoanalytic thinking no longer new, but the postmodern revolution has taken their insights to places these authors could not have dreamed of. In the hands of even their most devoted followers, Kohut's and Loewald's ideas have continued to evolve and mutate, leading to multiple new approaches to psychoanalysis and creating almost a rolling, late 20th-century revolution with no end in sight. Throughout this book, I have emphasized the continuity between Kohut's and Loewald's groundbreaking contributions and developments in postmodern psychoanalysis. But it seems that, even during the months it took me to write the previous 10 chapters, the field has evolved to an extent that disjunctions between older theories and new have become more striking. Thus, while in this chapter I consider further evidence of theoretical continuity, I also identify what may prove to be irreparable ruptures in analytic thinking as the 20th century draws to a close.

Postmodern psychoanalysis is multifaceted, with many voices and diverse emphases; it has its own continuum from moderate to radical. Just as Loewald and Kohut were responding to what they felt were the major errors, constraints, and weaknesses in Freud's theory, the postmoderns of today are responding to what they believe to be the errors, constraints, and weaknesses in Loewald's, Kohut's, and others' work that came before them. Change comes more quickly now than earlier in the century, and certain aspects of the postmodern sensibility are already in the process of being absorbed into mainstream psychoanalytic writing (i.e., Tyson, 1998). In some areas of theory and technique, earlier distinctions are beginning to blur.

We might even say that, in general, psychoanalysis is becoming a moderately postmodern endeavor. For instance, it is a rare analyst today who is not aware of the limits of her analytic knowledge and authority, who does not recognize (at least in theory) the ubiquity of her own subjectivity and transferences, and who is not familiar with the argument for a dynamic systems theory approach to the understanding of development and treatment. Although such terms as neutrality and abstinence are still clung to in some circles, the meaning of these concepts and their technical operation in practice are gradually shifting to allow for more self-expression by the analyst and more overt interaction in the analytic dyad. Most practicing analysts are now aware of multiple contributions to cure, with insight through interpretation giving up its claim to superordinacy and taking its place among interactive, relational, and experiential factors. At this level of abstraction, perhaps Kohut, Loewald, and the moderate postmoderns would have few substantive differences. But even as the more moderate aspects of postmodernism are being selectively integrated into mainstream psychoanalysis, more radical aspects of postmodern thought are being steadily introduced into analytic discourse from feminist, gender, and queer theories and from literary and cultural criticism. This influx of new ideas has created a new theoretical cutting edge of psychoanalysis that is progressively moving farther away from anything that either Kohut or Loewald could possibly have considered and far from anything that mainstream psychoanalysis has yet absorbed.

Perhaps most representative of the move beyond Kohut and Loewald is the fate of the concept of self as either supraordinate structure or center of experience, a concept introduced by Kohut only 25 years ago as central to human development. The notion of self has now fallen into disrepute; indeed, the self is rarely mentioned today, outside of self psychology, without reference to its disunity, its discontinuity, and its multiplicity. I have similarly noted that the concept of empathy has lost favor among postmodern writers both moderate and radical; it is now seen as running counter to efforts toward authenticity and spontaneity on the part of the analyst.

Thus, when we approach a discussion of what the analyst says and does, how she conceptualizes the analytic relationship, and what her basic attitudes toward the patient and the work are, the differences between older and newer theories take on greater significance. For instance, in turning from Freud's almost exclusive focus on interpretation and insight, Kohut and Loewald, independent of one another, introduced the notion that the analyst must convey an attitude that provides the patient with essential developmental experiences and must be available for aspects of relationship required for psychic growth. This attitude of "provision" and availability is at least implicitly rejected by some postmodern analysts, who emphasize the mutuality of the analytic relationship while downplaying its hierarchical aspects. In their eyes, the concept of an analyst who provides what the patient needs in the psychic realm or who makes herself available for the patient's use (as object or selfobject), implies a hierarchical arrangement between patient and analyst and threatens to foster undesirable idealization and compromise the patient's autonomy (see Renik, 1993, 1995, 1996). Analysts such as Mitchell, Aron, and Hoffman do address the necessary asymmetry of roles, tasks, and responsibility between patient and analyst, but they emphasize that such asymmetries (which imply hierarchy) coexist with important areas of mutuality in the analytic relationship.

But, while the postmoderns criticize Kohut for presuming to know what the patient might need (such as specific kinds of selfobject functioning on the part of the analyst), they themselves suggest that the patient needs an actual relationship with a distinctive other, even when such a relationship entails the patient's direct exposure to idiosynchratic (or psychopathological) elements in the analyst's character or the analyst's confrontation of the patient with the latter's "maladaptive" ways of relating. Thus, the moderate postmoderns seem to have changed the *content* of what the analyst can "know" but have not totally escaped a knowing position for the analyst, who may now let the patient know how his behavior affects the analyst. Contemporary analysts apparently assume that such "effects"—despite the analyst's unique subjectivity—will be generalizable to the patient's other relationships and that the patient can use such information without being hurt by it and without summoning even greater levels of self-protectiveness or defensiveness than those with which he began treatment.

Within each of the moderate postmoderns there does seem to be an ongoing struggle between old attitudes in which the analyst saw herself as "knowing" what the patient might need, and being able to provide it, and new attitudes in which the analytic relationship represents a meeting between two persons, in many ways two peers, who engage each other directly for the purpose of helping one of them with interpersonal and other problems of living. In the latter view, there is an emphasis on authenticity and spontaneity on the part of the analyst, with the analyst's claims of knowledge and authority—even knowledge concerning the needs of the patient—being seen as potential barriers to intimacy and engagement. Such engagement is the only mode of "work" through which the analyst can discover, first hand, the problematic aspects of the patient's interpersonal relationships. Mitchell (1996a), for instance, wrote that "Kohut was messianic; he often depicted empathy as if it were generic and easily achieved, a basic posture on the analyst's part that works for all patients" (p. 179). Instead, Mitchell advocates a process that he tentatively characterizes as the patient and analyst "[struggling] together to find a different kind of connection," a kind of connection that will inevitably be unique or "custom designed" to each patient/analyst pair (p. 184). Frequently, in the writings of the postmoderns, a dialectic between technique (or ritual) and spontaneity is the only way to balance the inner tensions of the analyst (see Hoffman, 1998) or the only way to contain the multiple paradoxes of the analytic situation (Paul Russell, 1990, personal communication; 1996, 1998; Pizer, 1998).

Just as the postmoderns have had difficulty escaping an updated version of the very problems they critique in the work of their forebears,

so Kohut and Loewald themselves had earlier placed an unacknowledged paradox at the heart of their writings. Trying to solve problems
that they found in Freud's classical approach, Kohut and Loewald
directed attention away from a conceptualization of the *patient's*
intrapsychic, drive-based fantasy as the sole determinant of the analytic
experience and toward the interactional realities of the *analyst's* behavior and unconscious processes. But simultaneously Kohut and Loewald
made it incumbent on the analyst to focus on accepting, elaborating,
and affirming the patient's view of reality (including that aspect of the
patient's reality involving the analyst's being, presence, and behavior).
Thus, Kohut and Loewald recognized that the analyst's own realities,
transferences, and countertransferences would necessarily intrude, but
at the same time they insisted that the analyst place the patient's reality above her own. For Kohut and Loewald, the tension lay between the
analyst's *recognition and acknowledgment* of the extent to which the analyst's own subjectivity might intrude and the analyst's *intention and
effort* to give as much weight as humanly possible to the subjectivity of
the patient.

The moderate postmoderns (especially Renik, 1993, 1995, 1996)
seem to have responded to this unintended paradox in Kohut's and
Loewald's work by insisting that the analyst present her own (subjective) reality to the patient, especially her opinions and emotional
responses to what the patient presents. Meanwhile, Hoffman (1996)
and Mitchell (1997) recognize that, at one level, the analyst's reactions
to her patients are no more than her uniquely subjective responses; but,
at the same time, they acknowledge that the inevitable authority attributed to analysts by their patients gives the analyst's words and feelings
a weight and significance that under optimal conditions can facilitate
the treatment. The tensions inherent in these dual recognitions by
Mitchell and Hoffman place a paradox at the center of the psychoanalytic work of the postmoderns as well, a newer version of the paradox
in the work of Loewald and Kohut.

One problem to watch for in discussions of treatments from an
interpersonal viewpoint is that the analyst's observations or responses
to the patient sometimes take on a hint of the old (and less ironic) kind
of authority (i.e., see Mitchell, 1992, who in discussing a case presented
by Trop and Stolorow, speaks of the patient's "opening gambit," as
noted earlier). This tendency may be an occasional and unintended side
effect of the value and importance currently assigned to the analyst's

subjectivity and will in time no doubt be struggled with and redressed in the literature.

But, in general, Kohut's attempted solution to the problem of the analyst's subjectivity was to give the *patient's* subjectivity all the attention, respect, and encouragement that the analyst could muster; whereas the postmodern solution to the problem of the analyst's subjectivity is to make it, at least at times, the focus of the analytic dialogue. Thus, the analyst is encouraged to articulate her subjective experience of and with the patient and also to invite the patient to elaborate on his own perceptions, interpretations, and fantasies concerning the analyst's subjectivity (Aron, 1996).

This latter act of bringing in the patient's perceptions of the analyst's subjectivity provides a counterbalance to the danger that the postmodern emphasis on the analyst's subjectivity will create a new and unwelcome "authority" in the analytic encounter, threatening to replace the analyst's earlier claim to objectivity with a new and opposite claim with regard to subjectivity. My point is that our patients may just as easily be tyrannized, and their treatments taken over just as surely, by the analyst's claim to subjectivity as they earlier were by the analyst's claim to objectivity. It is therefore important to acknowledge that, inevitably, both patient and analyst move back and forth between positions of relative objectivity and subjectivity (see also Fosshage, 1997).

Kohut and Loewald both saw the ability to recognize the subjectivity of others as a developmental achievement. But, even after this achievement is established developmentally, recognition and respect for the other's subjective viewpoint is not automatically accorded. Mutual respect must be *earned*, in either direction, on the basis of the ongoing interactive experience in any given treatment. Such respect will be earned when one perceives that one's feelings, opinions, and viewpoints are given a fair and reasonable hearing and when one feels that the other is making the best effort possible to register and communicate his or her subjective experience, while not claiming undue authority for that experience. That said for the mutuality of capacities, responsibilities, and goals in treatment, however, I have argued throughout—and I think that particularly Hoffman, Mitchell, and Aron would agree— that the analyst holds the lion's share of responsibility to struggle through the challenges and the impasses that arise in the therapeutic relationship. Likewise, the analyst must recognize and resolve countertransferences toward the goal of establishing or reestablishing broken connections within the patient and the analytic dyad. On this last point, continuity remains between Kohut and Loewald and at least some of the postmoderns.

We seem, so far, to have an interesting historical development with regard to attitudes toward analytic subjectivity and objectivity: Freud credited the analyst with being privy to an objective view of reality, which was to be presented to the patient as "the" undistorted truth of the patient's life and psychic organization and was to act as a corrective to the patient's inevitable distortions. Kohut and Loewald, on the other hand, saw the analyst's subjectivity and countertransferences as likely to interfere with her ability to see the patient's reality in any objective manner. To Kohut's way of thinking, in particular, it was often best for the analyst simply to affirm the patient's view of reality rather than to proffer her own, even when the patient's view starkly contradicted the analyst's own. This affirmation of the patient's subjective viewpoint (or in Loewald's, 1960, terms, this "centering" on the patient's experience) was understood by both Kohut and Loewald to be facilitative of psychic growth, hence therapeutic, especially in the early phases of treatment.

While the postmoderns have joined Kohut and Loewald in their recognition of the analyst's ubiquitous subjectivity, their response to this recognition is not to focus on an affirmation of the patient's subjectivity, in the manner of Kohut and Loewald, but rather to offer the analyst's distinctive subjectivity as an essential counterweight to the patient's own. They reject Freud's belief that the analyst has access to a view of reality more objective than the patient's. But they also reject Kohut's view that the analyst's inescapable subjectivity must lead her invariably to place the patient's subjectivity at the center of the analytic dialogue. Far more than either Kohut or Loewald, the moderate postmoderns *embrace* the analyst's inevitable subjectivity. They insist that she bring it into the articulated exchange with the patient, and use it to add to or counter the patient's subjectivity. In postmodern discourse, the analyst is more frequently encouraged spontaneously to express her authentic experience in the moment. Both Loewald (1960, 1986) and Kohut (1977a, 1982, 1984) strove to open up and relax the stance of the anonymous and abstinent analyst of classical theory; but among the moderate postmoderns the atmosphere is shifting further, from the naturally warm and friendly stance recommended by Kohut and Loewald to a potentially more emotionally charged (Renik, 1993, 1995, 1996) and confrontational relationship (Mitchell, 1992). I write "potentially" here, because the postmoderns clearly want us to expand our options concerning the ways that we may engage while they try to avoid general prescriptions.

I earlier noted that Kohut and Loewald anticipated postmodern attitudes partly by acknowledging the ubiquity of the analyst's subjectivity and countertransference. They differed from the moderate postmoderns who followed them not in recognizing the analyst's subjectivity, but in failing to advocate the revelation of the analyst's subjective experience to the patient. Kohut (1984) wrote that "objective truth does not exist in the psychology of complex mental states" (p. 36). Both Kohut and Loewald acknowledged the limits of the analyst's understanding and knowledge, Kohut referring to "at times well-nigh insurmountable difficulties that the (psychoanalyst) observer faces . . . due to his own shortcomings as an observing instrument." He went on to say that "these great difficulties . . . are due to the distorting influence of emotional biases in our empathy-based perception" (p. 38). Loewald (1986) took a step beyond Kohut's recognition of inevitable countertransference interferences in the analyst's perception of the patient to claim a general transference parity between patient and analyst and a bidirectionality of exchanges between transference and countertransference. He urged the analyst "to understand the patient's behavior as determined by the patient's past *and by the analyst's behavior with him . . .* ['T']he analyst's own words spoken and attitudes displayed . . . may have affected the patient and triggered the [very] behavior" the analyst is trying to understand (pp. 278–279). In this same passage, Loewald, speaking of the *patient's* countertransference to the *analyst's* transference, was echoing McLaughlin's (1981) earlier observations of these phenomena, now widely recognized as ubiquitous and bidirectional.

With Loewald's (1986) recognition of mutuality and bidirectionality in the analytic relationship, he yielded up the earlier authority that had automatically been granted to the analyst of classical writings. Yet he still tried to establish a basis on which the analyst might position himself as helper to the patient:

> Analysts differ from patients by the greater depth and scope of their understanding of the motivations and dynamics of psychic life and manifest behavior (their own and others), by their knowledge of the implications these motivations have for object relations, and by their hard-won ability to apply and use that

understanding and knowledge in the special object relationship establishing itself in the psychoanalytic encounter [pp. 275–276].

Here Loewald seems to have been pointing to the analyst's *training* to think psychoanalytically about her own and her patient's behavior, feelings, and interactions, but he made no further claims for differences between patients and analysts. This stance seems to represent a shift in his own thinking away from the idea that the analyst's ego would necessarily function at a higher level than would the patient's. But one thing that did not change in Loewald's writings was his reliance on Freudian terms, however imbued with a distinctive, even revolutionary, twist. For instance, while discussing "neutrality" in the context of transference–countertransference dynamics, he suggested that neutrality actually "*derives from* transference–countertransference dynamics," (p. 277, italics added), rather than affirming the more traditional notion that neutrality involves surmounting or *overcoming* transference–countertransference dynamics. Loewald went on to say that it is therefore only to "the extent to which the analyst achieves . . . neutrality vis-à-vis himself" and his countertransferences that she has any possibility of achieving neutrality toward the patient and his transferences (pp. 277–278).

Thus, Loewald idiosyncratically equated "neutrality" with the analyst's capacity to recognize, integrate, and master his own countertransference responses toward the patient. Although this was at the time a radical definition of neutrality, it now seems self-evident that the major interference with the analyst's neutrality is likely to be her own passions and countertransferences, especially her tendency to mistake her subjective perceptions and interpretations of the patient's behavior and verbalizations as objective observations. In passages such as these, Loewald manifests a postmodern sensibility as to the *limitations* of the analyst's neutrality and authority, while still insisting on the analyst's (in some ways old-fashioned) responsibility to the patient to struggle relentlessly with her own transferences and countertransferences.

Although Loewald recognized mutual transferences between patient and analyst, he also suggested that the patient's primitive transferences could "overstrain the soundness of the analyst's organization as a separate individual" (p. 284). This was a reference—unusual at the time—to the analyst's vulnerability, and such comments in Loewald's writings seem to have made it more acceptable for analysts to communicate about such difficulties. Indeed, both Kohut and Loewald acknowledged the need for ongoing self-analysis on the part of the analyst. But among the moderate postmoderns we find recommendations that the analyst go beyond her *private* struggles to gain intrapsychic and interpersonal understanding of her countertransferences, and that she solicit help from the *patient* in recognizing and resolving problematic aspects of the analyst's experience and behavior. Aron (1996) points out that the analyst's countertransference simply cannot be recognized without the observation and input of the second party to the relationship. Renik (1995) too recommends that the analyst involve the patient in such processes, partly as a strategy for diminishing the patient's unwanted idealization. Thus, by moving from Kohut and Loewald to the postmoderns, we move from the analyst's silent recognition of the ubiquity of her countertransference and sense of responsibility to struggle privately to contain it, to a direct engagement with the patient around the analyst's countertransference.

Meanwhile, the late 20th-century literature on enactment (e.g., Jacobs, 1986; Chused, 1991; Mclaughlin, 1991; Hirsch, 1993, 1998; Davies, 1997) now points to a clinical reality that often resembles neither the modern nor the postmodern scenario. It demonstrates how the analyst's countertransference may be unwittingly enacted, thereby becoming part of a trigger for painful struggles between patient and analyst long before the analyst can privately explore her experience or actively solicit the patient's observations concerning the analyst for the benefit of the treatment. In any event, the moderate postmodern discussions concerning the analyst's subjectivity and countertransference are not generally intended as a celebration of these phenomena but rather are a search for new ways to deal with aspects of the analyst's person that have always intruded into the work but have only rarely been acknowledged and addressed. Our theory as a whole seems now to be in transition between an earlier analytic attitude of knowing and providing what the patient needs (Kohut and Loewald) and an emergent attitude in which, even as we lend our personal and professional selves to the struggle involved in another person's psychic growth, we recognize and try to find ways of dealing with the limitations of our capacities to know either ourselves or others. Recently, it has been recognized that the patient's psychic growth in treatment sometimes rises or falls on the analyst's own capability to grow and change through the analytic relationship (Slavin and Kriegman, 1998).

But how much have more recent writers really moved beyond the farthest reaches of Loewald and Kohut's thought? Straddling the modern and postmodern both chronologically and conceptually, Loewald (1986) struggled, as do the postmoderns, with problems of hierarchy, and he emphasized duality and paradox in the analytic relationship as ways of dealing with certain of these challenges. His focus on countertransference tends toward the postmodern; his emphasis on the analyst's special responsibility to the patient less so. In trying to deal with the challenges of this duality, he seemed to anticipate the postmodern trend toward dialectical thinking. He suggested, for instance, that the analyst's countertransference reactions to the patient's transference have a "double sense of repetition and rapport [and] are themselves influenced by [the analyst's] displacement repetitions and by his rapport with the patient" (pp. 277–278). I submit that both the emphasis on the analyst's responsibilities to the patient and the evocation of the dialectic are today being employed to counter certain excesses associated with more radical postmodern views. Such attenuation of radical postmodern attitudes appears especially in the works of Hoffman, Mitchell, and Aron, and these authors in particular seem to suggest less a radical break than an evolutionary progression from Kohut and Loewald's writings to their own.

Of course, the most dramatic differences between Kohut and Loewald and contemporary authors can best be seen by comparing Kohut's and Loewald's work with the writings of queer theorists and cultural critics, whose ideas are increasingly represented and debated in the analytic literature. But, even without turning to the more radical postmoderns, an examination of Benjamin's (1998) recent work suggests how heretofore moderate postmoderns are being influenced by new and extra-analytic ways of thinking. In this context, Kohut and Loewald begin to seem more old-fashioned, even when we read Loewald's final publications or peruse the more "forward-looking" trends in post-Kohutian self psychology, such as intersubjective, relational, and dynamic systems theorizing (e.g., Stolorow et al., 1987; Stolorow and Atwood, 1992, 1997; Goldberg, 1988, 1990, 1995, 1997, 1998; Fosshage, 1989, 1995a; Lichtenberg, 1989, 1998; Bacal, 1995; Lachmann and Beebe, 1995, 1996a, b; Stolorow, 1995; Bacal and Thomson, 1996; Shane and Shane, 1996; Lichtenberg, Lachmann, and Fosshage, 1996a, b).

In chapter 4, we noted several areas of compatibility between Benjamin's (1988) earlier work and Kohut's (1984) later ideas. Both authors were eminently interested in the construction of the subject and both saw the subject's recognition of the other as central to psychic development. However, in Benjamin's (1998) more recent work, she is grappling with multiple issues that have been raised in feminist, cultural, and gender critiques. It is in her pursuit of these ideas that the departure from Kohut's and Loewald's concerns has taken a sharp turn. Benjamin positions herself at the crossroads between psychoanalysis and feminist theory, but at this crossroads, it seems, many additional pathways converge.

Benjamin's (1998) central concerns have to do with questions of similarity and difference in intersubjective relating, experiences she sees as necessary yet tending to be mutually exclusive of one another. In recognizing the other as a subject like oneself, one is threatened with the loss of the other as a uniquely different person. This is the problem that Benjamin sees in Kohut's emphasis on the selfobject aspects of relating. For Benjamin, negation and recognition, or sameness and otherness, must be constantly negotiated in every relationship in order for one to gain and regain a tenuous intersubjectivity that is always at risk (p. 96). The problem, as Benjamin sees it, is that without a distinctly different other we are alone in the universe; we tend to merge through identification with those we perceive in terms of their likenesses to ourselves. But, with too much emphasis on distinction and difference, we also lose the possibility for connection with others through shared experience, so that, even though we experience ourselves as living in a truly peopled world, we are again at risk of feeling alone.

Benjamin heralds *reciprocity of recognition* as the solution to this problem and as the basis of ethical living, and she believes that this goal is achieved through a constant two-way relational struggle to identify both "commonalities and precise points of difference" (Richard Bernstein, 1992, cited in Benjamin, 1998, p. 100). Kohut focused much more on recognition (through mirroring, twinship, and idealization) than on negation of commonalities, and he did so primarily with an eye on the analyst as a one-way provider of such recognition for the patient. This, in his view, was a developmental stepping stone to the emergent capacity for true mutuality: the mark of psychological maturity in which humor, wisdom, and empathy would prevail. But Benjamin no longer acknowledges a developmental progression in the movement toward mutuality of recognition. She thus sees Kohut— with whom she lumps Melanie Klein!—simply as failing the test of true intersubjectivity.

The rejection of the developmental viewpoint, a preeminently post-modern phenomenon, emerged in part to counter the historical use of developmental theory to support the destructive imposition of norms concerning sexual and other aspects of human behavior. A foremost example of such imposition is the use of Freud's psychosexual stages—which theoretically culminated in a normal and healthy heterosexual genitality for all—to justify negative stereotyping, hatred, and in some instances legalized punishment of nongenital and homoerotic sexuality. Although I would personally like to see psychoanalysis take an active and broad initiative to reverse the damage to individuals and groups that has historically been done in this regard, at the same time I recognize an ongoing neurological and psychological progression along a number of "developmental lines," which may result in the more or less predictable emergence of different needs and capacities over the course of a treatment or a life. Although certain capabilities are necessarily established initially in a predictable developmental sequence (i.e, language, or the paranoid and depressive positions), once established, many capabilities, and the needs associated with their waxing and waning, may shift transiently and bidirectionally. Thought of in this way, developmental sequences need not impose a rigid and normative gridlock on human behavior and experience. Kohut and Loewald both recognized different needs and capacities of the individual at different points in treatment or development, and these differences had important implications for the nature of the analyst's responsibility and her ways of relating. But such transient and bidirectional shifts in the patient's needs and capacities over time are not always allowed for today, even in the writings of the moderate postmoderns, where at times the analyst's subjectivity seems to prevail in a one-size-fits-all approach. I do not suggest that this is the meaning or intent of the moderate postmoderns, but it is sometimes the effect of bringing something to the fore that has heretofore been neglected or denied in psychoanalytic writings.

To return to Benjamin's (1998) work in particular: Still struggling for a basis of genuine intersubjectivity, she differs from earlier authors such as Kohut and Loewald, as well as from the other moderate post-moderns, in her focal interest in gender relations. This focus gives her version of intersubjectivity an original twist and separates it from the central concerns of other moderate postmoderns. Over the course of a full decade, for instance, Benjamin (1988, 1998) has worked at rescuing "woman" from her position and role in classical theory as object of man's desire. In Benjamin's view, this rescue is required if there is to be true intersubjectivity anywhere (excepting only a dyad consisting of two male subjects).

Within Benjamin's (1998) framework, intersubjectivity "requires that each subject own and enjoy her or his own desire as well as the activity that realizes it" (p. xvi). With this stress on the centrality of desire in the conceptualization of subjectivity, Benjamin departs radically from both Kohut and Loewald, who in the 1970s were trying to rescue psychoanalysis from what they felt was a too exclusive focus on sexuality in particular and on instincts in general. They therefore tended to avoid the language of desire. Now the ongoing cycle of psychoanalytic rescue efforts seems to have come full circle, and we find Benjamin (1994, 1998) following the lead of contemporary gender and queer theorists by returning psychoanalysis to its earlier focus on sexuality and desire (Teicholz, 1998b).

This return to sexuality is considered essential to the ongoing feminist project of resolving contradictions and correcting wrong thinking regarding women and female sexuality, contradictions and errors now felt to have been rampant throughout Freudian theory. It is also essential to the efforts of gender and queer theorists who continue to document the heterosexist bias in Freudian theory. Thus, the late 20th-century return to sexuality is, for the most part, anything but Freudian: it is undertaken in such a different spirit, and leads to conclusions so different from Freud's, that contemporary explorations of human sexuality seem at times to be about a different topic altogether. In any event, whereas Kohut and Loewald were instrumental in moving the psychoanalytic debate away from a focus on sexual anatomy and functions and toward explorations of self, object, selfobject, and relationship, Benjamin, along with other psychoanalytic feminists and the new gender theorists, are now once again bringing the penis and vagina back into psychoanalytic discourse.

Benjamin, for instance, speaks of the penis and the vagina as concrete objects with distinctive modes of activity—those of "active" expelling and "passive" holding and containing, respectively—and also as metaphors for different kinds of psychic experiences. Expelled or contained are tensions of all kinds, both sexual and psychological. But Benjamin does not agree with Freud that the nature of femininity is truly passive. Despite the different anatomy and modes of functioning of the genitals in men and women, she suggests, the polarities of masculinity and femininity, of activity and passivity, must be rethought. Women's so-called passivity, she tells us, encompasses its own mode of activity: that of holding and containing. Benjamin is herself actively struggling to get beyond the old complementarities without simply reversing the earlier dichotomies. In her words, gender "works through a mutual and symmetrical determination of opposing terms" (p. 66). This view resonates with the dialectical approach taken toward all the old classical dichotomies of psychoanalysis in the work of Hoffman, Mitchell, and others. Benjamin's discourse, in 1998 as in 1988, is original, detailed, elaborate, and complex; it cannot be adequately summarized here, other than my offering it as an example of how far psychoanalytic concerns have moved from the issues that preoccupied Kohut and Loewald.

Of course, we can only guess at how Kohut and Loewald might have responded to these innovations had they lived to see them and had they been able to continue developing their thinking in the context of our postmodern psychoanalytic world. The theories they left us have served as building blocks and stepping stones toward new ways of thinking, but those new ways of thinking seem now to be in the process of leaving the earlier concerns of Kohut and Loewald far behind. The moderate postmoderns are all, in their unique ways, grappling with and integrating the latest thinking from other fields. Change is accelerating at a pace unanticipated even a decade ago, as mainstream psychoanalysis swallows up innovations at the same time as new ideas from other fields provide a constant influx of stimulation and excitement at the boundaries between psychoanalysis and multiple academic disciplines. Some of these academic disciplines are newly emergent themselves but are exerting a powerful influence throughout academia and beyond. Perhaps starting with Kohut and Loewald, but proceeding far more rapidly now than when they were alive, radical new ideas are continually appearing at the outer edges of psychoanalysis and then inexorably making their way toward its center.

REFERENCES

Adler, G. (1984). Transitional phenomena, projective identification, and the essential ambiguity of the psychoanalytic situation. *Psychoanal. Q.*, 58:81–104.

——— (1989). Use and limitations of Kohut's self psychology in the treatment of borderline patients. *J. Amer. Psychoanal. Assn.*, 37:761–786.

Aichhorn, A. (1936). The narcissistic transference of the "Juvenile Imposter." In *Delinquency and Child Guidance: Selected Papers by August Aichhorn*, ed. O. Fleischamann, P. Kramer & H. Ross. New York: International Universities Press, 1964, pp. 174–191.

Aron, L. (1990). One-person and two-person psychologies and the method of psychoanalysis. *Psychoanal. Psychol.*, 7:475–486.

——— (1991). The patient's experience of the analyst's subjectivity. *Psychoanal. Dial.*, 1:29–51.

——— (1992). Interpretation as expression of the analyst's subjectivity. *Psychoanal. Dial.*, 2:475–507.

——— (1995). The internalized primal scene. *Psychoanal. Dial.*, 5:195–238.

——— (1996). *A Meeting of Minds*. Hillsdale, NJ: The Analytic Press.

——— & Harris, A. (1993). *The Legacy of Sandor Ferenczi*. Hillsdale, NJ: The Analytic Press.

Atwood, G. & Stolorow, R. (1984). *Structures of Subjectivity: Explorations in Psychoanalytic Phenomenology*. Hillsdale, NJ: The Analytic Press.

Bacal, H. (1988). Reflections on "optimum frustration." In *Learning from Kohut: Progress in Self Psychology, Vol. 4*, ed. A. Goldberg. Hillsdale, NJ: The Analytic Press, pp. 127–132.

——— (1989). Winnicott and self psychology: Remarkable reflections. In *Self Psychology: Comparisons and Contrasts*, ed., D. Detrick & S. Detrick. Hillsdale, NJ: The Analytic Press, pp. 259–271.

——— (1995). The essence of Kohut's work and the progress of self psychology. *Psychoanal. Dial.*, 5:353–366.

———— & Thomson, P. (1996). The psychoanalyst's selfobject needs and the effect of their frustration on the treatment: a new view of countertransference. *Basic Ideas Reconsidered: Progress in Self Psychology, Vol. 12*, ed. A. Goldberg. Hillsdale, NJ: The Analytic Press, pp. 17–35.

Balint, M. (1937). Early developmental states of the ego. Primary object-love. In *Primary Love and Psychoanalytic Technique*. New York: Liveright, 1953, pp. 90–108.

———— (1951). Love and hate. In *Primary Love and Psychoanalytic Technique*. New York: Liveright, pp.141–156.

———— (1953). *Primary Love and Psychoanalytic Technique*. New York: Liveright.

Barratt, B. (1993). *Psychoanalysis and the Postmodern Impulse: Knowing and Being Since Freud's Psychology*. Baltimore, MD: Johns Hopkins University Press.

———— (1995). Review essay: *Madness and Modernism: Insanity in the Light of Modern Art, Literature, and Thought*, by Louis Sass. Psychoanal. Dial., 5:113–121.

Beebe, B. & Lachmann, F. (1988a). Mother-infant mutual influence and precursors of psychic structure. In *Frontiers in Self Psychology: Progress in Self Psychology, Vol. 3*, ed. A. Goldberg. Hillsdale, NJ: The Analytic Press, pp. 3–26.

———— & ———— (1988b). The contribution of mother-infant mutual influence to the origins of self and object representations. *Psychoanal. Psychol.*, 5:305–337.

———— & ———— (1994). Representation and internalization in infancy: Three principles of salience. *Psychoanal. Psychol.*, 11:127–165.

———— ———— & Jaffe, J. (1997). Mother-infant interaction structures and presymbolic self and object representations. *Psychoanal. Dial.*, 7:133–182.

Benedek, T. (1959). Parenthood as a developmental phase. A contribution to the Libido Theory. *J. Amer. Psychoanal. Assn.*, 7:389–415.

Benjamin, J. (1988). *Bonds of Love: Psychoanalysis, Feminism, and the Problem of Domination*. New York: Pantheon.

———— (1990). An outline of intersubjectivity: The development of recognition. *Psychoanal. Psychol.*, 7 (Suppl.):33–46.

———— (1991). Father and daughter: Identification with a difference—a contradiction to gender heterodoxy. *Psychoanal. Dial.*, 1:277–300.

———— (1994). What angel would hear me?: The erotics of transference. *Psychoanal. Inq.*, 14:535–557.

———— (1995a). *Like Subjects, Love Objects: Essays on Recognition and Sexual Difference*. New Haven, CT: Yale University Press.

———— (1995b). Sameness and difference: Toward an "overinclusive" model of gender development. *Psychonanal. Inq.*, 15:125–142.

———— (1996). In defense of gender ambiguity. *Gender & Psychoanal.*, 1:27–45.

———— (1998). *Shadow of the Other: Intersubjectivity and Gender in Psychoanalysis.* New York: Routledge.

Bernstein, D. (1983). The female superego: A different perspective. *Internat. J. Psycho-Anal.*, 64:187–202.

———— (1990). Female genital anxieties, conflicts and typical mastery modes. *Internat. J. Psycho-Anal.*, 71:151–166.

———— (1993). *Female Identity Conflict in Clinical Practice.* Northvale, NJ: Aronson.

Bird, B. (1972). Notes on transference: Universal phenomenon and hardest part of analysis. In *Classics in Psychoanalytic Technique*, ed. R. Langs, pp. 51–68.

Bollas, C. (1989). *Forces of Destiny.* London: Free Association Books.

———— (1992). *Being a Character.* New York: Hill & Wang.

———— (1993). An interview with Christopher Bollas. *Psychoanal. Dial.*, 7:401–430.

Bowlby, J. (1958). The nature of the child's tie to its mother. *Internat. J. Psycho-Anal.*, 39:350–373.

Brandchaft, B. (1983). The negativism of the negative therapeutic action and the psychology of the self. In *The Future of Psychoanalysis*, ed. A. Goldberg. New York: International Universities Press, pp. 327–359.

Brodsky, J. (1995). *On Grief and Reason: Essays.* New York: Farrar, Straus & Giroux.

Bromberg, P. (1980). Empathy, anxiety, and reality: A view from the bridge. *Contemp. Psychoanal.*, 16:223–236.

———— (1996). Standing in the spaces: The multiplicity of self and the psychoanalytic relationship. *Contemp. Psychoanal.*, 32:509–535.

Brook, A. (1995). Explanation in the hermeneutic science. *Internat. J. Psycho-Anal.*, 76:519–532.

Buie, D. (1981). Empathy: Its nature and limitations. *J. Amer. Psychoanal. Assn.*, 29:281–308.

Butler, J. (1990). Gender trouble, feminist theory, and psychoanalytic discourse. In *Feminism/Postmodernism*, ed. D. Fuss. New York: Routledge, pp. 324–340.

———— (1995). Melancholy gender—refused identification. *Psychoanal. Dial.*, 5:165–180.

Chasseguet-Smirgel, J. (1964). *Female Sexuality: New Psychoanalytic Views.* London: Karnac Books, 1985.

———— (1975). Freud and female sexuality: The consideration of some blind spots in the exploration of the "dark continent." In *Sexuality and Mind.* New York: New York Universities Press, 1986, pp. 9–28.

———— (1986). *Sexuality and Mind: The Role of the Father and Mother in the Psyche.* New York: New York Universities Press.

Cherazi, S. (1986). Female psychology: A review. *J. Amer. Psychoanal. Assn.*, 34:141–162.

Chodorow, N. (1978). *The Reproduction of Mothering: Psychoanalysis and the Sociology of Gender.* Berkeley: University of Califorinia Press.

———— (1989). *Feminism and Psychoanalytic Theory.* New Haven, CT: Yale University Press.

———— (1994). *Femininities, Masculinities, Sexualities.* Lexington: University Press of Kentucky.

———— (1995). Multiplicities and uncertainties of gender: Commentary on Ruth Stein's "Analysis of a case of transexualism." *Psychoanal. Dial.*, 5:291–300.

Chused, J.F. (1991). The evocative power of enactments. *J. Amer. Psychoanal. Assn.*, 39:615–640.

Coates, S. (1990). Ontogenesis of boyhood gender identity disorder, *J. Amer. Psychoanal. Assn.*, 18:414–438.

———— (1997). Is it time to jettison the concept of developmental lines? Commentary on de Marneffe's paper "Bodies and words." *Gender & Psychoanal.*, 2:35–54.

———— Friedman, R., & Wolfe, S. (1991). The etiology of boyhood gender identity disorder: a model for integrating temperament, development, and psychodynamics. *Psychoanal. Dial.*, 1:481–524.

———— & Wolfe, S. (1995). Gender identity in boys: The interface of constitution and early experience. *Psychoanal. Inq.*, 15:6–38.

———— & Moore, M. S. (1997). The complexity of early trauma: Representation and transformation. *Psychoanal. Inq.*, 17:286–311.

Cocks, G., Ed. (1994). *The Curve of Life: Correspondence of Heinz Kohut.* Chicago: University of Chicago Press.

Cooper, S. (1996). The thin blue line of the interpersonal-intrapsychic dialectic: Commentary on papers by Gerson and Spezzano. *Psychoanal. Dial.*, 6:647–670.

Corbett, K. (1997). Discussion: L.M. Lothstein, "Pantyhose fetishism and self cohesion" (Vol.2, no.1). *Gender & Psychoanal.*, 2:259–272.

Davies, J. M. (1997). Dissociation, therapeutic enactment, and transference-countertransference processes. A discussion of papers on childhood sexual abuse. *Gender & Psychoanal.*, 2:241–257.

de Beauvoir, S. (1949). *The Second Sex.* New York: Vintage Books, 1974.

de Marneffe, D. (1997). Bodies and words: A study of young children's genital and gender knowledge. *Gender & Psychoanal.*, 2:3–34.

Demos, E. V. (1988). Affect and the development of the self: A new frontier. In *Frontiers in Self Psychology: Progress in Self Psychology, Vol. 3*, ed. A. Goldberg. Hillsdale, NJ: The Analytic Press, pp. 27–54.

———— (1989). A prospective constructionist view of development. In *Annual of Psychoanalysis*, 17:287–342. Hillsdale, NJ: The Analytic Press.

———— & Kaplan, S. (1986). Motivation and affect reconsidered: Affect biographies of two infants. *Psychoanal. Contemp. Thought*, 10:147–221.

Dimen, M. (1991). Deconstructing difference: Gender, splitting, and transitional space. *Psychoanal. Dial.*, 1:335–358.

Dinnage, R. (1996). The rise and fall of a half-genius. *New York Review of Books*, Nov. 14, pp. 30–34.

Doane, J. & Hodges, D. (1982). Looking for Mrs. Goodmother: D. W. Winnicott's "Mirror role of mother and family in child development." *enclitic*, 1:52–56.

———— & ———— (1992). *From Klein to Kristeva: Psychoanalytic Feminism and the Search for the "Good Enough Mother."* Ann Arbor: University of Michigan Press.

Domenici, T. & Lesser, R., ed. (1995). *Disorienting Sexuality: Psychoanalytic Reappraisals of Sexual Identities.* New York: Routledge.

Eagle, M. (1987). Theoretical and clinical shifts in psychoanalysis. *Amer. J. Orthopsychiat.*, 57:175–185.

Eagleton, T. (1996). *The Illusions of Postmodernism.* Cambridge, MA.: Blackwell.

Elliott, A. & Spezzano, C. (1996). Psychoanalysis at its limits: Navigating the postmodern turn. *Psychoanal. Q.*, 65:52–83.

Emde, R. (1980). A developmental orientation in psychoanalysis: ways of thinking about new knowledge and further research. *Psychoanal. Contemp. Thought*, 3:213–235.

———— (1981). Changing models of infancy and the nature of early development: remodeling the foundation. *J. Amer. Psychoanal. Assn.*, 29:179–219.

———— (1983). The prerepresentational self and its affective core. *The Psychoanalytic Study of the Child*, 38:165–192. New Haven, CT: Yale University Press.

———— (1988). Development terminable and interminable: I. Innate and motivational factors from infancy. *Internat. J. Psycho-Anal.*, 69:23–42.

———— (1990). Mobilizing fundamental modes of development: Empathic availability and therapeutic action. *J. Amer. Psychoanal. Assn.*, 38:881–914.

Fairbairn, D. (1941). A revised psychopathology of the psychoses and psychoneuroses. In *Psychoanalytic Studies of the Personality*. London: Routledge & Keagan Paul, 1952, pp. 28–58.

Fast, I. (1979). Developments in gender identity: gender differentiation in girls. *Internat. J. Psycho-Anal.*, 60:443–454.

———— (1984). *Gender Identity: A Differentiation Model.* Hillsdale, NJ: The Analytic Press.

———— (1990). Aspects of early gender development: Toward a reformulation. Psychoanal. Psychol., 7 (Suppl.):105–118.

Ferenczi, S. (1933). Confusion of tongues between adults and the child. In *Final Contributions to the Problems and Methods of Psycho-Analysis*, ed. M. Balint. New York: Brunner/Mazel, 1980, pp. 156–167.

Fogel, G., ed. (1991). *The Work of Hans Loewald: An Introduction and Commentary*. Northvale, NJ: Aronson.

Fosshage, J. (1989). The developmental function of dreaming mentation: Clinical implications. In *Dimensions of Self Experience: Progress in Self Psychology, Vol. 5*, ed. A. Goldberg. Hillsdale, NJ: The Analytic Press, pp. 3–12.

———— (1995a). Countertransference as the analyst's experience of the analysand: influence of listening perspectives. *Psychoanal. Psychol.*, 12:375–391.

———— (1995b). Interaction in psychoanalysis: A broadening horizon. *Psychoanal. Dial.*, 5:459–478.

———— (1997). Listening/experiencing perspectives and the quest for a facilitating responsiveness. In *Conversations in Self Psychology: Progress In Self Psychology, Vol. 13*, ed. A. Goldberg. Hillsdale, NJ: The Analytic Press, pp. 33–55.

Foucault, M. (1980). *The History of Sexuality, Vol. 1*. New York: Vintage.

———— (1984). *The Care of the Self: The History of Sexuality, Vol. 3*, trans R. Hurley. New York: Vintage Books, 1988.

Freud, S. (1898). Sexuality in the aetiology of the neuroses. *Standard Edition*, 3:263–286. London: Hogarth Press, 1962.

———— (1905). Three essays on the theory of sexuality. *Standard Edition*, 7:130–243. London: Hogarth Press, 1953.

———— (1908). "Civilized" sexual morality and modern nervous illness. *Standard Edition*, 9:181–204. London: Hogarth Press, 1959.

———— (1910). A special type of object choice made by men (contributions to the psychology of love I). *Standard Edition*: 11:163–176. London: Hogarth Press, 1957.

———— (1911–1915). Papers on technique. *Standard Edition*, 12:89–171. London: Hogarth Press, 1958.

———— (1912a). On the universal tendency to debasement in the sphere of love (contributions to the psychology of love II). *Standard Edition*, 11:177–190. London: Hogarth Press, 1957.

———— (1912b). Recommendations to physicians practising psycho-analysis. *Standard Edition*, 12:111–120. London: Hogarth Press, 1958.

———— (1913). On beginning the treatment (further recommendations on the technique of psychoanalysis I). *Standard Edition*, 12:121–144. London: Hogarth Press, 1958.

———— (1914). On narcissism: An introduction. *Standard Edition*: 14:73–102. London: Hogarth Press, 1957.

———— (1916). Introductory lectures on psychoanalysis. *Standard Edition*, 16:243–463. London: Hogarth Press, 1963.

———— (1917). General theory of the neuroses. *Standard Edition*: 16:234–463. London: Hogarth Press, 1963.

————— (1918). The taboo of virginity (contributions to the psychology of love III). *Standard Edition*, 11:191–208. London: Hogarth Press, 1957.

————— (1920). The psychogenesis of a case of homosexuality in a woman. *Standard Edition*, 18:145–174. London: Hogarth Press, 1955.

————— (1923a). The ego and id. *Standard Edition*, 19:13–66. London: Hogarth Press, 1961.

————— (1923b). The infantile genital organization: An interpolation into the theory of sexuality. *Standard Edition*, 19:141–148. London: Hogarth Press, 1961.

————— (1924). The economic problem of masochism. *Standard Edition*, 19:159–172. London: Hogarth Press, 1961.

————— (1925). Some psychical consequences of the anatomical distinction between the sexes. *Standard Edition*: 19:248–260. London: Hogarth Press, 1961.

————— (1933). New introductory lectures on psychoanalysis. *Standard Edition*, 22:112–135. London: Hogarth Press, 1964.

Friedman, L. (1991). On the therapeutic action of Loewald's theory. In *The Work of Hans Loewald: An Introduction and Commentary*, ed. G. Fogel. Northvale, NJ: Aronson, pp. 91–104..

————— (1996). Editorial : The Loewald phenomenon. *J. Amer. Psychoanal. Assn.*, 44:671–672.

Gadamer, H. (1970). *Truth and Method*. New York: Crossroads.

Galenson, E. & Roiphe, H. (1976). Some suggested revision concerning early female development. *J. Amer. Psychoanal. Assn.*, 24 (Suppl.):20–57.

Gedo, J. (1981). *Advances in Clinical Psychoanalysis*. New York: International Universities Press.

————— (1989). Self pscyhology: A post-Kohutian view. In *Self Psychology: Comparisons and Contrasts*, ed. D. Detrick & S. Detrick. Hillsdale, NJ: The Analytic Press, pp. 415–428.

————— (1997). Ferenczi as the orthodox visier. *Psychoanal. Inq.*, 17:428–436.

————— & Goldberg, A. (1973). *Models of the Mind*. Chicago: University of Chicago Press.

Gerson, S. (1996). Neutrality, resistance, and self-disclosure in an intersubjective analysis. *Psychoanal. Dial.*, 6:623–646.

Gilligan, C. (1982). *In a Different Voice*. Cambridge, MA: Harvard University Press.

Goldberg, A. (1983). On the nature of the "misfit." *In The Future of Psychoanalysis*, ed. A. Goldberg. New York: International Universities Press, pp. 309–326.

————— (1985). Discussion: The definition and role of interpretation. In *Progress in Self Psychology, Vol. 1*, ed. A. Goldberg. Hillsdale, NJ: The Analytic Press, pp. 62–68.

——— (1988). *A Fresh Look at Psychoanalysis: The View from Self Psychology.* Hillsdale, NJ: The Analytic Press.

——— (1990). *The Prisonhouse of Psychoanalysis.* Hillsdale, NJ: The Analytic Press.

——— (1995). *The Problem of Perversion: The View from Self Psychology.* New Haven, CT: Yale University Press.

——— (1996). It is all interaction. *Psychoanal. Inq.,* 16:96–106.

——— (1997). Three forms of meaning and their psychoanalytic significance. *J. Amer. Psychoanal. Assn.,* 45:491–506.

——— (1998). Self psychology since Kohut. *Psychoanal. Q.,* 67:240–255.

Goldner, V. (1991). Toward a critical relational theory of gender. *Psychoanal. Dial.,* 1:249–272.

——— (1997). Introduction [to commentaries on *Disorienting Sexuality*]. *Gender & Psychoanal.,* 2:173–176.

Gottlieb, A. (1996). The new science. *New York Times Book Review.* Nov. 17, p. 28.

Greenberg, J. (1996). Psychoanalytic interactions. *Psychoanal. Inq.,* 16:25–38.

——— & Mitchell, S. (1983). *Object Relations in Psychoanalytic Theory.* Cambridge, MA: Harvard University Press.

Greenson, R. (1967). *The Technique and Practice of Psychoanalysis, Vol. 1.* New York: International Universities Press.

Guntrip, H. (1952). The schizoid personality and the external world. In *Schizoid Phenomena, Object Relations and the Self.* New York: International Universities Press, 1995, pp. 17–48.

Habermas, J. (1971). *Knowledge and Human Interest.* Boston: Beacon Press.

Harris, A. (1991a). Gender as contradiction. *Psychoanal. Dial.,* 1:197–224.

——— (1991b). A symposium on gender: Introduction. *Psychoanal. Dial.,* 1:243–248.

——— (1997). Aggression, envy, and ambition: circulating tensions in women's psychic life. *Gender & Psychoanal.,* 2:291–325.

Hartmann, H. (1939). Psychoanalysis and the concept of health. In *Essays on Ego Psychology.* New York: International Universities Press, 1964, pp. 3–18.

——— (1950). Comments on the psychoanalytic theory of the ego. In *Essays in Ego Psychology.* New York: International Universities Press, 1964, pp. 131–141.

Harvey, D. (1990). *The Condition of Postmodernity.* Cambridge, MA: Blackwell.

Heinz, R. (1976). J. P. Sartre's existentielle Psychoanalyse. *Archiv fur Rechtsund Sozialphilosophie,* 62:61–88.

Hirsch, I. (1993). Countertransference enactments and some issues related to external factors in the analyst's life. *Psychoanal. Dial.,* 3:343–366.

——— (1998). The concept of enactment and theoretical convergence, *Psychoanal. Q.,* 67:78–101.

Hoffman, I. Z. (1983). The patient as the interpreter of the analyst's experience. *Contemp. Psychoanal.*, 19:389–422.

——— (1987). The value of uncertainty in psychoanalytic practice. *Contemp. Psychoanal.*, 23:205–215.

——— (1991). Toward a social-constructivist view of the psychoanalytic situation. *Psychoanal. Dial.*, 1:74–105.

——— (1992). Some practical implications of a social-constructivist view of the psychoanalytic situation. *Psychoanal. Dial.*, 2:287–304.

——— (1994). Dialectical thinking and therapeutic action in the psychoanalytic process. *Psychoanal. Q.*, 63:187–218.

——— (1996). The intimate and ironic authority of the psychoanalyst's presence. *Psychoanal. Q.*, 65:102–136.

——— (1998). *Ritual and Spontaneity in the Psychoanalytic Process: A Dialectical-Constructivist View*. Hillsdale, NJ: The Analytic Press.

Horney, K. (1924). On the genesis of the castration complex in women. In *Feminine Psychology*. New York: Norton, 1967, pp. 37–53.

——— (1926). The flight from womanhood. In *Feminine Psychology*. New York: Norton, 1967, pp. 54–70.

——— (1932). The dread of women. *Internat. J. Psycho-Anal.*, 13:359– 370.

——— (1933). The denial of the vagina. In *Feminine Psychology*. New York: Norton, 1967, pp. 147–162.

Jacobs, T. (1986). On countertransference enactments. *J. Amer. Psychoanal. Assn.*, 34:289–308.

Jacobson, L. (1997). The soul of psychoanalysis in the modern world: Reflections on the work of Christopher Bollas. *Psychoanal. Dial.*, 7:81–116.

Jones, E. (1927). The early development of female sexuality. *Papers on Psychoanalysis*. Boston: Beacon Press, 1961.

——— (1933). Early female sexuality. In *Papers on Psychoanalysis*. Boston: Beacon Press, 1961.

Jordan, J. (1984). Empathy and boundaries. Work In Progress #16. Wellesley, MA: Stone Center Working Papers Series.

——— (1986). The meaning of mutuality. Work in Progress#23. Wellesley. MA: Stone Center Working Paper Series.

——— (1987). Clarity in connection: Empathic knowing, desire, and sexuality. Work in Progress #29. Wellesley, MA: Stone Center Working Papers Series.

Joseph, B. (1992). Psychic change: some perspectives. *Internat. J. Psycho-Anal.*, 73:237–244.

Kernberg, O. (1976). *Object Relations Theory and Clinical Psychoanalysis*. New York: Aronson.

Kestenberg, J. (1956). On the development of maternal feelings in early childhood. The *Psychoanalytic Study of the Child*, 11:275–291. New York: International Universities Press.

———— (1968). Outside and inside, male and female. *J. Amer. Psychoanal. Assn.*, 16:457–520.

———— (1976). Regression and reintegration in pregnancy. *J. Amer. Psychoanal. Assn.*, 24(Suppl.):213–250.

Khan, M. (1974). *The Privacy of the Self.* New York: International Universities Press.

Kleeman, J. (1976). Freud's views on early female sexuality in the light of direct child observation. *J. Amer. Psychoanal. Assn.*, 24(Suppl.):3–27.

Klein, G. (1976). *Psychoanalytic Theory: An Exploration of Essentials.* New York: International Universities Press.

Klein, M. (1928). Early states of the Oedipus complex. *Int. J. Psycho-Anal.*, 9:167–180.

———— (1937). Love, guilt, and reparation. In *Love, Guilt, and Reparation and Other Works 1921–1945.* New York: Free Press, 1975, pp. 306–343.

———— (1952). Some theoretical conclusions regarding the emotional life of the infant. In *Envy and Gratitude and Other Works 1946–1963.* New York: Free Press, 1975, pp.61–93.

Kohut, H. (1959). Introspection, empathy, and psychoanalysis. *J. Amer. Psychoanal. Assn.*, 7:459–483.

———— (1966). Forms and transformations of narcissism. *J. Amer. Psychoanal. Assn.*, 14:243–272.

———— (1970). Psychoanalysis in a troubled world. In *The Search for the Self,* Vol. 2., ed. P. Ornstein. New York: International Universities Press, 1978, pp. 511–546.

———— (1971). *The Analysis of the Self.* New York: International Universities Press.

———— (1972). Thoughts on narcissism and narcissistic rage. *The Psychoanalytic Study of the Child,* 27:360–400. New Haven, CT: Yale University Press.

———— (1973). The analyst in the community of scholars. *Annual of Psychoanalysis,* 3:341–370. Chicago: University of Chicago Press.

———— (1974). Remarks about the formation of the self: Letter to a student regarding some principles of psychoanalytic research. In *The Search for the Self, Vol. 2,* ed. P. Ornstein. New York: International Universities Press, 1978, pp. 737–770.

———— (1977a). *The Restoration of the Self.* New York: International Universities Press.

———— (1977b). The two analyses of Mr. Z. *Internat. J. Psycho-Anal.*, 60:3–27.

———— (1978a). *The Search for the Self, Vols. 1 & 2,* ed. P. Ornstein. New York: International Universities Press.

———— (1978b). *The Psychology of the Self: A Casebook,* ed. A. Goldberg. New York: International Universities Press.

———— (1978c). The self in history. In *The Search for the Self, Vol. 2*, ed. P. Ornstein. New York: International Universities Press, 1978, pp. 771–782.

———— (1980). Reflections. In *Advances in Self Psychology*, ed. A. Goldberg. New York: International Universities Press, pp. 473–554.

———— (1982). Introspection, empathy, and the semi-circle of mental health. *Internat. J. Psycho-Anal.*, 63:395–407.

———— (1984). *How Does Analysis Cure?* ed. A. Goldberg & P. Stepansky. Chicago: University of Chicago Press.

———— & Wolf, E. (1978). The disorders of the self and their treatment: An outline. *Internat. J. Psycho-Anal.*, 59:413–425.

Kristeva, J. (1987). *In the Beginning Was Love*. New York: Columbia University Press.

———— (1996). *Julia Kristeva, Interviews*, ed. R. M. Guberman. New York: Columbia University Press.

Kubie, L. (1974). The drive to become both sexes. *Psychoanal. Q.*, 43:349–426.

Kulish, N. M. (1991). The mental representation of the clitoris: The fear of female sexuality. *Psychoanal. Inq.*, 11:511–536.

Lacan, J. (1977). *Ecrits: A Selection*, trans. A. Sheridan. New York: Norton.

Lachmann, F. (1990). On some challenges to clinical theory in the treatment of character pathology. In *The Realities of Transference: Progress in Self Psychology, Vol. 6*, ed. A. Goldberg. Hillsdale, NJ: The Analytic Press, pp. 59–68.

———— (1991). Three self psychologies or one? In *The Evolution of Self Psychology: Progress in Self Psychology, Vol. 7*, ed. A. Goldberg. Hillsdale, NJ: The Analytic Press, pp. 167–174.

———— & Beebe, B. (1992). Reformulations of early development and transference: Implications for psychic structure formation. In *Interface of Psychoanalysis and Psychology*, ed. J. Barron, M. Eagle & D. Wolitzky. Washington, DC: American Psychological Assn., pp. 133–153.

———— & ———— (1995). Self psychology today, *Psychoanal. Dial.*, 5:375–384.

———— & ———— (1996a). Three principles of salience in the organization of the patient-analyst interaction. *Psychoanal. Psychol.*, 13:1–22.

———— & ———— (1996b). The contribution of self- and mutual regulation to therapeutic action: A case illustration. In *Basic Ideas Reconsidered: Progress in Self Psychology, Vol. 12*, ed. A. Goldberg. Hillsdale, NJ: The Analytic Press, pp. 123–140.

Laing, R. D. (1970). *Knots*. New York: Vintage Books.

Lang, J. (1984). Notes toward a psychology of the feminine self. In *Kohut's Legacy: Contributions to Self Psychology*. ed. P. Stepansky & A. Goldberg. Hillsdale, NJ: The Analytic Press. pp. 51–70.

Lasch, C. (1978). *The Culture of Narcissism*. New York: Norton.

Lax, R. (1994). Aspects of primary and secondary genital feelings and anxieties in girls during the preoedipal and early oedipal phases. *Psychoanal. Q.*, 63:271–296.

Layton, L. (1997). The doer behind the deed. *Gender & Psychoanal.*, 2:131–156.

Lichtenberg, J. (1983a). Is there a weltanschauung to be developed from psychoanalysis? In *The Future of Psychoanalysis*, ed. A. Goldberg. New York: International Universities Press, pp. 203–240.

——— (1983b). *Psychoanalysis and Infant Research.* Hillsdale, NJ: The Analytic Press.

——— (1987). Infant studies and clinical work with adults. *Psychoanal. Inq.*, 7:311–330.

——— (1988). Infant research and self psychology. Frontiers in Self Psychology: Progress in Self *Psychology, Vol. 3.*, ed. A. Goldberg. Hillsdale, NJ: The Analytic Press, pp. 59–63.

——— (1989). *Psychoanalysis and Motivation.* Hillsdale, NJ: The Analytic Press.

——— (1990). Rethinking the scope of the patient's transference and the therapist's counter-responsiveness. In *The Realities of Transference: Progress In Self Psychology, Vol. 6*, ed. A. Goldberg. Hillsdale, NJ: The Analytic Press, pp. 23–33.

——— (1998). Experience as a guide to psychoanalytic theory and practice. *J. Amer. Psychoanal. Assn.*, 46:17–35.

——— Lachmann, F. & Fosshage, J. (1996). *The Clinical Exchange: Techniques Derived from Self and Motivational Systems.* Hillsdale, NJ: The Analytic Press.

Loewald, H. (1960). On the therapeutic action of psychoanalysis. In *Papers on Psychoanalysis.* New Haven, CT: Yale University Press, 1980, pp. 221–256.

——— (1962). Internalization, separation, mourning, and the superego. In *Papers on Psychoanalysis.* New Haven, CT: Yale University Press, 1980. pp. 257–276.

——— (1973a). Book review: Heinz Kohut, The Analysis of the Self. In *Papers on Psychoanalysis.* New Haven, CT: Yale University Press, 1980, pp. 342–351.

——— (1973b). On internalization. In *Papers on Psychoanalysis.* New Haven, CT: Yale University Press, 1980, pp. 69–86.

——— (1975). Psychoanalysis as an art and the fantasy character of the psychoanalytic situation. In *Papers on Psychoanalysis.* New Haven, CT: Yale Uniersity Press, 1980, pp. 352–371.

——— (1976). Perspectives on memory. In *Papers on Psychoanalysis.* New Haven, CT: Yale University Press, 1980, 148–173.

——— (1977). Book review essay on The Freud/Jung Letters. In *Papers on Psychoanalysis.* New Haven, CT: Yale University Press, 1980, pp. 405–418.

——— (1978a). Primary process, secondary process, and language. In *Papers on Psychoanalysis.* New Haven, CT: Yale University Press, 1980, pp. 178–206.

——— (1978b). Instinct theory, object relations, and psychic structure formation. In *Papers on Psychoanalysis.* New Haven, CT: Yale University Press, 1980, pp. 207–218.

——— (1979a). Reflections on the psychoanalytic process and its therapeutic potential. In *Papers on Psychoanalysis.* New Haven, CT: Yale University Press, 1980, pp. 372–383.

——— (1979b). The waning of the Oedipus complex. *J. Amer. Psychoanal. Assn.*, 27:751–776.

——— (1986). Transference-countertransference. *J. Amer. Psychoanal. Assn.*, 34:275–289.

Lyons-Ruth, K. (1991). Rapprochement or approachment: Mahler's theory reconsidered from the vantage point of recent research. *Psychoanal. Psychol.*, 8:1–24.

Mahler, M., Pine, F. & Bergman, A. (1975). *The Psychological Birth of the Human Infant.* New York: Basic Books.

Maurensig, P. (1997). *Lunenberg Variations.* New York: Farrar, Straus, & Giroux.

Mayer, E. L.. (1985). "Everybody must be just like me": Observations on female castration anxiety. *Internat. J. Psycho-Anal.*, 66:331–347.

——— (1991). Towers and enclosed spaces: A preliminary report on gender differences in children's reactions to block structures. *Psychoanal. Inq.*, 11:280–510.

——— (1995). The phallic castration complex and primary femininity: Paired developmental lines toward female gender identity. *J. Amer. Psychoanal. Assn.*, 43:17–38.

——— (1996a). Psychoanalytic stories about gender: Moving toward an integration of mind and body. *Gender & Psychoanal.*, 1:239–248.

——— (1996b). Changes in science and changing ideas about knowledge and authority in psychoanalysis. *Psychoanal. Q.*, 65:158–200.

McDougall, J. (1964). Homosexuality in women. In *Female Sexuality*, ed. J. Chasseguet-Smirgel. London: Karnac Books, 1970, pp. 171–212.

McGuire, W., ed. (1974). *The Freud-Jung Letters: The Correspondence Between Sigmund Freud and C.G. Jung*, trans. R. Mannheim & R. F. C. Hull. Princeton, NJ: Princeton University Press.

McLaughlin, J. (1981). Transference, psychic reality, and countertransference. *Psychoanal. Q.*, 50:639–664.

——— (1991). Clinical and theoretical aspects of enactment. *J. Amer. Psychoanal. Assn.*, 39:595–614.

Meluk, T. (1976). Discussion of "Freud and female sexuality." *Internat. J. Psycho-Anal.*, 57:307–310.

Mensch, J. (1996). *After Modernity: Husserlian Reflections on a Philosophical Tradition.* Albany: State University of New York.

Miller, H. L. (1997). *Science and Dissent in Post-Mao China: The Politics of*

Knowledge. Seattle: University of Washington Press.

Miller, J. B. (1976). *Toward a New Psychology of Women.* Boston: Beacon Press.

Mitchell, J. (1974). *Psychoanalysis and Feminism.* New York: Pantheon Books.

Mitchell, S. (1988). *Relational Concepts in Psychoanalysis.* Cambridge, MA.: Harvard University Press.

———— (1991). Wishes, needs, and personal negotiations. *Psychoanal. Inq.,* 11:147–170.

———— (1992). Commentary on Trop and Stolorow's "Defense analysis in self psychology." *Psychoanal. Dial.,* 3:441–453.

———— (1993). *Hope and Dread in Psychoanalysis.* New York: Basic Books.

———— (1996a). When interpretations fail: A new look at the therapeutic action of psychoanalysis. In *Understanding Therapeutic Action: Psychodynamic Concepts of Cure,* ed. L. Lifson. Hillsdale, NJ: The Analytic Press, pp. 165–186.

———— (1996b). Constructions of gender and sexuality, sandcastles on the shore: A response to Mayer and Schwartz. *Gender & Psychoanal.,* 1:261–270.

———— (1997). *Influence and Autonomy in Psychoanalysis.* Hillsdale, NJ.: The Analytic Press.

———— & Black, M. (1995). *Freud and Beyond: A History of Modern Psychoanalytic Thought.* New York: Basic Books.

Modell, A. (1968). *Object Love and Reality.* New York: International University Press.

———— (1992). The private self and private space. *Annual of Psychoanal.,* 20:1–24.

———— (1993). *The Private Self.* Cambridge, MA: Harvard University Press.

Money, J. & Ehrhardt, A. (1972). *Man and Woman, Boy and Girl.* Baltimore, MD: Johns Hopkins University Press.

———— Hampson, J. G. & Hampson, J. L. (1955a). An examination of some basic sexual concepts: The evidence of human hermaphroditism. *Bull. Johns Hopkins Hosp.,* 97:301–310.

———— ———— & ———— (1955b). Hermaphroditism: Recommendations concerning assignment of sex, change of sex, and psychologic management. *Bull. Johns Hopkins Hosp.,* 97:284–300.

Ogden, T. (1982). *Projective Identification and Psychotherapeutic Technique.* New York: Aronson.

———— (1986). *The Matrix of the Mind.* Northvale, NJ: Aronson.

———— (1992a). The dialectically constituted/decentered subject of psychoanalysis. I: the Freudian subject. *Internat. J. Psycho-Anal.,* 73:517–526.

———— (1992b). The dialectically constituted/decentered subject of psychoanalysis. II: the contributions of Klein and Winnicott. *Internat. J. Psycho-Anal.,* 73:613–626.

———— (1994). *Subjects of Analysis.* Northvale, NJ: Aronson.

Ornstein, A. (1988). Optimal responsiveness and the theory of cure. In *Learning from Kohut: Progress in Self Psychology, Vol. 4*, ed. A. Goldberg. Hillsdale, NJ: The Analytic Press, pp. 155–159.

―――― (1990). Selfobject transferences and the process of working through. In *The Realities of Transference: Progress in Self Psychology, Vol. 6*, ed. A. Goldberg. Hillsdale, NJ: The Analytic Press, pp. 41–58.

―――― (1992). The curative fantasy and psychic recovery: contribution to the theory of psychoanalytic psychotherapy. Revised version of paper presented in Distinguished Lecture Series, American Psychiatric Assn., San Francisco, May 9, 1989.

Ornstein, P. (1991). Why self psychology is not an object relations theory: Clinical and theoretical considerations. In *The Evolution of Self Psychology: Progress in Self Psychology, Vol. 7*, ed. A. Goldberg. Hillsdale, NJ: The Analytic Press, pp. 17–30.

―――― (1993a). Sexuality and aggression in pathogenesis and in the clinical situation. In *The Widening Scope of Self Psychology: Progress In Self Psychology, Vol. 9*, ed. A. Goldberg. Hillsdale, NJ: The Analytic Press, pp. 109–128.

―――― (1993b). Chronic rage from underground: Reflections on its structure and treatment. In *The Widening Scope of Self Psychology: Progress in Self Psychology, Vol. 9*, ed. A. Goldberg. Hillsdale, NJ: The Analytic Press, pp. 143–157.

―――― & Ornstein, A. (1985). Clinical understanding and explaining: The empathic vantage point. In *Progress In Self Psychology, Vol. 1*, ed. A. Goldberg. Hillsdale, NJ: The Analytic Press, pp. 43–61.

Panel (1996). A classic revisited: Loewald on the therapeutic action of psychoanalysis. G. Fogel, Chair; P, Tyson; J. Greenberg; J.T. McLaughlin; E.R. Peyser. *J. Amer. Psychoanal. Assn.*, 44:863–924.

Parens, H., Pollock, L., Stern, J. & Kramer, S. (1976). On the girl's entry into the Oedipus complex. *J. Amer. Psychoanal. Assn.*, 24 (Suppl.):79–107.

Person, E. (1990). The influence of values in psychoanalysis: The case of female psychology. In *Essential Papers on the Psychology of Women*, ed., C. Zanardi. New York: New York University Press, pp. 305–331.

―――― & Ovesey, L. (1983). Psychoanalytic theories of gender identity. *J. Amer. Psychoanal. Assn.*, 11:203–226.

Pizer, S. (1996). Negotiating potential space: Illusion, play, metaphor, and the subjunctive. *Psychoanal. Dial.*, 6:689–712.

―――― (1998). *Building Bridges: The Negotiation of Paradox in Psychoanalysis*. Hillsdale, NJ: The Analytic Press.

Protter, B. (1996). Classical, modern, and postmodern psychoanalysis: Epistemic transformations. *Psychoanal. Dial.*, 6:533–562.

Racker, H. (1972). The meanings and uses of countertransference. In *Classics in Psychoanalytic Technique*, ed., R. Langs. Northvale, NJ: Aronson, pp. 177–200.

Renik, O. (1993). Analytic interaction: conceptualizing technique in the light of the analyst's irreducible subjectivity. *Psychoanal. Q.*, 62:553–571.

——— (1995). The ideal of the anonymous analyst and the problem of self-disclosure. *Psychoanal. Q.*, 64:466–495.

——— (1996). The perils of neutrality. *Psychoanal. Q.*, 65:495–517.

Resenau, P. (1992). *Post-Modernism and the Social Sciences*. Princeton, NJ: Princeton University Press.

Richards, A. K. (1992). The influence of sphincter control and genital sensation on body image and gender identity in women. *Psychoanal. Q.*, 61:331–351.

——— (1996). Ladies of fashion: Pleasure, perversion, or paraphilia. *Internat. J. Psycho-Anal.*, 77:337–351.

Ricoeur, P. (1970). *Freud and Philosophy: An Essay on Interpretation*. New Haven, CT: Yale University Press.

——— (1992). *Oneself as Another*. Chicago: University of Chicago Press.

Ritvo, S. (1976). Adolescent to woman. *J. Amer. Psychoanal. Assn.*, 24 (Suppl): 127–138.

Roiphe, H. & Galenson, E. (1981). *Infantile Origins of Sexual Identity*. New York: International Universities Press.

Rubin, G. (1975). The traffic in women. In *Toward an Anthropology of Women*, ed. R. R. Reiter. New York: Monthly Review Press.

Russell, P. (1996). Process with involvement: The interpretation of affect. In *Understanding Therapeutic Action*, ed. L. Lifson. HIllsdale, NJ: The Analytic Press, pp. 201–216.

——— (1998). *Trauma, Repetition, and Affect Regulation: The Work of Paul Russell*, ed. J. Teicholz & D. Kriegman. New York: The Other Press.

Rycroft, C. (1966). Causes and meaning. In *Psychoanalysis and Beyond*, ed. P. Fuller. Chicago: Chicago University Press, 1985.

Sander, L. (1975). Infant and caretaking environment. In *Explorations in Child Psychiatry*, ed. E. J. Anthony. New York: Plenum.

Sandler, J. (1976). Countertransference and role-responsiveness. In *Classics of Psychoanalytic Technique*, ed. R. Lang. Northvale: NJ, pp. 273–278.

Santner, E. (1996). *My Own Private Germany: Daniel Paul Schreber's Secret History of Modernity*. Princeton, NJ: Princeton University Press.

Sartre, J. (1968). *Being and Nothingness*, trans. H. Barnes. New York: Washington Square Press.

Sass, L. (1995). Review essay: *Psychoanalysis and the Postmodern Impulse: Knowing and Being Since Freud's Psychology*, by Barnaby Barratt. *Psychoanal. Dial.*, 5:123–136.

Schafer, R. (1974). Problems in Freud's psychology of women. *J. Amer. Psychoanal. Assn.*, 22:459–485.

——— (1976). *A New Language for Psychoanalysis*. New Haven, CT: Yale University Press.

———— (1978). *Language and Insight*. New Haven, CT: Yale Universities Press.

———— (1993). *Retelling a Life: Narration and Dialogue in Psychoanalysis*. New York: Basic Books.

Schwartz, A. (1997). *Disorienting Sexuality*: A Commentary [on the book by Thomas Domenici and Ronnie C. Lesser, New York: Routledge, 1995]. *Gender & Psychoanal.*, 2:191–202.

Schwartz, J. (1995). What does the physicist know? Thraldom and insecurity in the relationship of psychoanalysis to physics. *Psychoanal. Dial.*, 5:45–62.

Shane, E. & Shane, M. (1990). Object loss and selfobject loss: A consideration of self psychology's contribution to understanding mourning and the failure to mourn. *Annual of Psychoanalysis*, 17:115–131. Hillsdale, NJ: The Analytic Press.

Shane, M. & Shane, E. (1988). Pathways to integration: Adding to the self psychology model. In *Learning from Kohut: Progress In Self Psychology, Vol. 4*, ed. A. Goldberg. Hillsdale, NJ: The Analytic Press, pp. 71–78.

———— & ———— (1996). Self psychology in search of the optimal: A consideration of responsiveness, optimal provision, optimal gratification, and optimal restraint in the clinical situation. In *Basic Ideas Reconsidered: Progress in Self Psychology, Vol. 12*, ed. A. Goldberg. Hillsdale, NJ: The Analytic Press, pp. 37–53.

Shapin, S. (1996). *The Scientific Revolution*. Chicago: University of Chicago Press.

Slavin, M. (1997). Discussion of keynote address, "Whose self is it anyway?: The analyst's use of self" by J. G. Teicholz. Fall Conference, Boston Institute for Psychotherapy: *The Balancing Act: Walking the Tightrope of Two Selves in the Service of One*, Boston, Nov. 8.

———— & Kriegman, D. (1992). *The Adaptive Design of the Human Psyche: Psychoanalysis, Evolutionary Biology, and the Therapeutic Process*. New York: The Guilford Press.

———— & ———— (1998). Why the analyst needs to change: Toward a theory of conflict, negotiation, and mutual influence in the therapeutic process. *Psychoanal. Dial.*, 8:247–284.

Slochower, J. (1991). Variations in the analytic holding environment. *Internat. J. Psycho-Anal.*, 72:709–718.

———— (1996). Holding and the fate of the analyst's subjectivity. *Psychoanal. Dial.*, 6:323–353.

Spence, D. (1982). *Narrative Truth and Historical Truth*. New York: Norton.

Spezzano, C. (1993). *Affect in Psychoanalysis: A Clinical Synthesis*. Hillsdale, NJ: The Analytic Press.

———— (1996). The three faces of two-person psychology: development, ontology, and epistemology. *Psychoanal. Dial.*, 6:599–622.

Stack, C. (1995). The lesbian patient: narratives of subjectivity, gender, and sexual identity. In *Lesbians and Psychoanalysis: Revolutions in Theory and*

Practice, ed. J. Glassgold & S. Iascuza. New York: Free Press, pp. 327–342.

Stechler, G. (1983). Infancy research: A contribution to self psychology. In *Reflections on Self Psychology*, ed. J. Lichtenberg & S. Kaplan. Hillsdale, NJ: The Analytic Press, pp. 43–48.

———— & Kaplan, S. (1980). The development of the self: A psychoanalytic perspective. The *Psychoanal. Study of the Child*, 35:85–106.

Steiner, R. (1995). Hermeneutics or Hermes-mess? *Internat. J. Psycho-Anal.*, 76:435–445.

Stepansky, P. (1989). Adler, Kohut, and the idea of a psychoanalytic research tradition. In *Self Psychology: Comparisons and Contrasts*, ed. D. Detrick & S. Detrick. Hillsdale, NJ: The Analytic Press, pp. 49–74.

Stern, D. B. (1996). The social construction of therapeutic action. *Psychoanal. Inq.*, 16:265–293.

Stern, D. N. (1983). The early development of schemas of the self, other, and self with other. In *Reflections on Self Psychology*, ed. J. Lichtenberg & S. Kaplan. Hillsdale, NJ: The Analytic Press, pp. 49–84.

———— (1985). *The Interpersonal World of the Infant*. New York: Basic Books.

Stiver, I. (1983). The meanings of "dependency" in male-female relationships. Work in Progress #11. Wellesley, MA: Stone Center Working Papers Series.

———— (1986). Beyond the Oedipus complex: Mothers and daughters. Work in Progress #26. Wellesley, MA: Stone Center Working Papers Series.

Stoller, R. (1964). A contribution to the study of gender identity. *Internat. J. Psycho-Anal.*, 45:220–226.

———— (1968). The sense of femaleness. *Psychoanal. Q.*, 37:42–55.

———— (1976). Primary femininity. *J. Amer. Psychoanal. Assn.*, 24 (Suppl.):59–78.

Stolorow, R. (1980). Discussion of "Self psychology and the concept of health" by Paul Ornstein. In *Advances in Self Psychology*, ed. A. Goldberg. New York: International Universities Press, pp. 161–165.

———— (1995). An intersubjective view of self psychology. *Psychoanal. Dialogues*, 5: 393–400.

———— & Atwood, G. (1979). *Faces in a Cloud: Subjectivity in Personality Theory*. Northvale, NJ: Aronson.

———— & ———— (1992). *Contexts of Being*. Hillsdale, NJ: The Analytic Press.

———— & ———— (1997). Deconstructing the myth of the neutral analyst: An alternative from intersubjective systems theory. *Psychoanal. Q.*, 66:431–449.

————, ———— & Brandchaft, B., ed. (1994). *The Intersubjective Perspective*. Northvale, NJ: Aronson.

————, Brandchaft, B. & Atwood, G. (1987). *Psychoanalytic Treatment: An Intersubjective Approach*. Hillsdale, NJ: The Analytic Press.

———— & Lachmann, F. (1980). *Psychoanalysis of Developmental Arrests*. Madison: International Universities Press.

Strozier, C. (1980). Heinz Kohut and the historical imagination. *Advances in Self Psychology*, ed. A. Goldberg. New York: International Universities Press, pp. 397–406.

Sucharov, M. (1994). Psychoanalysis, self psychology, and intersubjectivity. In *The Intersubjective Perspective*, ed. R. Stolorow, G. Atwood & B. Brandchaft. Northvale, NJ: Aronson, pp. 187–202.

———— (1997). Secret conversations with my father: The human contextualization of theoretical discourse. Presented at 20th Annual International Conference on the Psychology of the Self: *Challenges in Self Psychology*. Nov. 15, Chicago.

Sullivan, H. S. (1947). *Conceptions of Modern Psychiatry*. New York: Norton.

———— (1953). *The Interpersonal Theory of Psychiatry*. New York: Norton.

Surrey, J. (1984). The "self-in-relation": A theory of women's development. Work in Progress #13. Wellesley, MA: Stone Center Working Paper Studies.

Sweetnam, A. (1996). The changing contexts of gender: Between fixed and fluid experience. *Psychoanal. Dial.*, 6:437–460.

Symposium (1994). Therapeutic Action. MIP Fourth Annual Symposium, October 15, Cambridge, MA. Opening remarks: Elizabeth Loewald.

Teicholz, J. G. (1978). A selective review of the psychoanalytic literature on theoretical conceptualizations of narcissism. *J. Amer. Psychoanal. Assn.*, 26:831–862.

———— (1989). Broadening the meaning of empathy for work with primitive disorders. Presented at spring meeting of Div. 39, American Psychological Association, Boston.

———— (1990). Two strands of internalization: curative factors in psychoanalysis. Presented at Harvard Medical School/Mass. General Hospital Grand Rounds. Nov. 12, Boston.

———— (1995). Loewald's "positive neutrality" and the affirmative potential of psychoanalytic interventions. *The Psychoanalytic Study of the Child*, 50:48–75. New Haven, CT: Yale University Press.

———— (1996). Optimal responsiveness: its role in psychic growth and change. In *Understanding Therapeutic Action: Psychodynamic Aspects of Cure*, ed. L. Lifson. Hillsdale, NJ: The Analytic Press, pp. 139–161.

———— (1998a). Self and relationship: Kohut, Loewald, and the postmoderns. In *The World of Self Psychology: Progress in Self Psychology, Vol.14*, ed. A. Goldberg. Hillsdale, NJ: The Analytic Press, pp. 267–292.

———— (1998b). Psychoanalysis, postmodernism, and the construction of the sexual subject: Discussion of papers by J. McCarroll & L. Nguyen. Presented at spring meeting of Div. 39, American Psychological Association. Boston, April 24th.

Terman, D. (1980). Object love and the psychology of the self. In *Advances in Self Psychology*, ed. A. Goldberg. New York: International Universities Press, pp. 349–362.

—————— (1988). Optimum frustration: Structuralization and the therapeutic process. In *Learning from Kohut: Progress in Self Psychology, Vol. 4*, ed. A. Goldberg. Hillsdale, NJ: The Analytic Press, pp. 113–126.

Tolpin, M. (1977). Self objects and Oedipal objects: A crucial developmental distinction. *The Psychoanalytic Study of the Child*, 33:167–184. New Haven, CT: Yale University Press.

—————— (1983). Corrective emotional experience: A self psychological reevaluation. In *The Future of Psychoanalysis*, ed. A. Goldberg. New York: International Universities Press, pp. 363–380.

—————— (1993). The unmirrored self, compensatory structure, and cure: The exemplary case of Anna O. *Annual of Psychoanalysis*, 21:157–178. Hillsdale, NJ: The Analytic Press.

Tolpin, P. (1983). Self psychology and the interpretation of dreams. In *The Future of Psychoanalysis*, ed. A. Goldberg. New York: International Universities Press, pp. 255–272.

Torok, M. (1964). The significance of penis envy in a woman. In *Female Sexuality*, ed., J. Chasseguet-Smirgel. Ann Arbor: University of Michigan Press, 1985, pp. 135–170.

Trop, J. & Stolorow, R. (1992). Defense analysis in self psychology: a developmental view. *Psychoanal. Dial.*, 2:427–441.

Tyson, P. (1982). A developmental line of gender identity, gender role, and choice of love object. *J. Amer. Psychoanal. Assn.*, 30:61–86.

—————— (1994). Bedrock and beyond: An examination of the clinical utility of contemporary theories of female psychology. *J. Amer. Psychoanal. Assn.*, 42:447–468.

Winnicott, D. W. (1945). Primitive emotional development. In *Through Paediatrics to Psycho-Analysis*. New York: Basic Books, 1975, pp. 145–156.

—————— (1947). Hate in the countertransference. In *Collected Papers: Through Paediatrics to Psycho-Analysis*. New York: Basic Books, pp. 194–203.

—————— (1951). Transitional objects and transitional phenomena. In *Collected Papers: Through Paediatrics to Psycho-Anal*. New York: Basic Books, 1975, pp. 229–242.

—————— (1954). The depressive position in normal emotional development. In *Collected Papers: Through Paediatrics to Psycho-Analysis*. New York: Basic Books, 1975, pp. 262–277.

—————— (1955). Clinical varieties of transference. In *Collected Papers: Through Paediatrics to Psycho-Analysis*. New York: Basic Books, 1975, pp. 295–299.

—————— (1958). The capacity to be alone. *The Maturational Processes and the Facilitating Environment*. New York: International Universities Press, 29–36.

—————— (1960a). Ego distortion in terms of true and false self. In *The Maturational Processes and the Facilitating Environment*. New York: International Universities Press, 1965, pp. 140–152.

———— (1960b). The theory of the parent-infant relationship. In *The Maturational Processes and the Facilitating Environment*. New York: International Universities Press, 1965, pp. 37–55.

———— (1963). Communicating and not communicating leading to a study of certain opposites. In *The Maturational Processes and the Facilitating Environment*. New York: International Universities Press, 1965, pp.179–192.

———— (1965). *The Maturational Processes and the Facilitating Environment*. New York: International Universities Press.

———— (1971). *Playing and Reality*. New York: Basic Books.Wolf, E. (1983). Empathy and countertransference. In *The Future of Psychoanalysis*, ed. A. Goldberg. New York: International Universities Press, pp. 309–326.

Wolf, E. (1983). Empathy and countertransference In *The Future of Psychoanalysis*, ed. A. Goldberg. New York: International Universitites Press, pp. 309–326.

———— (1988). Problems of therapeutic orientation. In *Learning from Kohut: Progress in Self Psychology, Vol. 4*, ed. A. Goldberg. Hillsdale, NJ: The Analytic Press, pp. 168–172.

———— (1989). Therapeutic experiences. In *Dimensions of Self Experience: Progress in Self Psychology, Vol. 5*, ed. A. Goldberg. Hillsdale, NJ: The Analytic Press, pp. 105–120.

———— (1991). Heinz Kohut Memorial Lecture: Toward a level playing field. In *The Evolution of Self Psychology: Progress in Self Psychology, Vol. 7*, ed. A. Goldberg. Hillsdale, NJ: The Analytic Press, pp.185–200.

———— (1992). On being a scientist or a healer: reflections on abstinence, neutrality, and gratification. *Annual of Psychoanalysis*, 20:115–130. Hillsdale, NJ: The Analytic Press.

———— (1993). The role of interpretation in therapeutic change. In *The Widening Scope of Self Psychology: Progress in Self Psychology, Vol. 9*, ed. A. Goldberg. Hillsdale, NJ: The Analytic Press, pp. 15–30.

Young-Bruehl, E. (1991). Rereading Freud on female development. *Psychoanal. Inq.*, 11:427–440.

———— (1996). Gender and psychoanalysis: An introductory essay. *Gender & Psychoanal.*, 1:7–18.

INDEX

A

Adler, G., 23, 129
affective tracking, 154
aggression, innate destructive,
    40–41, 98
Aichhorn, A., 32
ambiguity, postmodern embrace of,
    23–24
analyst. *See also* blank screen
    metaphor; postmodern
    analysts; *specific topics*
  expanding participation and
    repertoire, 189–191
  immersion in patient's experience,
    141
  narcissistic needs and shadow side,
    64, 65, 161
  as new object, 16, 155–156, 204
  roles of, 147–148
  subjectivity of, xxii, 26–28, 69–70,
    72, 92, 107, 189–191,
    245–247. *See also* analyst's
    self-expression; empathy,
    critiques of, postmodern
    impact on analyst's theories,
    126–127
    implications for analytic situation,
    122–128
    and mutual influence, 152–157,
    182, 191–194
    negative effects of trying to "put

aside" or transcend, 70, 71
    patients' experience of, 143, 189
    patients' interpretation of, 124
    vs. selfobject function, 71
    shift from patient's subjectivity
    to, 118–120
    suspension *vs.* nonarticulation
    of, 148
analyst's self-expression, 136–138,
    140–142, 190
  vs. containment, 142–151, 158,
    161–162, 200
    of annoyance, 145–146
    "bracketing," 148, 152
    breakdown of self-containment,
    149–150
    dangers of expression, 158, 173
    held in abeyance early in treatment,
    141
analytic authority, 128, 191–196, 245
analytic interaction, 193. *See also*
    analyst, subjectivity of,
    implications; intersubjective
    dyad; *specific topics*
  focus on conscious experience in, 22
  patient's subjectivity and analyst's
    codetermining influence on,
    178–181
analytic third, 175–176, 184
Aron, L., xxiv, 4, 6, 7, 9, 18, 21–23,
    37, 54, 57–58, 63, 65–67, 70,

277

18689857R00172

Printed in Great Britain
by Amazon